Regulating Privacy

Regulating Privacy

Data Protection and Public Policy in Europe and the United States

Colin J. Bennett

Cornell University Press

ITHACA AND LONDON

First published 1992 by Cornell University Press.

International Standard Book Number 0-8014-2611-1
Library of Congress Catalog Card Number 91-30559

Printed in the United States of America

*Librarians: Library of Congress cataloging information
appears on the last page of the book.*

⊗ The paper in this book meets the minimum requirements
of the American National Standard for Information Sciences—
Permanence of Paper for Printed Materials, ANSI Z39.48-1984.

Contents

Preface

As information technology has been applied to modern organizations, personal information has become far easier to collect, store, manipulate, and disseminate. By the late 1960s this development had raised within postindustrial democratic states a complex but common set of fears that crucial individual rights and liberties were being compromised. States then responded with data protection statutes, designed to regulate the collection, storage, use and disclosure of recorded information relating to identifiable individuals and thus protect the value of personal privacy. This book is a comparative study of the data protection policies of four countries—Sweden, the United States, West Germany, and the United Kingdom.

A multitude of works exists on this overall subject. There are polemical books designed to alert the general public to the privacy problem; there are legalistic analyses of complicated and esoteric doctrinal and statutory questions; there are philosophical works on the various ethical and moral dimensions of privacy; there are more technical treatments from the computer scientists and information systems experts; there are official and unofficial reports from national commissions, international working parties, civil liberties groups, and professional associations. Many conferences, seminars, and colloquia have been held; and all these have been accompanied by a steady flow of journalism. As yet, however, no systematic and comparative work has appeared to answer the questions that the political scientist would pose: How have different countries with divergent institutional arrangements and cultural traditions tried to solve this common problem? And more particularly, why have they responded as they have? Those are the central questions of this book.

The way in which different political systems have regulated the collection, storage, and communication of personal information may tell us much about their cultural, ideological, and institutional settings as well. The work is built around the concepts "convergence" and "divergence"; how have broad transnational forces for convergence confronted domestic forces for divergence? We may expect significant pressures for cross-national conformity. The task is to assess how these pressures have influenced the political debates in each country, and how, if at all, they have been filtered, diluted, obstructed, or overwhelmed by the distinctive structures and cultures within our four states. Five plausible explanations for convergence are suggested: technological determinism (where there is no alternative given the nature of information technology); emulation (the copying or adaptation of legislation passed elsewhere); elite networking (convergence through the common perceptions and interaction of a cross-national policy community); harmonization (through authoritative action by international organizations); and penetration (a more coercive process where states are forced to conform to legislative action taken elsewhere).

The extent to which states do not converge depends on a series of obstacles and constraints peculiar to the particular countries. Five possible reasons for divergence are postulated: the formal structures of the state, the preferences of dominant social groups, the role of political parties in linking social preferences to state institutions, the position and power of bureaucracy, and economic constraints. This framework for convergence and divergence guides the choice and interpretation of the empirical evidence.

After elaborating on this analytical framework and approach in the Introduction, I next discuss the nature of the policy problem, how it arose, and how it became politicized. It is unequivocally a problem of the "postindustrial" or "information" society. Just as postindustrialism has been accompanied by some profound transformations, so the "information revolution" has brought not only challenges and opportunities but also dangers. This book analyzes one of the most significant problems associated with the modern information society. It is a problem not simply for the postindustrial state, however, but more specifically for the *democratic* postindustrial state. Democratic theory, and especially liberal democratic theory, stresses the definition of, and respect for, a private domain of behavior with which government cannot interfere. Information technology has the potential to alter the boundaries between the realms of social and individual action. What at first glance seems a technical and esoteric issue therefore raises some of the central and ancient questions of political theory.

In the late 1960s the realization emerged that the application of information technology to the public organization—and we are principally dealing with the *public* sector—may also entail a qualitative change in the relationship between the individual and the state. Personal information systems employing the latest information technology were associated with excessive surveillance, with a reduction in individualism and human dignity, and with the "Big Brother" symbolism of the "1984" society. A sprinkling of horror stories circulated about the adverse consequences that can arise from the abuse and misuse of automatically processed personal information. The nature of the problem is complex and multidimensional, and the purpose of Chapter 1 is to explore the various aspects of the issue with a view to understanding how it was defined and perceived in each country.

Chapter 2 traces the development and formation of data protection policy on two levels of analysis. I first track the diffusion of data protection policy throughout all Organization for Economic Cooperation and Development (OECD) countries that have so far legislated. This aggregate cross-sectional approach is then combined with a more detailed and contextual analysis of the smaller four-nation sample. The development of the 1973 Swedish Data Act, the 1974 United States Privacy Act, the 1977 West German Data Protection Act and the 1984 British Data Protection Act is then thoroughly discussed. Chapter 3 presents those aspects of the policies which appear most similar. Evidence from content analysis and certain secondary impressions demonstrates that, on basic questions of principle, there has been a high degree of policy convergence. Over time, states have resolved to deal with the problem by enacting a remarkably similar set of statutory provisions. In Chapter 4 I examine this convergence against my analytical framework.

Chapter 5 reviews the elements of data protection policy that appear the most divergent. The major differences center on the policy instruments chosen to enforce the respective laws. I first note the international repertoire of potential instruments that could conceivably be brought to bear, and I then describe the choice of each state: Sweden opted for a licensing system, the United States relied on self-help and judicial enforcement, West Germany established a data protection commissioner, and the United Kingdom adopted a registration approach. The differences among these various methods of implementation are analyzed and the advantages and disadvantages examined. In Chapter 6 I explain these different choices.

The comparison of national responses to the same stimulus is a fruitful and long-standing research tradition in comparative politics. Moreover, the very novelty of the issue, and the fact that it has rarely been examined through the lens of the political scientist, provides an opportunity to examine whether generalizations about policy making derived from the analysis of other substantive issues also hold true for data protection. Inasmuch as this book describes how four states have grappled with the social and political implications of information technology, it should contribute to the continuing debate about the protection of personal privacy in information societies. Chapter 7 reviews the findings, compares the different styles of policy making and implementation, explores the implications for the autonomy of contemporary democratic states, and evaluates the prospects for data protection in an era of rapid technological innovation.

My analysis reflects a recognition that these questions are inherently complex and that the answers will be qualified and contingent. My overriding conviction, however, is that the intellectual rewards of cross-national comparison far outweigh the practical, methodological, and theoretical difficulties which inevitably arise. Only through cross-national comparison can we distinguish the persistent, generic, and transnational from the conditional, particular, and country-specific. To expose this contrast, probably no more essential question could be studied than one that asks how different democracies have attempted to protect the personal privacy of their citizens against the intrusiveness and impersonality of the postindustrial society.

I am indebted to many people for their help and encouragement over several years. Certainly the advice of graduate teachers and supervisors at the University of Illinois at Urbana-Champaign is reflected in these pages. In particular, I thank Fred Wirt for initally stimulating my interest in policy analysis and patiently guiding me along the difficult path of developing and then executing a comparative research design. David Linowes, the former chair of the U.S. Privacy Protection Study Commission, provided much essential research material and useful contacts. Moreover, as Boeschenstein Chair of Public Policy and Political Economy, he financially supported a significant part of my graduate career at the University of Illinois.

I am also grateful to David Flaherty of the University of Western Ontario, who allowed me access to the library of his Privacy Project and who has continually offered advice and encouragement. Much of David Flaherty's pioneering work on data protection is cited throughout this book, and there is no doubt that my analysis would have been more difficult had he not paved the way. Others who read and commented on parts or versions of the manuscript include Philip Monypenny, Marvin Weinbaum, Harvey Choldin, and John Bradfield. At the University of Victoria, my colleague Anthony Birch provided useful suggestions and insights that contributed significantly to the quality of the final work.

Funding for this project came from several sources. The Dean S. Dorman Award from the University of Illinois provided the initial opportunity to conduct interviews with policy makers and specialists in both the United States and Europe. Since then my work has been supported by the Social Science and Humanities Research Council of Canada (SSHRC 410-87-1383) and by the Faculty Research and Travel Committee of the University of Victoria. It is my sincere hope that, although Canada is not included here as a case study, this analysis provides some important international lessons for the Canadian system of data protection.

Earlier versions of parts of the argument have appeared elsewhere. Papers on convergence theory were given at the annual meetings of the American Political Science Association in 1987 and the Canadian Political Science Association in 1988. Portions of the analysis are also found in two earlier articles: "Different Processes, One Result: The Convergence of Data Protection Policy in Europe and the United States," *Governance* 1 (1988): 415–41; and "Regulating the Computer: Comparing Policy Instruments in Europe and the United States," *European Journal of Political Research* 16 (1988): 437–66.

I much appreciate the help that Martin Thorn gave with the translation of certain key documentary sources. The research assistance of David McDonald and Tom Nixon is also noted with gratitude. The task of typing (and retyping my typing) fell to Laurel Barnes, whose perseverance despite my handwriting and my ineptitude on the word processor deserves much praise and thanks. I am also indebted to Doris Lam for other secretarial assistance.

Finally, I wish to express my appeciation to the experts and officials who have been involved with the challenges of protecting personal data and who helped me in this study. I have much admiration for the efforts of these few men and women who have tried to develop a set of practical principles for the protection of personal information in the face of enormous bureaucratic and technological forces. I have interviewed many of them over the years, and without their assistance this book would be a lot weaker. Their privacy is respected in these pages, but they nevertheless responded to my questions with candor and with much genuine interest.

COLIN BENNETT

Victoria, British Columbia

Abbreviations

ACLU	American Civil Liberties Union
ADP	Automatic Data Processing
AFIPS	American Federation of Information Processing Societies
BDSG	Bundesdatenschutzgesetz (German Federal Data Protection Act)
BfD	Bundesbeauftragte für den Datenschutz (Federal Commissioner for Data Protection)
CNIL	Commission Nationale de l'Informatique et Libertés (French Commission on Informatics and Freedom)
CPUs	Central Processing Units
DALK	Parliamentary Commission on Revision of the Data Act (Sweden)
DIB	Data Inspection Board (Sweden)
DvD	Deutsche Vereinigung für Datenschutz (German Association for Data Protection)
EC	European Communities
FOIA	Freedom of Information Act (United States)
GAO	General Accounting Office (United States)
GSA	General Services Administration (United States)
HEW	Department of Health, Education, and Welfare (United States)
ICCP	Information Computer Communications Policy Unit (OECD)
ISDN	Integrated Services Digital Networks
ITAP	Information Technology Advisory Panel (United Kingdom)
NCCL	National Council for Civil Liberties (United Kingdom)
NTIA	National Telecommunications and Information Administration (United States)
OECD	Organization for Economic Cooperation and Development
OIRA	Office of Information and Regulatory Affairs (United States)

ABBREVIATIONS

OPM Office of Personnel Management (United States)
OTA Office of Technology Assessment (United States)
PPSC Privacy Protection Study Commission (United States)
SCB Central Bureau of Statistics (Sweden)

Regulating Privacy

Introduction

This book falls within that general category of political science known as comparative policy analysis. In probably the pioneering work in this subfield, Arnold Heidenheimer defined it as "the study of how, why, and to what effect different governments pursue particular courses of action or inaction."[1] In this case, the course of action is the attempt to protect individual privacy rights against the dangers stemming from the collection, storage, manipulation, and dissemination of personal data by the modern organization employing the latest information technology. The analysis focuses on the "how" and "why" questions and for most part leaves the "to what effect" aspect to other scholars and later works.[2]

Comparative public policy research arose in the early 1970s from a combination of the policy analyst's quest for relevance and the comparativist's search for middle-range theory about the processes and structures of government. The underlying assumption is that by comparing policy *output* in different national settings, we can better understand the range of social, economic, environmental, and political variables that might account for that output. The policy is the starting

1. Arnold J. Heidenheimer, Hugh Heclo, and Carolyn T. Adams, *Comparative Public Policy: The Politics of Social Choice in Europe and America*, 2d ed. (New York: St. Martin's Press, 1983), pp. 2–3.
2. For the most comprehensive evaluation of data protection law, see David H. Flaherty, *Protecting Privacy in Surveillance Societies: The Federal Republic of Germany, Sweden, France, Canada, and the United States* (Chapel Hill: University of North Carolina Press, 1989). Although implementation is not a central part of my analysis, comments on the "to what effect" question are presented in Chapter 7.

1

point. Asking the "why here, and not there" or "why like this here, and that there" questions leads to wider generalizations about the causes of public policy and to a richer set of insights into our own and foreign political systems.

There is now a substantial body of theoretical and empirical literature that could fall under the general rubric of "comparative policy analysis." Most, however, deals with fairly traditional policy problems that are defined by established policy sectors—economic, social, health, education, environmental, and so on. Moreover, much of this work tends to stay within those sectors, drawing upon and speaking to literature about the same broad policy issue. This progress of comparative policy analysis within the convenient yet atheoretical set of sectoral policy categories has probably restricted our understanding about "how, why, and to what effect different governments pursue particular courses of action or inaction."

One way to break away from the confines of sectorization is to study a completely new policy problem, one not subject to either established wisdom within the political science literature or to a long and institutionalized legacy of policy development. Information privacy, or "data protection" as it will be termed throughout, is a problem that has been with us only since the 1960s. It emerged on the political agendas of advanced industrial states as a result of the development and application of computers. The issue is most often considered one of civil liberties and analyzed within the pages of law journals. Yet it is clearly a policy problem amenable to analysis using the theoretical and methodological tools of the political scientist. On one level, this book is an attempt to integrate literature on comparative public policy with that on computers and privacy.[3] Thus it examines whether insights and generalizations drawn from the comparative analysis of other policy sectors also hold true for this new problem.

The combination of two principal and common elements of postindustrial society, bureaucracy and information technology, has created both quantitative and qualitative changes in the ways that both public and private organizations treat personal information. Sooner or later in every advanced industrial democracy, a complex set of fears arose

3. For the most complete bibliography, see David H. Flaherty, ed., *Privacy and Data Protection: An International Bibliography* (London: Mansell, 1984).

about the implications for the personal privacy of citizens, and the policy area known as "information privacy" or "data protection" emerged. By the end of the 1980s, the protection of personal data had taken on a momentum of its own as a separate and significant issue of public policy. Some seventeen members of the Organization for Economic Cooperation and Development (OECD), now have legislation designed to protect personal data from unreasonable and intrusive surveillance practices. I have chosen four representative laws for comparison and analysis: the Swedish Data Act of 1973; the American Privacy Act of 1974; the West German Data Protection Act of 1977; and the British Data Protection Act of 1984.

While we should keep in mind that many other legislative provisions have a bearing on the protection of personal data, the focus on these four provides the cross-national equivalence that enhances the comparative endeavor and, I hope, yields a richer set of insights. The equivalence of the research problem in different contexts, so often an insurmountable hurdle in comparative research, is less of an issue here. Data protection policy, by its very nature, holds some inherent advantages that mitigate several of the enormous theoretical, conceptual, and methodological problems that haunt other comparative research.

It is, first of all, new. The policy problem has been created by technological developments. So we are spared having to track and understand a long process of policy development during which bureaucratic norms and vested interests have become institutionalized and entrenched. Data protection constitutes an example of a fresh problem requiring a high degree of government innovation. It is in a way a pure test of different policy-making processes. Second, the policy problem is the same and, as we shall see in Chapter 1, is defined as the same in each of the four states. It reached the agenda at the same time (the late 1960s and early 1970s) in similar international economic and social conditions. Third, just one law tends to capture the major part of the policy activity in each country. Data protection policy (as defined and limited to public agencies) has a discrete and uncomplicated quality. There is no complex set of intervening interests or intricate process of resource allocation made through multiple administrative layers and transmitted to remote geographical locations. The policy-making effort aims to protect the relationship between the

3

citizen and the agencies of the democratic state, a classical liberal form of policy making.

So how have Sweden, the United States, West Germany, and Britain responded to this problem, and why have they responded in the way they have? The point of departure is the argument that there will be strong pressures for these states to respond in similar ways—there will be a policy *convergence* in other words. This result flows from a familiar thesis that technological and economic development has a leveling impact on diverse social structures, cultural traditions, and public policies. The "convergence thesis" says that modernization brings processes and implications in its wake: an emphasis on planning and rationalization; a replacement of an ideological with a pragmatic imperative; a centrality for a technocratic elite; and a pervasive role for high technology.[4]

General theories of convergence often result, however, in formulations that are imprecise about what is supposed to be converging and that obscure the different processes through which convergence might occur. The logic of the convergence thesis is overly deterministic; policy responses will supposedly converge because states at the same level of development face similar problems. The common "policy problem" plays the role of independent variable. Policy analysis that relies too heavily on this logic may easily collapse into an apology for economic or technological determinism, may lead to a premature rejection of no less important explanations for convergence, and may obscure some critical divergences.[5] It is an empirical question whether the same problems predetermine the same solution. The *technological determinism* hypothesis is the first, but only one, possible explanation for policy convergence in this area.

The second is *emulation,* because policy makers imitate or adapt the efforts of other countries. Data protection is an example of policy innovation, and as several studies have demonstrated, the incentives to copy or at least draw lessons from the pioneers in such circumstances can be strong. When innovation is required, there may be no readily

4. The convergence literature is reviewed and evaluated in Clark Kerr, *The Future of Industrial Societies: Convergence or Continuing Diversity?* (Cambridge: Harvard University Press, 1983).

5. For a more complete discussion of these problems, see Colin J. Bennett, "Review Article: What Is Policy Convergence and What Causes It?" *British Journal of Political Science* 21 (1991): 215–33.

available solution within the existing repertoire of policy and procedural techniques. Without the opportunity to learn from one's own experience, there is a natural tendency to look abroad, to see how other states have responded, to share ideas, and to bring foreign evidence to bear on the domestic decision-making process. Convergence is then the result of a pressure to conform in an insecure and tentative policy-making climate.

A third, and related, explanation may be termed *elite networking*. Here, convergence results from the shared beliefs of a relatively coherent and enduring network of elites bound by expertise on an issue and a common concern for its resolution. Convergence is the result not of constraints imposed by the problem or of collective insecurity but of a consensus among members of a transnational "policy community" or "issue network." This interaction occurs at first above the fray of domestic politics, the point at which a consensus of motivation and concern crystallizes. The participants then go forth to spread the word to their respective societies and governments. Similar responses then emanate as the result of the presentation and debate of similar evidence.

The fourth explanation is *harmonization*. Explicit attempts to harmonize policy require not only a coherent group of transnational actors, a broad consonance of motivation and concern, and regular opportunities for interaction, they also require authoritative action by an international organization or regime. The harmonization of policy by intergovernmental organizations is driven by a recognition of interdependence and of the need to avoid unnecessary discrepancies and incompatibilities. Convergence occurs because international regimes recognize this interdependence, realize that the problem cannot be properly or completely resolved at the national level, and decide that the benefits of convergence outweigh these alternatives.

One final possibility, which contrasts with the seemingly cooperative relations under harmonization, is that states may be forced to conform to the actions of others. This process is termed *penetration*. It is based on the assumption that policy action within one jurisdiction (either a nation-state or an international organization) may carry certain costs that are then exported to those which have not yet responded. In a penetrative process foreign officials participate in the domestic policy processes of another state, consulting, advising, and giving the strong message that the country concerned has no alternative but to follow the lead taken elsewhere.

I have conceptualized these different factors as processes to emphasize the dynamic qualities of the phenomenon. Convergence should not be used as a synonym for "similarity" or "uniformity." It should denote a pattern of development over time, a process rather than a condition. The essential theoretical dimension is not only spatial (other countries) but also temporal, a state of divergence or variability at some former point in time. The time frame of this study is from the mid-1960s until the mid-1980s. This theoretical framework, the hypotheses that it generates, and the evidence it demands are more fully discussed in Chapter 4.

The central theoretical argument is that these forces for convergence confront and interact with distinctively Swedish, German, American, and British beliefs and institutions. The extent to which states do not converge depends on obstacles or constraints peculiar to these particular states. The familiar metaphor of the prism is helpful here. A common problem with common properties flows around advanced democratic countries and is then confronted with a set of obstacles to be overcome in each state, some of which might block the dispersal, some of which might refract it in peculiar and interesting ways. The familiar conditions of postindustrialism (bureaucracy and information technology) have created a frequently recognized problem that enters four different prisms at roughly the same time. Whether, and in what ways, the resulting outcomes converge because of some or all of these transnational forces, or diverge because of distinctive cultural, constitutional, economic, or bureaucratic factors, is another way of stating the central question of this book.

The main finding, which structures the presentation of the later chapters, is that states have converged around the statutory principles of data protection; a common set of "fair information principles" forms the basis of all data protection law, as will be demonstrated in Chapter 3. Despite this similarity, however, there is a wide variation in the policy instruments selected to implement and enforce them: Sweden has a licensing system for all automated data processing systems storing personal data; the Americans rely on the assertion of individual rights through the courts with oversight roles for Congress and the Office of Management and Budget (OMB); the West Germans appointed a kind of ombudsman (the Federal Data Protection Commissioner); and the United Kingdom has a registration process.

This interesting divergence allows us to confront a central hypothesis of the "policy instruments" literature, which suggests that states have a basic repertoire of tools they can apply in any problem-solving situation. Is it true, as Christopher Hood asserts, that "the same basic set of tools appears again and again as governments face up to 'new' problems, such as computer privacy, glue-sniffing, micro-light aircraft and hang-gliders"?[6] Do governments have fairly limited imagination and apply the same instruments to new problems as were applied to old ones? If so, a fixed understanding of a repertoire of tools, perhaps mandated by constitutional norms, which varies from state to state, may account for the variation in the instruments employed to implement data protection. Or do other factors play a role, such as interest group pressure or the partisan complexion of governments of the day? Government bureaucracy may also assert itself on this issue. A weaker policy instrument may be expected where bureaucracy has the autonomy to express its own interest in maintaining control over personal information. Some instruments require the commitment of more public funds than do others. Do, therefore, economic constraints have an impact in some states?

A convergence on statutory principles may thus be explained through five different processes. The divergence at the level of policy instruments may be understood according to the analysis of five domestic characteristics of the countries under consideration: the repertoire of policy instruments within the state; the preferences of the dominant social groups; the role of political parties in electoral competition; the position and power of bureaucracy; and economic constraints. When we delve beneath the common socioeconomic and technological forces that have produced this problem and investigate what Hugh Heclo calls the "detailed twists and turns" of the "substantive policy content,"[7] we will find that a combination of influences accounts for the particular outcomes in each state. The events are not random and unpatterned, but they are complex. Only through

6. Christopher C. Hood, *The Tools of Government* (Chatham, N.J.: Chatham House, 1986), p. 8.
7. Hugh Heclo, *Modern Social Politics in Britain and Sweden* (New Haven: Yale University Press, 1974), p. 287.

a careful specification and comparison of policy content can we identify the convergences and divergences and investigate a range of alternative explanations.

The concepts of convergence and divergence have also been associated with questions about the relative autonomy of the democratic state. Some have assumed that evidence of convergence is also evidence that states have been forced to conform to an inexorable set of transnational forces. What does the evidence of convergence and divergence in data protection policy tell us about the relative autonomy of these four states? Which has been able to fashion a policy independently and in response to its own agenda? Which have been more influenced by forces beyond their control? The central conclusion here is that evidence of convergence per se should not be interpreted as evidence of a lack of autonomy. The key evidence is the *reason* for that convergence, hence the need in any study of this nature to explore various propositions that rest on different assumptions about the behavior and autonomy of state actors. Closely associated with this question is that of "policy style." Which were more anticipatory, which more reactive? In which was the process more conflictual, in which more consensual? How do generalizations about policy style drawn from other cases stand up to examination here?

How, in conclusion, do these observed patterns affect implementation? This analysis does not purport to provide a systematic evaluation of how these laws have been implemented. Nevertheless, it would be remiss simply to leave the story at the point of enactment, without looking into the different national experiences of applying these data protection principles. Chapter 7 suggests the most important determinants for the success of data protection agencies in the light of the statutory, political, technological, and international legacies left by this movement.

The methodological approach I adopt has gone under a number of related names: the "comparable-cases strategy," "the most similar systems design," or, most notably, John Stuart Mill's "method of concomitant variation."[8] The critical distinction from my point of

---

8. Arend Lijphart, "The Comparable-Cases Strategy in Comparative Research," *Comparative Political Studies* 8 (1975): 158–77; Adam Przeworski and Henry Teune, *The Logic of Comparative Social Inquiry* (New York: Wiley, 1970); John Stuart Mill, *A System of Logic*, 8th ed. (New York: Harper, 1893). The logic of this methodology is summarized by

view is between a case study as the intensive analysis of one scientific observation, and a strategy where a number of comparable cases are analyzed in order to introduce an element of *control*. In common with authors of other recent works in the genre, I have chosen to use a small number of comparable country cases to explain observed variations or nonvariations of policy content and policy instruments in their transnational and domestic contexts. What is critical for this endeavor is not only a careful specification of the research problem and the analytical framework but also a selection of appropriate, comparable cases.

At an aggregate level, the analysis can cover the majority of countries that have so far legislated on this policy issue. Also, to discern broad cross-national policy differences, comparisons can be made with those where data protection has not emerged as an issue. The more profound effort, however, will be to get inside the process and study the interaction of transnational and domestic forces on the policy choices of our four-nation sample.

I have several theoretical justifications for choosing the United States, Britain, Sweden, and West Germany from among the seventeen democracies that have so far enacted data protection laws. First, the chosen countries are all advanced democratic societies in North America and Western Europe. (Indeed, few countries elsewhere have considered such legislation). They share the same policy problem, because their private and public organizations have introduced computer technology, and because a respect for individual liberties is supposedly basic to their national life. They have acted within the same time frame, which means the identical international conditions of the 1970s and early 1980s. From a theoretical standpoint, I can justifiably argue that the choice of countries (and of this policy area) in effect allows for the control of a variety of situational factors that might be critically important in other research contexts.

A corresponding justification for my choice is that these countries appear inferentially to display a wide and interesting range of features that are hypothesized to be significant forces for the divergence of

---

Lijphart, p. 164: "the method of testing hypothesized empirical relationships among variables on the basis of the same logic that guides the statistical method, but in which the cases are selected in such a way as to maximize the variance of the independent variables and to minimize the variance of the control variables."

policy. In terms of formal legal/constitutional differences, we have three parliamentary and one presidential system, two unitary and two federal states. More significantly, we have two countries (the United States and Britain) whose legal systems are based on common law, one (West Germany) based on the continental civil or Roman law model, and the other (Sweden) with the Nordic law tradition. Moreover, the four have strikingly different administrative systems. Both Germany and Britain have a coordinated, hierarchical civil service that, in theory at least, is expected to be instrumental, anonymous, and not prone to engaging in political transactions. These contrast sharply with the decentralized and fragmented bureaucratic structure in the United States and with the system of policy-making through autonomous boards in Sweden.

The inclusion of the United States also counteracts some of the universalistic tendencies in both American and Eurocentric studies. Most European comparativists exclude analysis of the United States from their work, whereas many American social scientists tend to assume that lessons and conclusions of relevance to other countries can be drawn from specifically U.S.-based research. This book is representative of a growing body of work that argues the benefits of transatlantic comparison to dispel, on the one hand, notions of American exceptionalism, and, on the other, temptations to universalistic judgments.

The task is to understand the relationship between content and context in each country and to investigate the interaction between the transnational context motivating convergence and the domestic context forcing divergence. The endeavor, like Heclo's, will depend, as he said, "less on statistically unearthing and more on inductively building up generalizations from detailed if somewhat less tidy accounts." We will look "not at isolated, timeless factors in many settings but at strands of development in a few settings."[9] The approach demands the search for what Charles Anderson calls "contextual and experiential knowledge."[10] It is more messy, more inductive, less definitive, but probably more faithful to political reality.

9. Heclo, *Modern Social Politics*, p. 12.
10. Charles W. Anderson, "System and Strategy in Comparative Political Analysis: A Plea for Contextual and Experiential Knowledge," in *Perspectives in Public Policy-Making*, ed. William B. Gwyn and George C. Edwards III (New Orleans: Tulane Unversity Press, 1975), p. 222.

I have employed a variety of data sources to paint the fullest possible picture of both content and context and thus to determine the major influences on policy makers in each country. First, a rich store of valuable official documentary sources exists. These include the laws themselves, legislative floor debates, legislative committee reports and hearings, official governmental policy statements, and national and international study commission reports. I also utilize some less official documentary sources including reports from outside pressure groups such as civil liberties organizations. Second, the newness and complexity of the data protection issue has motivated policy makers from many countries to put their views and experiences in writing for the benefit of their counterparts overseas. Hence, those in the very center of the process have published a large number of articles on privacy, data protection, and computers. The lively (and for the most part public) debate among officials and specialists is an unusually rich body of data that provides important clues to the main influences in each country.

Finally, I conducted interviews with noted figures in the field. My aim was to tap into the policy community of data protection, so I interviewed as many people within that community as time and resources allowed.[11] Questions were directed toward gaining an appreciation of the specific reasons that brought the issue to the agenda, of the most important actors in the policy-making process, and of the impact of wider international and domestic factors on the countries in question. This evidence provides a useful background to the personalities and the conflicts and fills in some crucial gaps. Throughout one should bear in mind that what is treated here in objective academic terms was once a passionate intellectual and political effort to devise a solution to a new and challenging problem.

11. I chose respondents by two methods. First, I identified certain key figures in the movement from documentary sources: members of study commissions; leading officials within data protection authorities or the equivalent implementing agencies; and writers, academics, journalists, and other knowledgeable outside commentators. I then asked these respondents to identify others who should be interviewed, thus expanding the sample. I have conducted approximately fifty interviews, making visits to Washington, D.C. in December 1984, August 1987, and August 1988; to London in January 1986, June 1987, and December 1988; to Bonn in January 1985 and May 1987; and to Stockholm in January 1985 and June 1987. I also acquired data from written correspondence and telephone conversations from those I could not meet in person. Much of this research was conducted for a Ph.D. dissertation: Colin J. Bennett, "Regulating the Computer: A Comparative Study of Personal Data Protection Policy" (Ph.D. diss., University of Illinois at Urbana-Champaign, 1986).

1

The Policy Problem

For studies of more established economic and social issues, the policy problem tends to be self-defining; we can see the visible and direct effects of poverty, environmental pollution, urban decay, homelessness, and the like. It is not immediately obvious, however, what harm results from the computerized collection, use, and disclosure of personal data. The purpose of this first chapter is to describe the scope and nature of the data protection problem. Initially, I have to justify the use of the term and distinguish it from the wider value of privacy. I then examine the context that propelled the issue to the political agenda—the combined effects of information technology and bureaucratization.

An analysis of political rhetoric, the privacy literature, and the "horror stories" from a number of countries will reveal that the issues raised by data protection, while more focused than those surrounding privacy, are still complex and multifaceted. There is not one problem, but several. The aim is to distill these different concerns from the debate and to discover how they have been conceived and expressed in political rhetoric, scholarly discourse, and public consciousness in the four countries.

The Name: Privacy or Data Protection?

On a very general level the policy addressed here is part of the broad value called "privacy." But as many have remarked, privacy is a notoriously vague, ambiguous, and controversial term that embraces a confusing knot of problems, tensions, rights, and duties. In the name of privacy are defended such diverse concerns as the right to be free from intrusive police searches, from wiretapping, from persistent journalists, and so on; the right to make private decisions, particularly in relation to intimate family concerns (abortion or contraception, for instance); and the right to have some control over the collection, storage, and disclosure of personal information (by government, financial institutions, medical organizations, educational establishments, and others). Thus privacy has referred to the exclusiveness of physical space around an individual, to the autonomy of decision making without outside interference, and to the right to control the circulation of personal information.

It is impossible to list a definitive and exhaustive set of concerns encompassed by the word "privacy," though some have tried. Privacy is a highly subjective notion, whose interpretation changes over time and space. It clearly has a very different meaning for the modern middle-class professional with a bank account, numerous credit cards, medical, auto and life insurance, a mortgage and several magazine subscriptions, from that which it had for the rural farmer living in a small village in the last century. These complexities led Alan Westin to conclude that the concept is "part philosophy, some semantics and much pure passion."[1] They lead us to conclude that privacy may hold much emotive and symbolic appeal, but it is inadequate to conceptualize and frame the policy problem to be addressed here.

A more accurate appellation for the group of policies designed to regulate the collection, storage, use, and transmittal of personal information is *data protection,* the European nomenclature (translated from the German *Datenschutz).* This term, too, is not without problems. It is more technical and esoteric and means little to the average citizen. For this reason, most English-speaking nations have retained the word "privacy" to add popular appeal to statutes that essentially perform the same functions as European data protection laws. It is also unusual to talk about data protection in relation to information that is not contained in computers. And yet, as we shall see, some laws

1. Alan F. Westin, *Privacy and Freedom* (New York: Atheneum, 1967), p. x.

13

cover both automated and manual (paper) files, regulating the filing cabinet along with the computer.

"Data protection" is nevertheless a more precise term, and it distinguishes the policy problem that has arisen since the late 1960s from the broad social value that has such a rich tradition and important place in the liberal democratic heritage. Data protection is broadly analogous to the concept "information privacy," the classic definition of which is given by Westin: "the claim of individuals, groups or institutions to determine for themselves when, how and to what extent information about them is communicated to others."[2] Westin's definition provides as good a formulation for the concerns of this book as any other.

The Information Revolution in Postindustrial Society

The issue of data protection rose to the political agenda at a time when advanced industrial democracies were undergoing some profound transformations in their social and economic infrastructures. For many the changes have been as radical as the emergence of industrialism from feudalism. Popular literature has regarded this transition as a "megatrend"[3] that is generating a new "third wave" civilization.[4] James Beniger has reviewed contemporary social commentary and counted some seventy different "major societal transformations" identified from 1950 until 1984.[5] An assumption seems to be that we have only to find the correct name for this new communications/information/telematic/wired/technological/technetronic society in order to understand the fundamental essence of our times.

The more scholarly debate has centered on the concept of "postindustrialism," a word coined in the late 1960s to characterize the

2. Ibid., p. 7. Westin's definition embraces the claim of collectivities (groups and institutions) to privacy rights. This controversial philosophical question does not concern us here. Our focus, and indeed the principal aim of all data protection legislation, is the protection of the individual.

3. John Naisbitt, *Megatrends* (New York: Warner Books, 1982).

4. Alvin Toffler, *The Third Wave* (New York: Bantam Books, 1980).

5. James R. Beniger, *The Control Revolution: Technological and Economic Origins of the Information Society* (Cambridge: Harvard University Press, 1986), pp. 4–5.

various visions of the future that authors sought to extrapolate from the most startling social trends. The central elements of the postindustrial society are the predominance of the service sector and the white-collar labor force; advancing levels of education, affluence, and leisure time; a new "postbourgeois" value structure; the replacement of work and capital by knowledge as the driving force behind human productivity; and, most interesting from our point of view, the central role of information as the currency of the postindustrial economy,[6] meaning that the sources of innovation are increasingly derived from research and development, and that, by the standard measures of individual and societal wealth, knowledge and information are becoming more important relative to labor and capital. Marc Porat devised an empirical measure to substantiate the growing significance of the "information sector" to the postindustrial economy as a whole; he concluded that about half the work force is now engaged in the processing of information. A later report from the Organization for Economic Cooperation and Development confirmed a steady rise in the share of information occupations as a percentage of the economically active population in all member countries.[7]

Under this theory, information is conceptualized as a resource that has rapidly become easier to collect, store, retrieve, and communicate. Just as steel and fossil fuels were indispensable to the transition from an agricultural to an industrial society, so information is central to the shift from industrialism to postindustrialism. But any resource viewed in the abstract means little unless tied to the notion of ownership. It is here that more radical theorists question the assumptions of the postindustrial thesis and point out wider and arguably more profound

6. The central work is Daniel Bell, *The Coming of Post-Industrial Society* (New York: Basic Books, 1973). These themes are also found in John K. Galbraith, *The New Industrial State* (Boston: Houghton Mifflin, 1971), and Alan Touraine, *The Post-Industrial Society* (New York: Random House, 1971). The principal evidence for a new "postmaterialistic" value structure is found in Ronald Inglehart, *The Silent Revolution* (Princeton: Princeton University Press, 1977). It is important to distinguish between "knowledge" and "information." Knowledge, as Bell uses it, refers to a general understanding of the nature and causes of phenomena. Information is more transitory and contextual; it has value to somebody at a particular time. Information technology, therefore, by increasing the quantity of information that can be stored, manipulated, and communicated, enhances the value of information to individuals, to organizations, and to society as a whole.

7. Marc U. Porat, *The Information Economy: Definition and Measurement* (Washington, D.C.: Department of Commerce, 1977); OECD, *Trends in the Information Economy* (Paris: OECD, 1986), p. 9.

trends, notably capital accumulation, commodification, and social control.[8] Thus the change in the nature of the key resource may not be a profound social force if the forms and structures of resource ownership and control remain unchanged. So the "information revolution" is probably not a "revolution" at all but a culmination of changes in material processing set in motion more than a century ago.[9]

What seems incontrovertible, however, is the central place that information technology holds in postindustrial society. Nowadays, if we were describing the nature of the information society, we would be forced to consider a large selection of new communication and information technologies, all with privacy implications: interactive cable television, videotext, remote sensing, hidden cameras, electronic fund transfers, transponders, smart cards, and many others. Technological developments in microelectronics, particularly the miniaturization and enhanced capabilities of semiconductors, have led to dramatic reductions in physical size and substantial increases in robustness, computing speed, memory capability, reliability, and ease of use. These advances have coincided with rapid developments in communications, principally satellite technology, fibre optics cable, and digital telephony. The combination of these different technologies has meant that greater quantities of information can now be stored and transmitted by a greater number of people, at higher speeds, at lower costs, to multiple remote locations.

Even though the policies considered here were generally conceived in response to an earlier, more basic, and thankfully more understandable generation of computers, there is still considerable confusion about how to describe this technology. "Databank" is now considered an outdated concept as it implies the *storage* of data rather than its transmittal or retrieval. "Computer" is also a misnomer given the fact that most computers do far more than compute. The generic term "information technology" will be used throughout to describe the hardware and software associated with all features of automatic digital data processing and communication. Generally speaking, technological developments in the societies studied have been strikingly uniform. Subtle technological distinctions are not a salient factor in the explanation of cross-national policy choices.

8. See Vincent Mosco, *The Pay-per Society: Computers and Communication in the Information Age* (Toronto: Garamond, 1989).
9. Beniger, *The Control Revolution*.

It is also evident that information technology includes substantially more than the basic machinery. The most helpful definition in this respect is perhaps that by James Danziger and his colleagues in their study of computers in local government: "Computer technology encompasses a complex, interdependent system composed of *people* (e.g. users, computer specialists, managers), *equipment* (e.g. hardware such as computer mainframes and peripherals; software, such as operating systems and applications programs; and data), and *techniques* (e.g. procedures, practices, organizational arrangements)."[10] They talk of a "computer package" to denote this interdependence of people, equipment, and techniques. The problems associated with computers stem also from the interaction of the technology with these other elements.

Instantaneous access to vast quantities of information from multiple and remote locations has changed the character of the modern organization and of the society in which it is embedded. This change is probably more a revolution in the nature of communication than in the nature of information itself. Paul Sieghart describes the information society as follows:

> More transactions will tend to be recorded; the records will tend to be kept longer; information will tend to be given to more people; more data will tend to be transmitted over public communication channels; fewer people will know what is happening to the data; the data will tend to be more easily accessible; and data can be manipulated, combined, correlated, associated and analyzed to yield information which could not have been obtained without the use of computers.[11]

These new and more complicated relationships between the individual and those with the power to manipulate information are at the root of the data protection issue.

Bureaucratic Use of Personal Data

The "information society" provides the context for the data protection problem. It does not provide the cause. To appreciate fully the

10. James N. Danziger, et al., *Computers and Politics: High Technology in American Local Governments* (New York: Columbia University Press, 1982), pp. 4–5.
11. Paul Sieghart, *Privacy and Computers* (London: Latimer, 1976), pp. 75–76.

nature of the problem, we must explore the role that personal information plays in the modern organization, especially the public organization, and understand the impact that it has had on these structures.

As will be demonstrated in Chapter 2, the principal fears in all countries arose from the public sector. Of course, information about identifiable individuals, whether in automated or manual record-keeping systems, exists in a wide variety and increasing number of public and private organizations. The potential for privacy invasion is present wherever large quantities of personal data are collected and stored, in both the public and private sectors. Most national policies recognize this and regulate both. For the purposes of this book, however, I will concentrate mainly on data protection policy as it relates to national governments and give less emphasis to that relating to local or state authorities or to private industry. This focus allows the organizational equivalence necessary for comparative analysis among nation states. It also exposes the more interesting dimension of the problem for the political scientist: the changing relationship between the citizen and government, a connection that is generated by this new tension between personal privacy rights and the information needs of administrators and policy makers.

Record keeping on individuals is as old as civilization itself. Historical research has traced the notion of a system of personal records to most of the ancient civilizations of the Far and Near East, Central and South America, and the Mediterranean. With few exceptions, however, such as William the Conqueror's renowned Domesday Book, the collection and keeping of personal records were localized and unsystematic. It was only with the development of the modern state in Western Europe, with a codification of the mutual responsibilities of the government and those it governs, with the development of a centralized administration, and ultimately with the levying of taxes, that the relationship between citizen and state took on a different character. The expansion and institutionalization of state power over the last three hundred years brought with it the need for more formal, more discriminating, and more complex record-keeping systems.[12] As the functions and responsibilities of the state expanded with industrialization and the subsequent provision of social services in the

12. Charles Tilly, ed., *The Formation of National States in Western Europe* (Princeton: Princeton University Press, 1975).

twentieth century, so the relationship between citizen and state assumed all the formalized, routine, institutionalized, and impersonal characteristics that we come to associate with bureaucracy.[13]

On one level, therefore, the increase in the number and complexity of policies that we expect the modern welfare state to administer has meant a quantitative increase in the amount of information collected from individuals. We normally think nothing about supplying such information. Most citizens of advanced industrial states expect the provision of a variety of social services to counteract income vulnerability, old age, infirmity, and a variety of other social ills; we expect fully effective and well-funded educational institutions; we expect a subsidized, if not a nationalized, health service; and we expect a properly functioning criminal justice system. The performance of these functions requires the collection of masses of accurate information about the circumstances of individuals.

On a more qualitative level, there has also been a change in the nature of the information collected. As programs have become increasingly refined, more sensitive and discriminating information on the financial, employment, health, and educational histories of a citizen has been required. Moreover, the ability to assemble information selectively, or to correlate existing information, can be functionally equivalent to the ability to create new information. This capacity, obviously facilitated by information technology, enables agencies to identify, target, and perhaps manipulate a certain segment of the population that has common background characteristics. The twin techniques of "computer matching" (the comparison of different computer tapes to expose instances of fraud, waste, and abuse) and "computer profiling" (the derivation of classes of individuals most likely to engage in activities of interest to the agency in question) are the most modern manifestations of this power.[14]

Three types of personal records can be identified.[15] *Administrative* records are those generated by a transaction with an agency—

13. H. H. Gerth and C. Wright Mills, *From Max Weber: Essays in Sociology* (New York: Oxford University Press, 1946), pp. 196–244.

14. U.S. Congress, Office of Technology Assessment (OTA), *Federal Government Information Technology: Electronic Record Systems and Individual Privacy* (Washington, D.C.: Government Printing Office, 1986).

15. U.S. Department of Health, Education, and Welfare (HEW), *Records, Computers, and the Rights of Citizens*. Report of the Secretary's Advisory Committee on Automated Personal Data Systems (Washington, D.C.: HEW, 1973), p. 5.

applying for a license; reporting your taxable income; getting married; applying for grants, supplements, welfare assistance, a passport, and the like. This information tends to be self-reported and is usually granted because people feel they are exchanging information for a more important benefit. *Intelligence* records serve an investigative purpose; police criminal files or consumer credit reports are typical examples. The information is normally collected from sources other than the individual to whom the record pertains, and is inherently less innocuous. Finally, *statistical* records are created through a census or through survey research. Their purpose is to provide aggregate information for general policy making rather than for finely tuned decisions about individuals. Generally, the identity of the record subject can be separated from the data in the record.

All three types of record were present before the advent of the computer. All entail privacy implications. The advantages derived from the use of information technology for these purposes have been universally recognized: it can relieve officials of tedious tasks such as copying, filing, keeping records up-to-date, issuing certificates, and the like; it makes for more speed and efficiency in dealing with the public; it enhances the analytical capabilities of an organization; it helps rationalize administrative work; and it supposedly enables more accurate and fine-drawn decisions concerning clients and customers.

Some might add that a technological imperative is at work. Information technology helps add prestige and a sense of sophistication to an organization. As David Flaherty remarks: "Civil servants seek data on individuals to design and evaluate programs, to augment their prestige and power, and, as a product of a supposed technological imperative, to enable them to use the latest hardware and software programs."[16] The technology, however, should not be regarded as an autonomous force, subject to no independent human control. Nor should we see the problem as stemming solely from the pathologies of the modern organization, where the computer is a mere tool utilized to satisfy the expansionist, aggrandizing, manipulative tendencies of bureaucracy. Neither the technology nor the bureaucracy alone is the determining factor. Rather, there is a dynamic or interactive relationship between the two. The computer expands the horizons and pos-

16. Flaherty, *Protecting Privacy in Surveillance Societies*, p. 13.

sibilities for control, but within those parameters organizations may pursue a number of different directions, modifying their goals in terms of the different choices the technology presents. The direction of change, including the impact on privacy, is a result of the dynamic and interactive relationship between technological developments and social, administrative, and political decisions. The complexity of big government and the headway made by information technology have been two parallel and interdependent processes.

In the early 1960s, when computers first made their appearance in organizations, they were expensive and cumbersome, and they required considerable skill to operate; as a result their use was limited to a few public functions. The astounding progress made in microelectronics has now rendered the computer more manageable, less expensive, and more "user friendly." And these developments are undoubtedly also a cause of their spread throughout the agencies of government. The United States General Services Administration (GSA) has estimated that federal agencies would acquire half a million small computers by the beginning of the 1990s.[17] In terms of large central processing units (CPUs), federal agencies reported in 1989 some 45,000 CPUs and 330,000 peripherals. The total dollar value for automatic data processing equipment was reported as $8.5 billion.[18]

Reliable cross-national statistics on the numbers and types of computers in government are virtually impossible to collect, however, for a number of reasons: the decentralized nature of many administrative agencies means that computerization has been scattered; many large computers are leased rather than owned; the existence of others is shrouded in secrecy for security reasons; and the development of the personal computer and of widespread networking in recent years has made the notion of the discrete databank obsolete. Where one computer stops and another begins is a question that is becoming increasingly difficult to answer. Aggregate quantification of the computer population is misleading in another sense. Many of the purposes to which

17. GSA, *Purchase of Small Computers by the Federal Government in 1984* (Washington, D.C.: GSA, 1985).
18. GSA, Federal Equipment Data Center, *Automatic Data Processing Equipment in the U.S. Government*, First and Second Quarter FY 1989 Summary (Arlington, Va.: GSA, Federal Equipment Data Center, 1989).

information technology is put are irrelevant to the question of privacy protection—for example, where it is used solely for statistical, analytical, or financial management. Moreover, a considerable proportion of the expenditure on information technology by governments is for defense-related purposes (half in the statistics for CPUs quoted above). Aggregate figures on the numbers of machines and on expenditures can hardly be regarded as a full and commensurate representation of the increased danger to personal liberties.

As we shall see in Chapter 2, the issue rose to the agenda not through the abstract fears of massive computerization but through quite specific instances of perceived abuse. The catalysts that shifted the issue to the political agenda in all countries were more particular cases of the collection of data (e.g., censuses) or the concentration and centralization of data in new and potentially intrusive ways. Those specific instances, peculiar to the different countries, did more to accentuate the problem and focus the concern than did the general and gradual trends toward bureaucratization and computerization. These catalysts will be discussed in Chapter 2 in the context of the different countries under consideration.

Three Aspects of the Problem

It is commonly agreed, though rarely recognized, that the decision to adopt a technology often entails a complex set of entanglements and implications that are not immediately obvious to the adopter at the time. With most technologies the costs are readily apparent in the form of tangible, visible, and sometimes dramatic dangers. The advent of the computer, however, has not been accompanied by the sort of concerns that were associated with the automobile, the airplane, or nuclear power. Occasionally, the dangers are vividly displayed in mass culture, as with the neurotic HAL in the film *2001: A Space Odyssey* or more recently with the potential for "computer hacking" in *War Games*. Overall, though, the problems of information technology have existed at the periphery of public consciousness. Consequently, as Danziger and his colleagues observe, "the costs and benefits and the broader impacts of computer systems are largely perceived as indirect and subtle, if they are indeed perceived at all."[19] For the social scientist, therefore, the specification of the "policy problem" requires more careful and deliberate attention. Without evidence equivalent to a polluted atmosphere, an air disaster, or a nuclear meltdown, the legitimate question that can and should be asked is: What is the problem?

The initial response is that there is not one problem but several; thus the protection of personal information serves a number of different ends. A careful exploration of the debates and analysis surrounding the issue reveals several interrelated concerns that can best be analyzed on three levels: humanistic, political, and instrumental. The purpose is now to define and explain these three aspects of the data protection problem and to show how they rest on certain different assumptions about the nature and effects of personal information.

The Humanistic Dimension

Fundamentally, personal data protection serves a humanistic purpose. In this interpretation, the concern is essentially to protect or promote the dignity, individuality, integrity, or private personality of each one of us. The promotion of this value bolsters John Stuart Mill's basic principle of a liberal society that "over himself, over his own body and mind, the individual is sovereign."[20] For many modern advocates, the justification need only be made on this humanistic level. This notion also corresponds broadly to James Rule's concept "aesthetic privacy" or "the restriction of personal information as an end in itself."[21] At this level, arguments for data protection are virtually indistinguishable from those for privacy. We must, therefore, explore the nature and origins of this wider value to understand the humanistic justification for data protection.

Such concerns have been expressed by a number of people from diverse national backgrounds and ideological perspectives. One of the

19. Danziger et al., *Computers and Politics*, p. 1.
20. John Stuart Mill, "On Liberty," in *Utilitarianism*, ed. Mary Warnock (Glasgow: Fontana, 1962), p. 135.
21. James Rule et al., *The Politics of Privacy: Planning for Personal Data Systems as Powerful Technologies* (New York: Elsevier, 1980), p. 22.

first analyses of the subject in Britain by Justice (the British section of the International Commission of Jurists) states:

> To preserve his sense of identity and the integrity of his personality, to work out his personal relationships and find his way to his own salvation, each human being needs to be able to limit the area of his intercourse with others . . . . Above all we need to be able to keep to ourselves, if we want to, those thoughts and feelings, beliefs and doubts, hopes, plans, fears and fantasies, which we call "private" precisely because we wish to be able to choose freely with whom, and to what extent, we are willing to share them.[22]

Again from Britain, Ruth Cohen of the National Council for Civil Liberties (NCCL) stresses the dehumanizing qualities of automated record keeping, where "the individual is no longer a living, breathing person but a file with a name, number and label."[23] More recent British commentators, Duncan Campbell and Steve Connor, assert that "privacy is fundamental to personal integrity."[24]

We see similar rhetoric in the United States. Vance Packard's early attempt to arouse public attention to privacy, *The Naked Society*, talks of the "right to a private, unfettered life."[25] More scholarly justifications are found in the sociological analysis of Edward Shils, who traces the growth in the sensitivity to privacy to the late nineteenth century: "The growth of individuality, the sense of one's identity as an individual, likewise supported the belief that one's actions and their history 'belonged' to the self which generated them and were to be shared only with those with whom one wished to share them."[26] Westin's seminal study, *Privacy and Freedom*, was the first analysis to root this humanistic justification of information privacy in empirical evidence. He surveys a wealth of social, psychological, and anthropological literature and identifies four interrelated values: protecting

22. Justice (the British section of the International Commission of Jurists), *Privacy and the Law* (London: Justice, 1970), p. 4.

23. Ruth N. Cohen, *Whose File Is It Anyway?* (London: National Council for Civil Liberties, 1982), p. 10.

24. Duncan Campbell and Steve Connor, *On the Record: Surveillance, Computers and Privacy* (London: Michael Joseph, 1986), p. 12.

25. Vance Packard, *The Naked Society* (New York: Pocket Books, 1964), p. 169.

26. Edward Shils, "Privacy in Modern Industrial Society," in *Censuses, Surveys, and Privacy*, ed. Martin Bulmer (London: Macmillan, 1979), p. 26.

personal autonomy or one's "core self," providing a sense of emotion-
al release, promoting self-evaluation and creativity, and limiting and
protecting communication.[27]

Others have disaggregated the value in different ways. Flaherty lists
thirteen "different privacy interests for which individuals ought to be
able to claim protection with respect to information about themselves": the right to individual autonomy; the right to be left alone;
the right to a private life; the right to control information about
oneself; the right to limit accessibility; the right to exclusive control of
access to private realms; the right to minimize intrusiveness; the right
to expect confidentiality; the right to enjoy solitude; the right to enjoy
intimacy; the right to enjoy anonymity; the right to enjoy reserve; the
right to secrecy.[28] All these interrelated values form the underlying
"premise for the more detailed information-control principles and
practices included in data protection activities."[29]

Attempts to define the concept of "privacy" have generally not met
with any success. The classic definition is the "right to be let alone,"
originally presented by Judge Cooley and later elaborated in a famous
article by Samuel Warren and Louis Brandeis.[30] The motivation for
this article was a spate of gossip in the Boston newspapers about the
social affairs of Mrs. Warren, especially the wedding of her daughter.
William Prosser suggests that "she must have been a very beautiful
girl. . . . This was the face that launched a thousand lawsuits."[31] At
any rate, this eloquent attack on the tasteless techniques of the Boston
press was based on the central assumption that the "right to be let
alone" is a part of a "more general right to the immunity of the
person—the right to one's personality."[32]

Building on this article, later writers who were trying to set some
limits to American civil and constitutional privacy law have presented
more precise formulations. Richard Parker, for example, is persuaded
that "privacy is control over when and by whom the various parts of

---

27. Westin, *Privacy and Freedom*, pp. 32–39.
28. Flaherty, *Protecting Privacy in Surveillance Societies*, p. 8.
29. Ibid., p. 7.
30. Thomas M. Cooley, *A Treatise on the Law of Torts*, 2d ed. (Chicago: Callaghan, 1888); Samuel Warren and Louis Brandeis, "The Right to Privacy," *Harvard Law Review* 4 (1890): 193–220.
31. William Prosser, "Privacy," *California Law Review* 48 (1960): 423.
32. Warren and Brandeis, "The Right to Privacy," p. 207.

us can be sensed by others."[33] Others see it as a form of power: "that aspect of social order by which persons control access to information about themselves"[34] or the "right of selective disclosure."[35] For others, privacy is principally a psychological condition of "being apart from others."[36] Westin himself disaggregated the concept into four states of privacy: solitude, intimacy, anonymity, and reserve.[37]

Authors have now given up trying to define privacy, and there is no generally accepted definition. Many have questioned whether there is anything distinctive about the values traditionally subsumed under the privacy rubric. Perhaps privacy is so hopelessly diffuse as to be virtually indistinguishable from the related concepts of liberty, autonomy, and freedom. Others question the search for an all-embracing definition either because privacy is clearly culturally relative or because it is dependent on one's position in the social or economic stratum.[38] For others, privacy is inappropriate because it connotes withdrawal and isolation, whereas the issues and relationships raised by information technology and bureaucracy are inherently social.[39] Much ink has been spilt trying to grapple with these intractable philosophical and semantic questions. It is not clear whether political or judicial decision making has been helped or hindered by this vast literature.

For virtually every commentator, however, the fundamental issue has been the loss of human dignity, autonomy, or respect that results from a loss of control over personal information. Furthermore, the

33. Richard B. Parker, "A Definition of Privacy," *Rutgers Law Review* 27 (1974): 281.
34. Charles Fried, "Privacy," *Yale Law Journal* 77 (1968): 493.
35. Elizabeth L. Beardsley, "Privacy: Autonomy and Selective Disclosure," in *Privacy*, ed. J. Roland Pennock and John W. Chapman (New York: Atherton, 1971), pp. 56–70.
36. Michael A. Weinstein, "The Uses of Privacy in the Good Life," in *Privacy*, ed. Pennock and Chapman, p. 94.
37. Westin, *Privacy and Freedom*, pp. 31–32. In a state of solitude "the individual is separated from the group and freed from the observation of other persons." In intimacy, "the individual is acting as part of a small unit that claims and is allowed to exercise corporate seclusion." Anonymity "occurs when the individual is in public places or performing public acts but still seeks, and finds, freedom from identification and surveillance." Reserve is the "creation of a psychological barrier against unwanted intrusions."
38. These problems are discussed in Ferdinand D. Schoeman, "Privacy: Philosophical Dimensions of the Literature," in *Philosophical Dimensions of Privacy: An Anthology*, ed. Ferdinand D. Schoeman (Cambridge: Cambridge University Press, 1984), pp. 1–33.
39. This assumption was central to the work of the United States Privacy Protection Study Commission, *Personal Privacy in an Information Society* (Washington, D.C.: Government Printing Office, 1977), p. 21.

conviction that information privacy is an essential component of humanity is found in the literature and rhetoric of every country that has addressed this issue. In English we use the word "privacy." The Germans apply the related notion of *Die Privatsphäre*—literally a private sphere, a boundary between individual autonomy and social life.[40] The French frame the problem as *la protection de la vie privée* with very direct references to the connection between *l'informatique* (information technology) and les *libertés* (human freedoms).[41] The Swedes use the word *integritet*, which embodies the connotation that individuals have the right to be judged according to a complete profile of their personalities.[42]

Despite these linguistic differences, it is difficult to distinguish any differences in objectives on this humanistic level. Flaherty systematically presents the goals of data protection in each of his country case studies; these goals are striking for their common reliance on basic Anglo-American conceptions of liberty. For instance, Jan Freese, the central figure in the Swedish data protection movement, preferred to define privacy in the language of Warren and Brandeis as the "right to be left alone."[43] Hans Peter Bull, a similarly influential figure in West Germany, noted that people "want to continue living as individuals, with all their personal characteristics and attitudes and, if they like, to be left alone." He also emphasized that the German Data Protection Law was not a law to protect data but to protect the citizen.[44]

On this basic humanistic level, it is impossible to distinguish any significant cross-national differences in either definition or emphasis. However the concern is formulated, information technology accentuates the dehumanizing and alienating aspects of modern mass society and information technology. The former deputy secretary general of

40. Spiros Simitis et al., *Kommentar zum Bundesdatenschutzgesetz*, 3d ed. (Baden-Baden: Nomos, 1981), p. 60.

41. The issue was probably first framed in this way in the "Tricot Report," *Informatique et Libertés* (Paris: Documentation Francaise, 1975). This report led to the permanent *Commission Nationale de l'Informatique et des Libertés* (the CNIL), which oversees the French data protection law.

42. Sweden, Commission on Publicity and Secrecy of Official Documents, *Computers and Privacy* (Stockholm: Ministry of Justice, 1972) (English translation of the report *Data och Integritet*).

43. Jan Freese, "The Right to Be Let Alone in Sweden," *Transnational Data Report* 6 (December 1983): 448.

44. Quoted in Flaherty, *Protecting Privacy in Surveillance Societies,* p. 34.

the Organization for Economic Cooperation and Development, Gerard Eldin, put this question to an international conference in 1977: "Might not the machine—or the system to which it gives rise—overwhelm man, standardizing him, pigeonholing him, labelling his every characteristic, and robbing him of that essential element of originality and unpredictability which is his nature?"[45] This question is reminiscent of Jacques Ellul's warning that the relentless pursuit of "la technique" confines man "to the role of a recording device; he will note the effects of techniques upon one another, and register the results."[46]

The very collection of personal information, regardless of how it is used and applied, contributes to the sense of alienation within all postindustrial societies. Information technology adds a new layer to the already impersonal character of bureaucracy. It contributes to an uneasy sense that "someone out there knows something about me." There is nothing particularly rational about concerns for privacy on this level. And most of the expressions of concern are vague and poorly formulated. This approach rests on a strong belief that the limitations placed on the application of information technology should be set by ethical rather than technical standards.[47] Simply because fears may be based on vague aesthetic values rather than on hard reason, however, does not excuse the political system from formulating protective measures. The British privacy expert, Paul Sieghart, summarized this first underlying dimension of the privacy question at a conference in 1976: "The whole issue arises because people have fears about their privacy. Now fears may be irrational—but that doesn't make them go away. Privacy itself is in one sense irrational: it is all about people's feelings. But feelings are *there,* they are facts. And if people's anxieties aren't relieved, they tend to find outlets which are likely to be painful."[48]

45. Quoted in Frank Carmody, "Background to Data Protection in Europe," *Information Privacy* 1 (1978): 25.
46. Jacques Ellul, *The Technological Society* (New York: Vintage Books, 1964), p. 93.
47. This view is expressed most persuasively by Joseph Weizenbaum, *Computer Power and Human Reason* (San Francisco: Freeman, 1976). See also Hubert Dreyfus, *What Computers Can't Do: A Critique of Artificial Intelligence* (New York: Harper and Row, 1972).
48. Paul Sieghart, "Background to the Issue and the Government White Paper," in *Privacy and the Computer*, Proceedings of the Online Conference, London, 23 February, 1976 (Uxbridge, Middlesex: Online, 1976), p. 8.

The Political Dimension

The second concern is that information technology could become a tool of tyranny. From the classical liberal belief in limited government springs a distrust of the effects of power. Information technology enhances the power of government to collect and manipulate vast quantities of information about individual citizens—an intrinsic cause for concern. The control over the collection, use, and communication of personal information by government may have political implications. Through their interests in privacy, citizens may place limits on the power of the state.

This political aspect is likewise apparent in both the scholarly and rhetorical argument in different countries. Britons Michael Stone and Malcolm Warner warned in 1969: "The computer has given bureaucracy the gift of omniscience, if not omnipotence, by putting into its hands the power to *know.* No fact unrecorded, nothing forgotten nor lost, nothing forgiven."[49] In 1986, Campbell and Connor claimed to demonstrate "the inequitable political power that major information databanks grant to an increasingly harsh and authoritarian public administration."[50]

United States Senator Sam Ervin, the architect of the 1974 Privacy Act, saw in 1972 that "officials at every level of our national life who make decisions about people for limited purposes seem possessed by a desire to know the "total man" by gathering every possible bit of information about him."[51] In a similar vein, Arthur Miller proposed a new "Parkinson's Law" of bureaucracy and information: "Technological improvements in information-handling capability have been followed by a tendency to engage in more extensive manipulation and analysis of recorded data. This in turn has motivated the collection of data pertaining to a larger number of variables, which results in more personal information being extracted from individuals."[52] Fear of overpowerful government is deeply ingrained in the American political experience. This fear is reflected in the fragmented and de-

49. M. G. Stone and Malcolm Warner, "Politics, Privacy, and Computers," *The Political Quarterly* 40 (1969): 260.
50. Campbell and Connor, *On the Record*, p. 15.
51. Senator Sam J. Ervin, Jr., "Privacy and Government Investigations," *University of Illinois Law Forum* (1971): 138.
52. Arthur R. Miller, *The Assault on Privacy: Computers, Data Banks, and Dossiers* (Ann Arbor: University of Michigan Press, 1971), p. 21.

centralized distribution of authority in American government, in the Madisonian tradition of checking the power of "faction," and in the "Lockean liberal consensus."[53] The "rise of the computer state" is regarded as a threat to the liberal values that have such a central place in the American heritage.[54]

In continental Europe, the more direct and immediate experience of totalitarian rule has motivated similar and just as potent fears: "The Western Europeans, recalling the havoc the Gestapo wrought with manila folders, are horrified at the persecution that could be perpetrated with the aid of computers."[55] A 1984 conference of data protection specialists concluded that "one of the prime motives for the creation of data protection laws in continental Europe is the prevention of the recurrence of experiences in the 1930s and 1940s with Nazi and fascist regimes."[56] It is significant that liberal assumptions normally associated with the Anglo-American tradition should find their way with such regularity into the writings of continental European scholars.

This pervasive belief in information privacy as a bulwark against tyranny is reflected in the universally potent meaning of George Orwell's *1984*. The actual year was accompanied by a revival of interest in privacy issues, a plethora of commentary (some very alarmist), and a number of conferences on the dangers of information technology. Writings in many cultures and languages contain "Big Brother" symbolism and other Orwellian imagery.[57] Alexander Solzhenitsyn's chilling portrayal in *Cancer Ward* is also cited with regularity:

> As every man goes through life he fills in a number of forms for the record, each containing a number of questions. A man's answer to one question on one form becomes a little thread, permanently connecting him to the local center of personnel records administra-

53. Louis Hartz, *The Liberal Tradition in America* (New York: Random House, 1983).

54. David Burnham, *The Rise of the Computer State* (New York: Random House, 1983).

55. Oswald H. Ganley and Gladys D. Ganley, *To Inform or to Control? The New Communications Networks* (New York: McGraw-Hill, 1982), p. 87.

56. David H. Flaherty, *Nineteen Eighty-Four and After*. Final Report of the Bellagio Conference on Current and Future Problems of Data Protection (London, Ontario: University of Western Ontario, Privacy Project, 1984), p. 5.

57. See, for example, Klaus Haefner, *Der Grosse Bruder: Chancen und Gefahren für eine Informierte Gesellschaft* (Düsseldorf: Econ-verlag, 1980); Antony A. Thompson, *Big Brother in Britain Today* (London: Michael Joseph, 1970); Ian Will, *The Big Brother Society* (London: Harrap, 1983).

tion. There are thus hundreds of little threads radiating from every man, millions of threads in all. . . . They are not visible, they are not material, but every man is constantly aware of their existence. The point is that a so-called completely clean record was almost unattainable, an ideal, like absolute truth. Something negative or suspicious can always be noted down against any man alive. Everyone is guilty of something or has something to conceal. All one has to do is to look hard enough to find out what it is. Each man, permanently aware of his own invisible threads, naturally develops a respect for the people who manipulate the threads . . . and for these people's authority.[58]

Orwell and Solzhenitsyn speak to that basic concern for human rights that is the foundation of liberal democratic theory. The political community is defined not in holistic but in atomistic terms—the state is nothing more than the individuals that comprise it. It has no superior role or organic quality. Government is constituted by citizens and should remain accountable to them, from the conduct of the most significant public policy down to the management of the most insignificant piece of personal information.

The right to information privacy is therefore rooted in Lockean liberalism: inalienable human rights, limited government, the rule of law, and a separation between the realms of state and civil society. The most articulate modern proponent of the view that privacy is a prerequisite for liberal democracy is Alan Westin: "A balance that ensures strong citadels of individual and group privacy and limits both disclosure and surveillance is a prerequisite for liberal democratic societies." But as Westin shows, privacy performs several functions within this general role: it prevents the total politicizing of life; it bolsters religious diversity and tolerance; it protects the membership of voluntary associations; it fosters free scholarly investigation; it protects the electoral process by forbidding government inquiries into a citizen's voting record; it establishes barriers against compulsory self-incrimination and intrusive police practices; and it protects the activities of the press and other institutions which operate to keep government accountable.[59]

58. Alexander Solzhenitsyn, *Cancer Ward* (New York: Farrar, Straus and Giroux, 1969), p. 192.
59. Westin, *Privacy and Freedom*, p. 24–25.

Naturally, privacy cannot be an absolute right as it is bound by correlative rights and duties to the community. Hence "the constant search in democracies must be for the proper boundary line in each specific situation and for an over-all equilibrium that serves to strengthen democratic institutions and processes."[60] In John Stuart Mill's words, there are certain "self-regarding" activities of private concern, contrasted with "other-regarding" activities susceptible to community interest and regulation. The application of computer technology has restricted the individual activities that can properly be defined as "self-regarding." Therefore, the boundary between the private and the public realms is shifted with implications for all the private concerns that Westin lists as essential defenses against absolute government.

It is important to keep in mind, however, that Locke, Mill, and Westin represent just one particular version of democratic theory, in both a normative and an empirical sense. It is essentially a *pluralistic* view. Privacy bolsters the boundaries between competing, countervailing, overlapping centers of power. It builds or supports barriers both between the individual and the state *and* within the contours of civil society.[61] Yet many would contend that this view represents just one view of democracy, one that is neither valid nor indeed desirable in contemporary postindustrial conditions. Equally important democratic values are cooperation, community consciousness and active participation, values that are not promoted by bolstering the "right to be let alone." One could even argue that some of the most creative civilizations in human history (the cultures of Greece, Renaissance Italy, Elizabethan England) flourished despite or maybe *because of* the lack of individual privacy.

Information privacy is, therefore, a precondition not of democracy per se but of a particular type of democracy, one that is individualistic, noncommunitarian, possessive, perhaps market-oriented. Privacy, like other values, is viewed as a scarce resource for which individuals and groups will compete and which may be used in mutually exclusive or conflicting ways. But an equally strong tradition states that the central test of democracy is *participation*, not the existence of constitutional

60. Ibid., p. 25
61. Edward Shils viewed privacy in these pluralistic terms as bolstering the separation *between* groups. See *The Torment of Secrecy* (Glencoe, Ill.: Free Press, 1956), pp. 154–60.

rules protecting individual rights or the degree of competition be-tween centers of power.[62] The intellectual antecedents of the theory of information privacy are, therefore, Locke and Madison rather than Rousseau.

The Instrumental Dimension

The above two functions of personal data protection are substantive social values. Promoting individual autonomy and democratic ac-countability is an end in itself and, for some people, sufficient justifi-cation for regulating the collection, storage, processing, and dis-semination of personal data. Yet data protection, or information privacy, can also serve as a means to advance other rights and inter-ests. The author of one of the first studies from the OECD argues that "privacy has a social value in itself; it can be regarded as a human right. Data confidentiality . . . is a means to an end. It has no intrinsic value."[63] Applying economic methods of analysis, Richard Posner agrees that data protection can best be regarded as an intermediate economic good used to acquire other utilities.[64]

The instrumental purpose of data protection corresponds to Rule's notion of "strategic privacy" as "the restriction of personal informa-tion as a means to some other end."[65] Sieghart phrases the concern in terms of ensuring that the "right" people use the "right" data for the "right" purposes: "The 'right' data will be those which are accurate, complete, relevant and timely; the 'right' purposes will be those to which the data subject expressly or impliedly agreed, or which are sanctioned by law; the 'right' people will be those who need to use the data for those purposes alone."[66] When any one of these conditions is absent, critical rights, interests, and services may be jeopardized.

Sieghart is an English data protection expert. But this instrumental purpose has been emphasized by commentators from many countries.

---

62. For a clear discussion of these two traditions within democratic theory, see Carole Pateman, *Participation and Democratic Theory* (Cambridge: Cambridge University Press, 1970).

63. Uwe Thomas, *Computerized Data Banks in Public Administration*, OECD Informatics Studies No. 1 (Paris: OECD, 1971), p. 62.

64. Richard A. Posner, "An Economic Theory of Privacy," in *Philosophical Dimensions of Privacy*, ed. Schoeman, pp. 333–45.

65. Rule et al., *The Politics of Privacy*, p. 22.

66. Sieghart, *Privacy and Computers*, p. 76.

Jane Yurow, a former American government official, observes two kinds of fear behind the pressure for data protection laws. The second is that computers might promote tyranny. The first is that "computerization might expose individuals' private lives to the view of impersonal institutions which could use the information to make adverse economic and social decisions about individuals."[67] The German data protection legislation begins by declaring that "the purpose of data protection is to ensure against the misuse of personal data during storage, communication, modification and erasure (data processing) and *thereby* prevent harm to any personal interest that warrants protection."[68] The individual has an interest in ensuring that his or her information is accurate, relevant, and timely; that it is being utilized by those with authorization; and that it is not communicated beyond those who "need to know." Frits Hondius, a central official within the Council of Europe, confirms that "public anxiety about data processing originated in the citizen's exclusion from the handling of data about himself by others who may make decisions affecting his rights and interests in areas such as salary, insurance, health, and credit, on the basis of that information."[69]

This aspect of the problem embodies a number of assumptions that require explicit articulation. First, this concern stems not so much from the collection of personal data as from its use and dissemination. The harm results not from the information but from the *context* of that information. Thus, attempts to define or even rank order those data that are potentially most harmful are inherently misguided.[70] This view is also Sieghart's:

> There are no harmless data. Or to put it another way, it is not the data that are harmless, it is what people do with them that is the problem

67. Jane H. Yurow, "National Perspectives on Data Protection," *Transnational Data Report* 6 (1983): 338.

68. *Bundesdatenschutzgesetz* (Federal Data Protection Act) Sec. 1 (1) (italics mine). English translations of foreign data protection legislation are taken from Ulrich Dammann, Otto Mallmann, and Spiros Simitis, *Data Protection Legislation: An International Documentation* (Frankfurt am Main: Metzner, 1977).

69. Frits W. Hondius, "Data Law in Europe," *Stanford Journal of International Law* 16 (1980): 95.

70. Jon Bing, the Norwegian data protection expert, tried to rank order data by sensitivity in "Classification of Personal Information with Respect to the Sensitivity Aspect," in *Databanks and Society*, The First International Symposium on Databanks and Society (Oslo: Tromso, 1972).

. . . . My name in the London telephone directory or the electoral roll is perfectly harmless, but my name in a list of potential subversives or bad credit risks is capable of doing me harm. There are no harmless data, there are no harmful data. A datum is a datum—it is that which is given. It is what data you string together and what you do with them . . . which may or may not do harm.[71]

In this view, the government can collect as much data as it likes provided there are adequate procedural safeguards to ensure that the right people use the right data for the right purposes.

The second implication relates to the computer. Many would argue that by increasing information collection and storage and by facilitating its transmittal to multiple remote locations, computers increase the chances that the "wrong" data will be used or that the "wrong" people will use it or that it will be used for the "wrong" purposes. In the same way that more cars mean more accidents, more computers mean more information transactions. More transactions will create more mistakes (both accidental and deliberate). The problem is analogous to a familiar children's party game. All the participants sit in a circle, and one whispers a sentence to his or her neighbor. The sentence is communicated in like manner around the entire circle; when it returns to its starting point, it usually bears little or no resemblance to its original form. Such dangers were mitigated in the past by the sheer inefficiency of information storage, retrieval, and transfer. The filing cabinet and manila folder reduced the number of people in the circle and limited the potential transactions. The speed, capacity, and flexibility of the modern computer, which can carry out millions of operations a second and store in one small place enormous amounts of data that are instantly retrievable by people in multiple remote locations, increases the circle and multiplies the potential dangers.

The privacy literature is liberally sprinkled with horror stories about inaccurate, incomplete, irrelevant, or derogatory information maintained in files; about personal information kept far longer than is necessary; about access by unauthorized people and organizations; about data in the files of private and public bodies not authorized to receive them; about data being used out of context, for purposes other

---

71. Paul Sieghart, "Information Privacy and the Data Protection Bill," in *Data Protection: Perspectives on Information Privacy*, ed. Colin Bourn and John Benyon (Leicester: University of Leicester, Continuing Education Unit, 1984).

than those for which they were collected; and about deliberate intrusion and misuse of data files by unauthorized and authorized personnel.[72] Two such stories, one from the United States, the other from Britain, will suffice to highlight these kinds of problems.

The first story concerns one Leonard Smith, a retired postal inspector from Los Angeles. One night in May 1977, he was arrested outside his home on charges of public drunkenness. He pleaded not guilty, and the judge ordered his release. But he was not let go for another six days. The computerized wants and warrants system had revealed another Leonard Smith, one who was wanted for violating his probation twenty-seven years earlier. Under this system, the authorities are allowed to detain someone if about 60 percent of the computerized identifiers match those of the suspect. Leonard Smith was one of thousands of Los Angeles citizens mistakenly taken into custody each year because of inaccurate, incomplete, or obsolete information contained in the wants and warrants system.[73]

Campbell and Connor report the chilling story of Jan Martin, who worked for an independent film company that had been asked to make public relations films by Taylor Woodrow, the builders. Ms. Martin was refused employment on the grounds that she was connected to the Baader-Meinhof gang and was, therefore, a "security risk." Fortunately, Martin's father was a former senior Scotland Yard official and was able to trace the origins of this report. She and her husband had apparently been traveling in the Netherlands soon after a Baader-Meinhof attack. Her husband was recognized as having a keen resemblance to one of the leaders of Baader-Meinhof whose photograph was being circulated at that time. Someone spotted that likeness, and took Martin's car registration number; the report was passed back to Scotland Yard and MI5. This report was never checked, but it remained on her police file against her name and

---

72. The following are the most important English-language works: Westin, *Privacy and Freedom*; Malcolm Warner and Michael Stone, *The Data Bank Society: Organizations, Computers, and Social Freedom* (London: Allen and Unwin, 1970); Miller, *The Assault on Privacy*; James B. Rule, *Private Lives and Public Surveillance: Social Control in the Computer Age* (New York: Schocken Books, 1974); Donald Madgwick and Tony Smythe, *The Invasion of Privacy* (London: Pitman, 1974); Aryeh Neier, *Dossier: The Secret Files They Keep on You* (New York: Stein and Day, 1975). The impact of these and other works is discussed more fully in Chapter 2.

73. Burnham, *The Rise of the Computer State*, p. 152.

national insurance number, the number used for employment purposes.[74]

These two cases are from the area of law enforcement. But many other persuasive illustrations exist on how the computerization of personal data can lead to the denial of civil liberties, to discrimination in employment, to the lowering of a person's esteem in the eyes of the community, and to unjustly adverse decisions regarding eligibility for the whole range of governmental services. This argument assumes that if you protect the data on which such decisions are made, you also protect the integrity, fairness, and effectiveness of the decision-making process.

Public Attitudes toward Privacy

These three aspects of the problem may be analytically distinct, but they are closely interrelated in political rhetoric, scholarly discourse, and public consciousness. Having investigated the rhetoric and the scholarship, we will now examine the public concern. There is persuasive poll evidence that the mass publics of all four states demonstrate strong, and possibly growing, concern on all three dimensions of the data protection issue. Survey research on privacy, however, is extremely difficult to interpret given the subjective nature of the issue and the enormous conceptual complications discussed earlier. Conclusions and comparisons should, therefore, be drawn with care.

There has been very little systematic cross-national polling—asking equivalent questions of equivalent samples—from which to compare the responses of different populations. One recent exception was a Gallup poll conducted in 1984 on whether or not Orwell's grim vision had been realized. When confronted with the statement, "there is no real privacy because the government can learn anything it wants about you," 47 percent of the Americans, 68 percent of the Canadians and 59 percent of the Britons responded that such a condition is "already happening."[75] Interestingly, only 18 percent of the German respondents agreed with the statement. For more reliable assessments, how-

---

74. Campbell and Connor, *On the Record*, p. 286.
75. Gallup, *Six-Nation Survey on Orwell's "1984"* (Princeton, N.J.: Gallup, 1984).

ever, we must abandon any hope of being able to draw accurate cross-national comparisons and concentrate on the more sensitive studies conducted within each of our four countries.

The American evidence, not surprisingly, is the most comprehensive and allows us to track responses over time. In 1970 the public concern about privacy on an abstract humanistic level was not that great. A poll conducted by Louis Harris and Associates asked: "Do you ever tend to feel that sometimes your sense of privacy is being invaded or not—that people are trying to find out things about you that are not any of their business?" Thirty-four percent said yes, 62 percent said no, and 4 percent were not sure.[76] A year later, a study of public opinion toward computers sponsored by the American Federation of Information Processing Societies (AFIPS) and *Time* magazine contained this question: "Nowadays, some organizations keep information about millions of people. How do you feel about this—are you very concerned, fairly concerned, or not too concerned at all?" Sixty-two percent replied that they were either very or fairly concerned.[77] These answers perhaps indicate that people are more worried when the organizational and technological context is given.

It is also clear that political intrusiveness strikes a more responsive chord with the American public than does anything else. A mail survey of constituent opinions in 1971 asked: "Do you think there has been more of a tendency recently for the government to infringe unnecessarily upon the average American's privacy than there was ten years ago?" Sixty-seven percent said yes.[78] While these, and other, results provide evidence of early concern, there is little support for the view that it was any more than a "solid minority concern." Certainly, when ranked against other issues, privacy was noted as significantly less important than more materialistic problems.[79]

The later evidence, however, is unambiguous. After Watergate, after numerous scandals, and after the computer had become an everyday sight, privacy becomes, as the Office of Technology Assessment (OTA) concludes, "a significant and enduring value held by the American

76. Cited in Alan F. Westin and Michael A. Baker, *Databanks in a Free Society: Computers, Record-Keeping, and Privacy* (New York: Quadrangle Books, 1972), p. 466.
77. Ibid.
78. Ibid., p. 468.
79. Ibid., p. 467.

public."[80] OTA also finds that general concern over privacy has increased over the last decade. In different surveys by Louis Harris and Associates, citizens were asked: "Do you feel that the present uses of computers are an actual threat to personal privacy in this country, or not?" In 1974, the number of respondents answering in the affirmative was 38 percent, and in 1977, it was 41 percent. This figure rose to 54 percent in 1978 and 51 percent in 1983. On a general question about threats to personal privacy, 47 percent in January 1978 stated that they were either very concerned or somewhat concerned about such threats. The comparable figure in December 1978 was 64 percent and in 1983, 77 percent.[81]

The Harris poll conducted in 1983 demonstrated that a significant majority of American citizens believed that personal files were kept without their knowledge, that they did not trust either private or public organizations to use that information fairly and properly, and that new federal laws were required to provide adequate safeguards. The overall picture is graphically presented by the responses to a question about the imminence of a "1984" type society: six percent of the public said we are already there, 23 percent said we were very close and 40 percent somewhat close.[82] The Harris organization found similar levels of concern in 1990. In particular, it found a growing reluctance on the part of Americans to reveal personal information; some 42 percent have refused to give personal information to a business or a company because they thought it was either too personal or not needed. By contrast, only 14 percent have refused information to a government agency for the same reasons. Nevertheless, nearly four Americans in five expressed general concern about privacy threats and would add privacy to "life, liberty, and the pursuit of happiness" if the Declaration of Independence were rewritten today.[83]

The British evidence is less comprehensive but equally compelling. The earliest major survey of attitudes toward privacy was that con-

---

80. OTA, *Federal Government Information Technology*, p. 26.

81. Louis Harris and Associates, *The Dimensions of Privacy: A National Opinion Research Survey of Attitudes toward Privacy* (Stevens Point, Wis.: Sentry Insurance, 1979), and *The Road after 1984: The Impact of Technology on Society* (New Haven, Conn.: Southern New England Telephone, 1984). The results are summarized in OTA, *Federal Government Information Technology*, pp. 26–29.

82. Harris, *The Road after 1984*, p. 12.

83. "American Consumers' Privacy in the Information Age," *Transnational Data and Communications Report* 13 (August–September 1990).

ducted by the first official study committee under the chairmanship of Kenneth Younger; it also presents evidence of anxiety about a range of privacy invasion, a new issue on the British agenda at that time. In comparison with other issues, the committee found that it was ranked lower than economic issues, such as inflation and unemployment. It was considered the most important of seven social or civil rights issues. Thirty-eight percent viewed the privacy issue as quite important, 29 percent said it was very important, and 16 percent called it extremely important.[84] Moreover, 58 percent of those interviewed agreed that people had *less* privacy than they used to have. Forty-four percent felt able to give an example of an invasion of privacy that they had personally experienced within the last year. These instances were of an extraordinarily diverse nature, from answering unnecessary questions on government forms to being pestered by Jehovah's Witnesses. When questioned specifically about government databanks, however, the possibility of recording personal details on a large central computer with information available to anyone who asked for it produced the strongest reaction. Eighty-seven percent said that this would be an invasion of privacy, 71 percent said that they would be very annoyed or upset, and 85 percent thought that such databanks should be prohibited by law.[85] This aggregation of disparate evidence prompted the Younger committee to conclude that "privacy is undoubtedly of consequence to many, and possibly most, people."[86]

In 1987, the Data Protection Registrar's office commissioned the most comprehensive survey of opinions on privacy ever conducted in Britain. There is evidence that the issue was more salient than in 1972, as 73 percent classified it as very important, a rate almost as high as those for "improving standards of education" and "unemployment." Sixty-four percent were either very concerned or quite concerned about personal information kept by organizations. The responses revealed that financial information (savings, earnings, and credit ratings) was generally the type about which people felt most sensitive. The survey revealed a consistently high level of support for a range of privacy rights and for corresponding legislative guarantees.[87] Follow-

84. Great Britain, Home Office, *Report of the Committee on Privacy*, Cmnd. 5012 (The Younger Committee) (London: HMSO, 1972), pp. 230–31.
85. Ibid., p. 239.
86. Ibid., p. 32
87. Data Protection Registrar, *Third Report* (London: HMSO, 1987), pp. 40–45.

up surveys demonstrated a maintenance of these high levels of concern.[88]

An analysis of public opinion in 1983 for a symposium of the Hessian government in Wiesbaden provides important and similar evidence of the anxieties in West Germany. Eighty-one percent felt that the protection of personal information through a data protection law was either important or very important. Interestingly, this compares with a response rate of 83 percent to the same question asked in 1975.[89] There is, however, evidence of an increase in concern: in 1976, 49 percent of the respondents agreed with the statement that the computer gives the state too much power and too much potential for control. The equivalent responses in 1980 and 1983 were 55 percent and 60 percent respectively.[90] The political dimension of the issue also seems to emerge from the German responses. In 1975, 36 percent felt that the state and its officials should know as little as possible about the private lives of individual citizens. This figure rose to 65 percent in 1984.[91] Seventy-six percent said the same about the private sector in 1984. An interesting breakdown of these aggregate statistics reveals that the people who say that data protection is very important to them are more likely to be younger (28 to 44 years old) rather than older, and better educated.[92] Data protection is one of those postmaterialist issues, of which the most newsworthy examples are in the environmental sector as is reflected in the astounding rise of Die Grünen (the "Green Party") in recent years.

The rise in public concern in Germany has also been caused by the enormous controversies surrounding the population censuses of 1983 and 1987. A 1983 poll indicated that 52 percent of the population were dissatisfied with the census questions and mistrusted how answers to these questions would be used.[93] The 1983 census form was declared unconstitutional by the Constitutional Court (*Bundesverfassungsgericht*) on the grounds that it violated a right to "informa-

88. Data Protection Registrar, *Fifth Report* (London: HMSO, 1989), p. 21, and *Sixth Report* (London: HMSO, 1990), p. 25.
89. Horst Becker, "Bürger in der Modernen Informationsgesellschaft," in *Informationsgesellschaft oder Uberwachungstaat*, Symposium of the Hessian government, 3–5 September 1984 (Wiesbaden: Hessendienst, 1984), p. 411.
90. Ibid., p. 414.
91. Ibid., p. 413.
92. Ibid., p. 416.
93. Flaherty, *Protecting Privacy in Surveillance Societies*, p. 79.

tional self-determination." When the census was finally conducted in 1987, there was a considerable degree of noncompliance. These controversies undoubtedly contributed to the growing salience of data protection in Germany. According to a 1989 poll, about two-thirds of the German public believed that the state knew too much about its citizens' private affairs.[94]

Finally, the Swedish Central Bureau of Statistics also took Orwell seriously and conducted a survey in 1984. To the statement that "authorities keep a lot of unnecessary information in their data files," 51 percent of Swedes polled agreed totally. Privacy issues also seem more noticeable in Sweden than in other countries. In 1976, the three highest ranked issues were reducing unemployment, stopping inflation, and protecting the privacy of the people. In 1984, protecting the environment was listed second, relegating the privacy problem to fourth. The Swedish concern, however, seems more instrumental; they are concerned with use and disclosure rather than collection. For instance, 59 percent do not feel threatened by taking part in governmental surveys. Eighty to 90 percent found it quite in order for governmental authorities to keep personal files. On the other hand, 45 percent felt frightened of the potential for authorities to control citizens with the help of computerized data files.[95]

In summary, these disparate studies seem to show clear evidence that privacy issues generally, and data protection more specifically, have been salient questions in each of our four sample states. Gradual exposure to and realization of the capabilities of computers has also meant an increase in the recognition of the potential dangers, especially in West Germany and the United States. But there is evidence of concern over all three aspects of the issue: most citizens seem to have a keen awareness of privacy as a key ingredient of human dignity; most fear the political implications; most have reservations about the use and disclosure of personal information held in computers.

It is undoubtedly very tempting to infer from these imperfect surveys that concerns for privacy are related to the more profound at-

94. "Einwag impressed by privacy awareness," *Transnational Data and Communications Report* 12 (March 1989).
95. Sweden, Data Inspection Board, "Public Attitudes to Data-Processing in the Information Society," English Summary of the Report from the Swedish Central Bureau of Statistics (Stockholm: Datainspektionen, January 1985).

tributes of political culture. We might postulate a direct relationship between wider sets of normative beliefs and orientations toward political authority and the kinds of concerns expressed in these various surveys. These results not only show that privacy is a significant value for most citizens but they also demonstrate deep-seated fears of the state and distrust in the ability of public officials to utilize personal information with care and propriety. As "trust in government" has been one of the central variables for those who try to compare political cultures, we might expect fears to be far greater in those societies in which citizens have typically displayed a less "deferential" or "subject" orientation toward public officials and the institutions in which these officials operate.[96]

The problems of defining generic differences in national political cultures and holding these as significant explanations for cross-national differences in attitudes, behavior, and public policy have long been recognized.[97] In this case, at least from the data we have so far, it is impossible to identify any clear and systematic cross-national differences. Everywhere, and among all classes, ages, genders, and races, we see a strong, if poorly articulated, concern about how information technology may be, and has been, used by private and, especially, public organizations. The sources of those concerns may be rooted in different historical experiences. But in their nature and extent, the public concern is more striking for its cross-national similarities rather than for its differences.

The Constants

The aim of this chapter has been to establish the context for the resolution of this problem. The issue has arisen because of the convergence of two major characteristics of the postindustrial state—bureaucratization and information technology. With only minor variations in timing and emphasis, these processes have been transnational. As computers were developed, governments of different political

96. Germany and Britain are two such societies; see the systematic but dated evidence in Gabriel A. Almond and Sidney Verba, *The Civic Culture* (Boston: Little Brown, 1965).
97. Gabriel A. Almond and Sidney Verba, eds., *The Civic Culture Revisited* (Boston: Little, Brown, 1980).

and ideological complexions realized their advantages: personal data could be used and disclosed for a variety of administrative, statistical, and investigative purposes.

The problem of data protection or information privacy thus arose. It is a complex and multifaceted issue, one riddled with contradictions, and the conceptual confusion has not yet been settled. There are at least three interrelated goals of data protection: to protect a sense of privacy, dignity, and anonymity from the increasingly intrusive organization; to enhance governmental accountability; and to improve the integrity and efficiency of administrative decision making. These values may or may not be promoted by other policies designed to promote privacy, such as controls over wiretapping and other forms of surveillance. But the wider dimensions of privacy are really not our concern. The collection, manipulation, and dissemination of personal information produces the problem, especially when information technology is utilized, and at least sets some boundaries to the issue.

Moreover, evidence from political rhetoric, scholarly analysis, and survey research suggests that there are no major differences in the way the problem was conceived or defined in each country, even though it is tempting to think that elite and mass attitudes toward privacy might provide some intriguing insights into different national cultures. Despite linguistic variations, and although the problem is multifaceted, the issue raised fears everywhere of a loss of human dignity, of an overpowerful state, and of the misuse and abuse of personal information. The striking features are the common perceptions of the problem and the lack of influence on these by distinctively national preoccupations and attitudes. With subtle variations, which will be discussed in due course, the context and definition of the problem have been broadly the same. There existed a common technological and bureaucratic context, common fears, a common time frame, a common problem. These are our "constants." Given these similarities, was there a common response?

2

The Politics of Data Protection

The mere existence of a policy problem, even a widely recognized one, is not enough to make it a political issue. Studies of agenda setting have made a distinction between a systemic or social agenda consisting of all issues commonly perceived to merit political attention, and an institutional or governmental agenda comprising those specific items that captivate the active and serious attention of authoritative decision makers. How issues move from one agenda to the other, how they become "issues whose time has come," is a fascinating question for political scientists.[1]

The purpose of this chapter is to demonstrate how data protection moved from an abstract intellectual concern to a contentious political issue. There were some common catalysts that had a similar impact in different states. I will begin with a discussion of these factors and then move to a broader treatment of the international diffusion of data protection policy among all countries that have so far legislated. This general picture is provided as a backdrop for the more intensive discussion of the development of data protection law in Sweden, the United States, West Germany, and the United Kingdom.

1. Roger W. Cobb and Charles D. Elder, *Participation in American Politics: The Dynamics of Agenda-Building* (Boston: Allyn and Bacon, 1972); John W. Kingdon, *Agendas, Alternatives, and Public Policies* (Boston: Little, Brown, 1984).

Common Catalysts for Political Action

The policy problem as discussed in Chapter 1 may be regarded as somewhat esoteric and not likely to capture the imagination of either politicians or their constituents. As it did with other issues, a confluence of various factors in the late 1960s made the problems more tangible and immediate and pushed data protection from the systemic to the institutional agenda. Four factors are responsible: specific plans for the centralization of population data in governmental agencies; the accompanying proposals for personal identification numbers; the occurrence of decennial censuses in many countries around 1970; and a spate of alarmist publications.

Plans for Centralized Databanks

No other development raised the specter of "1984" more dramatically than the proposals, in several countries, for the introduction of centralized and computerized population databanks. As never before, computers enabled the linkage of miscellaneous personal information held in disparate locations. Bureaucrats in several countries saw the advantages of assembling under one roof a diversity of personal data within the various agencies of national governments.

One of the first major proposals of this sort was put forward in the United States. In 1966 the Social Science Research Council submitted a proposal to the Bureau of the Budget to establish a "Federal Data Center . . . with the authority to obtain computer tapes and other machine readable data produced by all federal agencies." It was to have "the function of providing data and service facilities so that within the proper safeguards concerning the disclosure of information both Federal agencies and users outside of the government would have access to basic data."[2] The plan, which would have linked census data with that held by the Internal Revenue Service, the Social Security Administration, and other agencies, would have provided a store of valuable information for government planners and private researchers

---

2. U.S. House of Representatives, *The Computer and the Invasion of Privacy*, Hearings before the Special Subcommittee on Invasion of Privacy of the Committee on Government Operations, House of Representatives, 89th Cong., 2d sess. (Washington, D.C.: Government Printing Office, 1966), p. 195.

alike. It is probable that the planned network was to be used only for aggregate statistical analysis rather than for administrative decision making about identifiable individuals. When subjected to congressional scrutiny, however, the plan floundered amid a spate of hostile publicity. The Federal Data Center idea established an atmosphere of suspicion that permeated the American debate and sent alarm bells ringing in other countries too.[3] Technological advances in the United States were generally considered precursors to what could happen elsewhere.

The Swedes were also pioneers in the application of automatic data processing to governmental agencies. Plans for the development of databanks for population registration, vehicle registration, land records, police files, social services, and employment were underway as early as 1963. Much of this data was and is under the control of the Central Bureau of Statistics (*Statistiska Centralbyran* [SCB]). A great deal of the centralization of statistical activities for the Swedish government occurred during the 1960s with the substantial growth of the SCB.

It was the existence of a Register of the Total Population, however, facilitated by the highly developed system of personal identification numbers, that stirred the attention of reformers. It began in 1968 with a listing of 8 million individuals from county and parish population data. A Central Register of Taxpayers, containing data on 6.5 million persons, was also established from local sources.[4] All these data were collected for statistical purposes, and there is no evidence that they have been released in anything other than anonymous form. Nevertheless, as in the United States, the accumulation of this volume of information in a centralized repository aroused instinctive fears about the potential for surveillance and social control. In response, the Riksdag suspended the development of the Population Register in April 1972, pending the outcome of data protection legislation.

The collection of statistics in Britain has traditionally been less centralized than in Sweden. But there have been exceptions, most notably the Driver and Vehicle Licensing Center. Since 1973 all driver

3. See Warner and Stone, *The Data Bank Society*, p. 83, and Hans Peter Bull, *Datenschutz oder die Angst vor dem Computer* (Munich: Piper, 1984), p. 73, for the British and German reactions.
4. David H. Flaherty, *Privacy and Government Data Banks: An International Perspective* (London: Mansell, 1979), pp. 105–6.

and vehicle licensing has been coordinated from a central databank in South Wales, which now holds about 33 million records of drivers and issues about 900,000 new, amended, or renewed licenses each month. The previous system was decentralized, operating from some 183 offices throughout England and Wales. The centralization of records evoked considerable concern about the likelihood of abuses, the virtually unregulated access by law enforcement authorities, and the specter of computers making decisions and controlling lives. One Member of Parliament in 1968 could "picture the stage being reached when a button was pressed and if the computer gave the 'thumbs down' sign, he would never get a license."[5]

Many of the first applications directly affecting citizen records occurred at the state and local levels of government. In West Germany, where the data protection issue must always be seen in the context of a federal governmental structure, the first concerns were expressed at the *Land* (state) level. By the early 1970s, every Land had set up its own government data center for the day-to-day administration of the state, particularly for purposes of regional and urban planning. The state of Hesse, for instance, had established its own government databank (under the Hessenplan) by the late 1960s. In the course of developing this plan, the privacy implications were raised and discussed, leading to the world's first data protection law in 1970. In a similar vein, Bavaria had far-sighted goals to convert the large computer systems installed for the Munich Olympic Games for the use of the Bavarian Land Information System.

Similar developments were also taking place at the federal level. In 1968 an office was established to coordinate the acquisition and application of automatic data processing. The office was charged with integrating hardware and software acquisition to facilitate the networking of federal, *Länder*, and municipal governments.[6] At around the same time the *Bundeskriminalamt* (federal criminal office) began to establish an integrated information system of criminal justice data across Germany.[7]

---

5. Warner and Stone, *The Data Bank Society*, p. 105, and NCCL, *Privacy: The Information Gatherers* (London: NCCL, 1977).

6. Werner Liedtke, *Das Bundesdatenschutzgesetz: Eine Fallstudie zum Gesetzgebungsprozess* (Düsseldorf: Mannhold, 1980), p. 96.

7. Ibid., p. 102.

The above examples are those that motivated particular press and public attention in their respective countries. It is somewhat ironic that protest tended to focus on the collection of information for statistical rather than for administrative and investigative purposes. But all over Europe and North America, governments had begun planning their organizations and programs with automatic data processing in mind. The advantages of computers for planning, coordinative, analytical, budgetary, and management purposes were widely recognized and pursued with enthusiasm, even though some plans were, according to Frits Hondius, "over-ambitious and gave an exaggerated idea of the present state of the art."[8] These plans also inspired fears about the expanded power of central government vis-à-vis the legislature, the local administration, the private sector, and, most especially, the citizen.[9]

Personal Identification Numbers

Closely related to long-term plans for automatic data processing in government were proposals to introduce, or to develop more fully, personal identification numbers for every citizen. Automated information technology requires a personal numerical code for both identification and authentication. Many administrators and information systems analysts argued that efficiency in the management of all governmental services could be improved if such a code was universal—if it applied to everyone and could be used for all government purposes. The universal Personal Identification Number (PIN), a unique numerical code for each individual, would facilitate communication, linkage with other record-keeping systems, efficiency, and accuracy.

In some continental European countries, clergy had conducted population registration for centuries. In Sweden, for instance, primary population registration occurred at the parish level and provided the basis for a more systematic designation in 1947 of a ten-digit identity number, which incorporates information on gender and date of birth. These data are then fed to county offices where they are computerized

8. Frits W. Hondius, *Emerging Data Protection in Europe*, (Amsterdam: North Holland, 1975), p. 5.
9. Perhaps the most controversial scheme was presented in France. The publication of the government's plans in 1974 for a national data bank entitled "Safari" triggered a public outcry and marked the beginning of a data protection movement. See Philippe Boucher, "Safari, ou la chasse aux Français," *Le Monde*, 21 March 1974.

and sent to other regional and national authorities. The introduction of computers therefore proceeded with a system of universal identifiers already in place. The identity number is now used for a wider variety of public and private purposes, such as the registration of students and the billing of telephone calls.[10] Although the PIN is especially valuable in a nation with millions of Andersons, Eriksons, and Petersons, it contributed significantly to the recognition of the data protection problem in Sweden.

The PIN was also instrumental in the movement for data protection at the federal level in Germany. The federal Ministry of the Interior had an interest in improving registration for both German and foreign residents by introducing a twelve-digit PIN. The proposal for a Population Registration Bill (*Bundesmeldesgesetz*) was formulated in 1970 with a planned introduction in 1973. The simultaneous introduction of a data protection bill in the legislature was seen by some as a palliative necessary to smooth the enactment of such an extensive system. Whether the two measures were so closely linked is not clear. It was agreed, however, that no system of automatic record keeping using PINs should be introduced without corresponding safeguards.[11] These PINs even became something of an issue in the federal elections of 1976. In the end, the bill on the reform of personal registration was regarded as unconstitutional, and only the data protection law was considered and eventually enacted.

While the question of personal identifiers has a strong emotive appeal and was clearly at the forefront of attention in many countries, it is worth adding that no country has given its citizens *unique* numbers which follow the person from birth to grave and which are generally used for all administrative purposes. The most advanced systems are in countries, such as Sweden, where population registration has deep historical roots and where the process has been uninterrupted by periods of occupation by outside forces. Most countries, however, tend to have personal identifiers that were developed initially for the quite specific purposes of identification or authentication as part of the expansion of the welfare state. Examples include the American Social Security Number, the British National Health Service Number,

---

10. Flaherty, *Protecting Privacy in Surveillance Societies*, p. 98.
11. Bull, *Datenschutz oder die Angst vor dem Computer*, p. 193.

and the Canadian Social Insurance Number. The issue in these countries has been the incremental and surreptitious use of these numbers for ends unrelated to those for which they were created. Where proposals have been introduced for a new universal identifier accompanied by a personal identification card, such as in Germany and Australia,[12] they have been met with strong resistance because of the belief that nonuniformity and nonstandardization, with all the attendant problems for administration, are vital to the maintenance of personal privacy.

Population Censuses

The population census is, and will continue to be, a "flashpoint for public concerns over privacy, since responses are mandatory and cover the entire population."[13] Several censuses scheduled around 1970 served to bring privacy questions to public attention because of the entry of automation into the census procedure and the use of what were regarded as overly intrusive questions. The 1970 census in Sweden, for instance, prompted many complaints to the parliamentary commissioner for the judiciary (the ombudsman) and had a dramatic effect on the intensity of the debate in the press. The application of automatic data processing to a process as comprehensive as the census highlighted the risks and the inadequacy of existing law. Many criticized the specificity of the questions, especially those relating to standard of living. There was also considerable concern that owners of multiple dwellings were to handle the census forms of their tenants.[14] The unequaled conditions of openness in Sweden (under the Freedom of the Press Act, which treats all administrative documents as *public* documents) contributed to the alarm. Attention also focused on the

12. The Australian proposal to introduce a national identification card with a photograph of the holder, a personal identification number, and a central population register was particularly contentious. The proposal passed the House of Representatives but was stopped in the Senate in December 1986 after a major public outcry. An integral part of this legislation was the creation of a Data Protection Authority, which also floundered. The Australians finally passed a Privacy Act in 1988. See *Transnational Data and Communications Report* 10 (March 1987): 20.

13. David H. Flaherty, "Governmental Surveillance and Bureaucratic Accountability: Data Protection Agencies in Western Societies," *Science, Technology, and Human Values* 11 (1986): 17.

14. Flaherty, *Privacy and Government Data Banks*, p. 108.

process of selling census data to private concerns (particularly to direct-mail marketers).

Similarly, the 1971 census in Britain caused the biggest outpouring of public concern about privacy ever witnessed in that country. The results were intended to "make the Doomsday Book look like a slim paperback by comparison."[15] An army of 105,000 enumerators circulated throughout the country in April of that year bringing with them a more complicated and comprehensive form than ever before. The protests and questions, directed to the press, to civil liberties organizations, and to Members of Parliament, sought justification for some of the more intrusive and less relevant components of the census form. Many people objected to answering questions about ethnic origin, professional qualifications, and residents (including tenants) of the household. The 1971 census led to a large (though indeterminate) number of refusals to cooperate, to a few prosecutions, to an official inquiry into census procedures, and to the first widespread public suspicion about privacy invasions in Britain.

Article 1, Section 2 of the U.S. Constitution mandates a decennial census, principally in order to apportion seats in the House of Representatives. Over the decades, however, the census has expanded from a simple exercise in counting the population into an opportunity to gather a variety of information on the social and economic circumstances of Americans. As happened in Europe, the unprecedented extensiveness and intrusiveness of the questions in the census of 1970 raised public disquiet. There were significant congressional investigations into the activities of the Bureau of the Census, which led the bureau to take measures to restore public and legislative confidence.[16]

Similar protests have occurred from time to time in other countries, the most notable being in Germany in 1983 and 1987. The comprehensive and intense nature of the census effort provides an occasion for privacy and civil liberties advocates to focus public attention on the issues concerned. Information collection otherwise is a gradual and cumulative process. The act of filling out a comprehensive census form provides a more direct and immediate glimpse of what government knows, or what it wants to know. It raises, in one concentrated

---

15. Madgwick and Smythe, *The Invasion of Privacy*, p. 88.
16. Flaherty, *Privacy and Government Data Banks*, p. 263.

period, the issues of intrusiveness, fairness of use, and confidentiality. The seemingly irrelevant, clumsy, and invasive nature of some census questions allowed people to ask themselves whether this information was really necessary, how it was going to be used, and who could get hold of it.

The "Computers and Privacy" Literature

The final motivation for political action was the spate of literature published in many countries in the late 1960s and early 1970s that served to draw public, and particularly elite, attention to the privacy problem. Much of this literature was couched in the most foreboding language with a prolific use of "Big Brother" terms and symbols suggestive of the surveillance and intrusiveness of the "1984" society. The impact of such writing should not be exaggerated. But the sheer number of works and the volume of reported "horror stories" clearly helped to push the issue from the systemic to the institutional agenda.

The early works were principally American in origin and focus. Of special early significance in shaping the issue were *The Naked Society* (1964) by Vance Packard and *The Privacy Invaders* (1964) by Myron Brenton.[17] Both journalistic books were designed to arouse public awareness of a variety of new surveillance practices with an emphasis on the intrusion of hidden cameras, private detectives, polygraph examinations, and the like. The message was simple and direct: your privacy is being invaded; be vigilant! But no attempt was made to define privacy or to provide effective advocacy for policy makers.

The most influential book by far was Alan Westin's *Privacy and Freedom* (1967). This seminal and scholarly treatment of the meaning of privacy in a historical, sociological, and legal context also discusses how privacy was being eroded by developments in information technology. The conceptualization of four states of privacy (solitude, anonymity, reserve, and intimacy) and the classification of privacy threats in terms of physical surveillance (listening and watching devices), psychological surveillance (sensors, lie detectors), and data surveillance (automated record keeping) elevated the debate to a more sophisti-

17. Vance Packard, *The Naked Society* (New York: Pocket Books, 1964); Myron Brenton, *The Privacy Invaders* (New York: Coward-McCann, 1964).

cated level. It allowed us to see privacy not in isolationist, seclusionary terms but as one value competing with a variety of others in contemporary society.

Westin's prescriptions were widely influential, as will be demonstrated in later sections. James Rule and his colleagues observed that "since the publication of *Privacy and Freedom* nearly all of these measures have been either implemented or actively discussed in official circles," and some "have had especially far-reaching effects on subsequent legislation."[18] A similarly influential American study was Arthur Miller's *Assault on Privacy* (1971), which presented a more up-to-date evaluation of the "changing face of information handling." The book abounds with examples of the abuse of large record-keeping systems. The works of Westin and Miller were widely influential in Europe too; Miller's study was later translated into German.

These two works were accompanied or followed by several less important treatments that are nevertheless worthy of a brief note: *The Death of Privacy* (1969), by Jerry Rosenberg; *On Record: Files and Dossiers in American Life* (1969), by Stanton Wheeler; Alan Westin and Michael Baker's *Databanks in a Free Society*, the first major empirical analysis of the impact of record-keeping practices on civil liberties; James Rule's *Private Lives and Public Surveillance* (1974), the first attempt at a comparative treatment of record keeping in the United States and the United Kingdom; Arieh Neier's *Dossier: The Secret Files They Keep on You*(1975); and Alan Lemond and Ron Fry's *No Place to Hide*(1975).[19]

The early literature in Britain tended to adopt a similar civil libertarian focus. Two early books of note are *The Databank Society* (1970), by Malcolm Warner and Michael Stone, and *The Invasion of Privacy* (1974), by Donald Madgwick and Tony Smythe. The "Alan Westin" of the British privacy debate is probably Paul Sieghart, whose later book *Privacy and Computers* (1976) adopted a more objective and analytical perspective and served to advance the debate beyond the level of slogans and horror stories.

18. Rule et al., *The Politics of Privacy*, p. 76.
19. Jerry M. Rosenberg, *The Death of Privacy* (New York: Random House, 1969); Stanton Wheeler, ed., *On Record: Files and Dossiers in American Life* (New York: Russell Sage, 1969); Westin and Baker, *Databanks in a Free Society*; Rule, *Private Lives and Public Surveillance*; Neier, *Dossier*; Alan LeMond and Ron Fry, *No Place to Hide: A Guide to Bugs, Wiretaps, Surveillance, and Other Privacy Invasions* (New York: St. Martin's, 1975).

West German literature generally had a more scholarly and legalistic orientation. Examples include: *Datenschutz* (1973), edited by Wolfgang Kilian, Klaus Lenk, and Wilhelm Steinmuller; *Datenbanken und Datenschutz* ("Databanks and Data Protection," [1974]) by Ulrich Dammann et al.; and probably the most influential, *Numerierte Bürger* ("Numbered Citizens," [1975]) by Gerd Hoffmann, Barbara Tiedze, and Adalbert Podlech.[20] There was less literature of note in Sweden. As we shall see, the legislative process there went forward without a perceived need to stir the consciousness of the public. Parenthetically, we might speculate that public awareness may not have been considered as powerful a factor in West Germany and Sweden as in Britain and the United States. Hence, any written literature was directed more to elites than to the general public.

These works represent but a fraction of the writing on the subject. There were also press, periodical, and journal articles as well as conferences sponsored by legal groups, civil liberties organizations, and international bodies. The climate of rapid technological change caused the more analytical and reflective literature to be overshadowed by more urgent expressions of polemics, policy advocacy, and legal justification. And as the issue moved from one of social alarm to political interest, attention also moved to the various official inquiries set up to examine the problem. Democratic nations followed each other in recognizing the dangers, and each responded in a similar fashion by establishing national study commissions.

The Cross-National Diffusion of Data Protection

How and why policy innovations spread internationally is normally termed "diffusion analysis." With enough cases it is possible to test competing hypotheses about the reasons for a particular pattern of diffusion; those reasons may be spatial (i.e., related to geographical proximity), hierarchical (i.e., following lines from leaders to fol-

---

20. Wolfgang Kilian, Klaus Lenk, and Wilhelm Steinmuller eds., *Datenschutz* (Frankfurt: Athenaum, 1973); Ulrich Dammann et al., *Datenbanken und Datenschutz* (Frankfurt: Herder, 1974); Gerd E. Hoffmann, Barbara Tiedze, and Adalbert Podlech, *Numerierte Bürger* (Wuppertal: Hammer, 1975).

lowers), or socioeconomic (from most developed to least developed).[21] Most of this analysis centers on social security programs in which there are enough cases to allow reliable statistical tests of association. My presentation of the diffusion of data protection is necessarily more descriptive than analytical. The low number of cases precludes any attempt to divine an overall pattern to the spread of the policy, though there are certain interesting aspects of the timing that are worthy of discussion. Tracking the process cross-nationally will also serve to identify the pioneers and the laggards.

Table 1 presents a typology of the responses of all twenty-four OECD countries. These are classified according to the level of response as of January 1991: (1) those with legislation; (2) those where government bills have already been introduced into the legislature; (3) those that have received reports from study commissions; and (4) those where no official action has yet been taken. It is readily apparent that with the exception of Turkey there is now no OECD country in which there has not been some governmental attention to data protection. It should also be noted that in Spain and Portugal there are substantial constitutional provisions on data protection which are expected to presage the passage of statutory protections.

The restriction of this analysis to the OECD countries is misleading in only two senses. There is a 1985 Protection of Privacy Act in Israel, and more recently there has been a stirring of interest in data protection in Eastern Europe. In April 1990 an international conference was held in Budapest during which Western experts presented their views on data protection and privacy to representatives from Hungary, Bulgaria, Czechoslovakia, the German Democratic Republic, Poland, Romania, the Soviet Union, and Yugoslavia.[22] In 1989, Hungary began considering a data protection law and a revision of its constitution to "recognize every human being's right to the protection of personal

---

21. Harold Wilensky et al., "Comparative Social Policy: Theories, Methods, Findings," in *Comparative Policy Research: Learning from Experience*, ed. M. Dierkes, H. N. Weiler, and A. B. Antal (Aldershot: Gower, 1987), pp. 389–90; David Collier and Richard E. Messick, "Prerequisites Versus Diffusion: Testing Alternative Explanations of Social Security Adoption," *American Political Science Review* 69 (1975): 1299–1315; Colin J. Bennett, "Understanding Ripple Effects: Prerequisite Versus Diffusion Explanations of Innovations in Bureaucratic Accountability," Paper presented to the 1990 meeting of the Western Political Science Association, Newport Beach, Calif.

22. *Transnational Data and Communications Report* 13 (June/July 1990): 6.

Table 1. The status of data protection legislation in OECD countries as of January 1991

Country	Legislation or action	Date of passage
Sweden	Data Act	1973 (amended 1982)
United States	Privacy Act	1974
West Germany	Data Protection Act	1977
Canada	Privacy Act	1977 (amended 1982)
France	Law on Informatics & Liberties	1978
Norway	Personal Data Registers Act	1978
Denmark	Private Registers Act	1978
Austria	Data Protection Act	1978
Luxembourg	Data Protection Act	1979
Iceland	Act on the Systematic Recording of Personal Data	1981
New Zealand	Official Information Act	1982
United Kingdom	Data Protection Act	1984
Finland	Personal Data File Act	1987
Ireland	Data Protection Act	1988
Australia	Privacy Act	1988
Japan	Personal Data Protection Act	1988
The Netherlands	Data Protection Act	1988
Belgium, Portugal, Switzerland	Government data protection bills introduced in the Legislature	
Italy, Greece, Spain	Official study commissions established or draft legislation prepared	
Turkey	No official action	

Source: "Status of Data Protection/Privacy Legislation," *Transnational Data and Communications Report*, various issues.

data."[23] As German reunification proceeds, the Länder formerly in the territory of the German Democratic Republic are expected to pass data protection provisions compatible with those already in existence.

There has also been some interest in data protection in the more "developed" countries of the third world, such as Brazil. With few exceptions, this interest is confined to the perceived economic implications of the legislation. As we will see, fears that data protection could be used for trade protection have surfaced from time to time. An unfortunate ramification of the use of the term "data protection" is its

23. Laszlo Solyom, "Hungary: New Data Protection Rights," *Transnational Data and Communications Report* 12 (November 1989): 29–32.

"protectionist" connotations. Certain countries of the developing world that have been trying to establish their own communications and computer infrastructures fear that the protection of personal data could be used as a pretext for the curtailment of transborder data flows. The civil libertarian concerns, however, have not taken root. Data protection has been, at least for the time frame of this study, a subject for the rich, democratic countries.

The pace of enactment has increased over time within the OECD states. At first glance this increase might indicate a "bandwagon effect"; as more states legislate, the pressure to do so increases on those who have not. The above is one key interpretation of the regular finding in studies of the diffusion of innovations that the pattern often approximates the "S-shape" of the cumulative normal curve.[24] Innovations begin slowly; as others learn of this activity, an "interaction effect" occurs and produces a more frequent rate of adoption. This frequency then ultimately abates as the laggards bring up the rear. Lest the diffusion of data protection be interpreted simply as an exercise in imitation, it should be noted that all countries devoted considerable effort to analysis of the problem. Most (with the exception of West Germany) have seen the need to establish official commissions, study committees, or working parties. There was a sense of uncertainty everywhere regarding the nature of the danger as well as a strong belief that the newness of the problem required extensive analysis and investigation. Some conducted this analysis more quickly than did others.

Table 2 ranks the countries according to the date of the establishment of the first study commission (an indicator of the first official attention or response to the problem); the date of the legislation; and the difference between the two (an indicator of the speed of the policymaking process). The figures require some qualification before they can be interpreted.[25] The date of the first official interest is, in each

24. Virginia Gray, "Innovation in the States: A Diffusion Study," *American Political Science Review* 67 (1973): 1174–85.
25. The dates in the table in some cases are a little vague. Where the month is unclear, the time is calculated from midyear. The commissions in most cases are those set up by government to examine general data protection issues in either the public or the private sectors or in both. It should be noted that for the United States there had been attention from the Congress since the mid-1960s; the first serious executive initiative dates from February 1972. West Germany did not set up a study commission. The first official action occurred in September 1973 with the circulation of the first draft bill.

Table 2. Rank order of countries by speed of policy making

Rank order by date first government commission set up	Rank order by date of national legislation	Rank order by speed of policy making (gap in months between cols 1 & 2)	
Sweden, 1969	Sweden, July 1973	United States	34
United Kingdom, May 1970	United States, Jan. 1975	France	37
Denmark, Sept. 1970	West Germany, Jan. 1977	West Germany	39
Norway, Dec. 1970	Canada, Oct. 1977	Sweden	49
Canada, April 1971	France, Jan. 1978	Ireland	49
Austria, 1971	Norway, June 1978	New Zealand	54
United States, Feb. 1972	Denmark, June 1978	Luxembourg	69
The Netherlands, 1972	Austria, Oct. 1978	Canada	78
Luxembourg, 1973	Luxembourg, March 1979	Finland	82
West Germany, Sept. 1973	New Zealand, Dec. 1982	Austria	88
France, Nov. 1974	United Kindom, July 1984	Norway	90
Australia, 1975	Finland, April 1987	Denmark	93
New Zealand, May 1978	Ireland, July 1988	Japan	102
Japan, 1980	Australia, Dec. 1988	Australia	162
Finland, 1980	Japan, Dec. 1988	United Kingdom	170
Ireland, 1984	Netherlands, Dec. 1988	Netherlands	198

Source: Transnational Data and Communications Report, various issues; personal interviews and correspondence.

case, somewhat imprecise. In some instances, prior investigations had taken place within the secrecy of ministerial agencies (such as in France, where the Conseil d'État had been studying the issue since 1971). In other cases the interest in data protection grew out of investigations into related issues (such as the Freedom of the Press Act in Sweden). In the only presidential democracy in our sample (the United States), the date of executive action is less meaningful than in parliamentary regimes. Congress had been looking into the problem for at least eight years before the Department of Health, Education, and Welfare (HEW) began its studies, and had indeed legislated in the area of credit files in 1970. In the federal systems included, much of the necessary analysis had already been completed at the state or regional level. For example, the West Germans already had a model to work with in the form of the Hessian Data Protection Act of 1970.

The date of the establishment of the first commission is, however, a fixed moment in time and one that occurred in all countries (with the exception of West Germany). This date signifies an official commitment to a public investigation. It marks a time when executive officials formally realized that an issue existed and that demands for action either had to be met or mollified. In the absence of any clearer evidence of agenda setting, this date indicates the time when privacy and data protection moved from the systemic to the institutional agenda.

The date of the passage of legislation (marked at the time of royal assent or presidential signing) is a more precise indicator of the end of the policy formulation stage. One should note, however, that in both Canada and Sweden these first-generation statutes have been subsequently amended. In the case of Canada, the amendments to Part IV of the Canadian Human Rights Act of 1977 (in the form of the Federal Access to Information and Privacy Act of 1982) might more properly be dated as the beginning of data protection in Canada. One can also question whether New Zealand has full-fledged data protection legislation as the 1982 provisions were, as in Canada, part of a broader access to information law. The process of evaluation is an ongoing one in all countries; the possibility of amendment is keenly recognized everywhere. Amendments are presently being considered in Germany, Denmark, Sweden, New Zealand, and Australia. Given these caveats, we can now explore more intensively the policy-making processes in the four major countries of interest.

Table 2 clearly reveals that some countries (the United States, France, and Sweden) were able to act relatively quickly; the progress in others (e.g., the United Kingdom, the Netherlands, Australia, and several, such as Italy and Switzerland, that have yet to legislate) was far slower. The table also indicates that the pioneers at a national level were the Swedes.

The Formation of the Swedish Data Act

Some writers have referred to the Swedish data protection policy as a deliberate "experiment, a strategy for gaining experience"[26] that

26. Bing, "A Comparative Outline of Privacy Legislation," p. 150.

had "an enormous and direct influence on the development of data protection in Western European countries."[27] Hondius wrote later that the Swedish Data Act is "still remarkable for its brevity and foresight. If laws in other countries appear to be more sophisticated on certain points, it should be recognized that this would not have been possible without the Swedish prototype."[28]

That the testing ground for this legislation was Sweden, and not elsewhere, is attributable to a number of structural and contextual factors. First, Sweden has enjoyed a policy style that is "typically prospective and preventive in its intent, rather than retrospective and remedial."[29] This style may be stereotypical and outdated. It is, nevertheless, the style of problem solving favored by Jan Freese, the Director General of the Swedish Data Inspection Board from 1975 to 1986 and one of the foremost advocates and publicists for data protection in the world.

> I am not sure we can afford computerization of society to develop like a "happening." To me it is important to solve problems, and I prefer to do so before they occur. If you look into history you will probably realize that the information explosion or revolution, the first steps of which we are just now facing, has a dimension never seen before. There are good chances that developments will be positive. But there are risks. We have already faced some of them. We will find several more.[30]

This approach is fortified by two long-standing structures of consultation: royal commissions, which are institutionalized mechanisms for policy analysis and evaluation; and the *remiss* procedure, negotiation with affected groups prior to policy formulation, which ensures a wide degree of compliance with the resulting policy. More generally, scholars have depicted a Swedish policy process that is deliberative,

27. Flaherty, *Protecting Privacy in Surveillance Societies*, p. 94.
28. Frits W. Hondius, "Data Legislation on the March," *Information Privacy* 1 (1978): 4.
29. Richard Elmore, Gunnel Gustafsson, and Erwin Hargrove, "Comparing Implementation Processes in Sweden and the United States," *Scandinavian Political Studies* 9 (1986): 221.
30. Jan Freese, "Preserving the Open Flow of Information across Borders," in OECD, *Transborder Data Flows and the Protection of Privacy*, Proceedings of a Symposium held in Vienna, 20–23 September 1977 (Paris: OECD, 1979), p. 282.

rationalistic, consensual, anticipatory, and open.[31] Even though there is evidence of an erosion of this style,[32] it is highly suited to the identification and resolution of a problem like data protection.

There is a second set of contextual factors that explain why the Swedes were the pioneers in this area. Foremost is the fact that Sweden experienced a relatively early and more widespread computerized registration of its small population than did many other countries. Freese estimates that "on the average, the name of every adult, unmarried and conscientious Swede appears in at least 100 personal files. . . . With a population of roughly eight million, Sweden is one of the most computerized countries in the world."[33] A more recent estimate suggests that each individual is included in between fifty and three hundred personal registers.[34] As we have noted, this extensive computerization is facilitated by the highly developed system of personal identification numbers. By the late 1960s, it had become technically easier to monitor people in Sweden than in other countries.

Moreover, the uniquely open system of administration in Sweden explains why the problem was perceived as more acute at such an early stage; it also provides insights into the subsequent passage and content of the Data Act. The Freedom of the Press Act, passed in 1766, is the fourth major provision of the Swedish Constitution. The act not only guarantees freedom of speech and of the press (like the First Amendment to the United States Constitution), but it also uniquely allows free public access to official documents; those inspecting such documents are entitled to a copy of them as well. This "publicity principle" is qualified by the exemptions provided in the 1937 Secrecy Act, which stipulates that documents concerning national or internal security affairs, certain financial data, and some personal records (relating to medical, social welfare, or financial interests) may be kept from public view. The Secrecy Act has been amended several times. Nevertheless, it is commonly agreed that this long-standing

31. Thomas Anton, "Policy-making and Political Culture in Sweden," *Scandinavian Political Studies* 4 (1969): 88–102; Donald M. Hancock, *Sweden: The Politics of Postindustrial Change* (Hinsdale, Ill.: Dryden Press, 1972).
32. See Olof Ruin, "Sweden in the 1970s: Policy-making Becomes More Difficult," in *Policy Styles in Western Europe*, ed. Jeremy Richardson (London: Allen & Unwin, 1982).
33. Jan Freese, "The Swedish Data Act," *Current Sweden* 178 (November 1977): 6.
34. Gert Persson, "Computerised Personal Registers and the Protection of Privacy," *Current Sweden* 344 (February 1986): 2.

presumption of publicity has probably made the Swedish political system the most open in the world.[35]

The provisions of the Freedom of the Press Act originally related only to documents. This fact became problematic when, in the 1960s, more and more official information (and particularly personal information) was stored on magnetic tape. Initially, fears arose that citizens would not be able to exercise their constitutional rights of access without appropriate information technology. There was a belief that computerization should not obstruct the operation of the publicity principle. It was also realized that computerization entailed privacy risks. This problem was highlighted by a 1971 decision of the Supreme Administrative Court (the highest judicial body dealing with administrative law) that magnetic tapes were de facto documents. Hence, tapes were treated like other public documents, and made available on request, even to commercial enterprises that might stand to gain financially from the transaction. These peculiar factors persuaded many in government and industry that the combination of computerization and unequaled conditions of publicity had produced a new set of privacy problems, and that urgent action should be taken to investigate the proper balance between governmental openness and individual privacy in Sweden.

These initial dilemmas confronted the Royal Commission on Publicity and Secrecy,[36] the body established in 1969 that provided the analysis, the recommendations, and the initial drafting which culminated in the passage of the Data Act in 1973. The peculiar context of openness in which the privacy issue was debated directly influenced the way the problem was addressed and decided by the commission. The immediate problem concerned public access to government files and questions of how to limit or extend the scope and application of the Freedom of the Press Act. The 1970 census, however, and the many complaints that went to the ombudsman about census questions, shifted the concern from that of openness and confidentiality to the broader privacy implications of automatic data processing (ADP). Indeed, the government was so concerned that opposition to the cen-

---

35. See James Michael, *The Politics of Secrecy* (London: Penguin Books, 1982), chap. 9.
36. Sweden, Commission on Publicity and Secrecy of Official Documents, *Computers and Privacy*.

sus might invalidate its final results that the commission's charge was officially widened to address the growing concern.

The first conclusion (or, perhaps, assumption) of the Commission on Publicity and Secrecy was that "the ADP technique gives rise to quite new threats to personal privacy. Compared with information kept in documents it is principally a matter of degree, but the difference is such that the situation has changed in a decisive way."[37] In facilitating greater storage and speedier communication, therefore, the computer had rendered existing laws obsolete: Swedish rules for protection of privacy did not meet the problems arising through the development of computers. These problems could be met to some extent through amendments to the Secrecy Act, but this action was not sufficient. The commission therefore proposed the Data Act (*Datalagen*), applicable solely to computerized personal records.

What began as a constitutional issue of how to maintain the publicity principle in the computer age shifted to a problem of data protection with its own legal instrument, institutional mechanism, and subsequent momentum. The peculiar roots of the issue, however, precluded any attempt to define privacy in substantive terms and to fashion a full legal right based on the privacy principle. The commission noted the different dimensions of the concept with reference to American and British formulations and concluded that "the limits, therefore, cannot possibly be drawn distinctly, definitely or in detail."[38] The definitional problems are compounded by the fact that the rough translation for privacy in Swedish (*integritet*) also embodies the "individual's demand to be judged by relevant criteria."[39]

The reluctance to establish conceptual and legal boundaries resulted in a very flexible approach with the "starting-point that all information about the conditions of individuals may concern privacy."[40] This starting point, and the emphasis on computerized files, led to the enactment of a distinctive feature of Swedish data protection law—that no personalized information may be computerized without permission—to be granted and enforced through the newly created Data Inspection Board (DIB). Individual privacy would thus be pro-

37. Ibid., p. 6.
38. Ibid., p. 5.
39. Ibid., p. 4.
40. Ibid, p. 5.

tected through procedural safeguards, ones defined and monitored by this board.

The Royal Commission on Publicity and Secrecy published its report *Computers and Privacy* in July 1972. Less than a year later, in April 1973, the Riksdag passed the Data Act.[41] The parliamentary passage was mainly smooth, depoliticized, and uncontentious. The only major modification to the commission's draft concerned personal files created by government decree or by parliamentary decision; for constitutional and political reasons, it was not thought appropriate to give an agency acting on statutory authority (the DIB) licensing rights over other government files. The Social Democratic government argued (against opposition parties) that the Riksdag itself provides control of governmental systems, and if there are abuses, redress can be sought through the ombudsman. The DIB was therefore given advisory rather than regulatory powers in this area.[42] These responsibilities will be more fully discussed in Chapter 5.

The full legislation of data protection principles, however, also entailed an amendment to the Freedom of the Press Act. This constitutional reform required a more complicated procedure as well as the intervention of a general election. But this amendment was duly adopted in February 1974; thus the publicity principle from then on applied to automated records. The Credit Information Act and Debt Recovery Acts were passed at roughly the same time; these acts regulate computerized credit information, and the DIB again has licensing and supervisory responsibilities. When the Data Act came into full force on 1 July 1974, the world's first national system of personal data protection was in place.

The Emergence of the American Privacy Act

The "right to privacy" is widely considered to be American in both origin and development. The source is normally traced to the seminal

41. *Data Act* (Datalagen), SFS 1973: 289. English translation from Dammann et al., *Data Protection Legislation*, pp. 129–45.
42. Per-Gunnar Vinge, *Experiences of the Swedish Data Act* (Stockholm: Federation of Swedish Industries, 1975).

article by Samuel Warren and Louis Brandeis in the *Harvard Law Review* in 1890.[43] The definition of privacy upon which this article, and subsequent case law, was based was "the right to be let alone." In fact, this formulation was originally presented a year earlier by Judge Thomas M. Cooley in the second edition of his book on tort law.[44] Although these early writings were directed toward supposedly intrusive practices of newspaper reporters for the Boston gossip columns, they provided the philosophical and doctrinal basis for the extension of the right to privacy to other social relationships and modes of behavior as well as for the development in the early years of the twentieth century of a distinct area of common law.

The case law that developed, however, was incoherent and directionless. In 1960, William Prosser reexamined the area and concluded that there was no distinct right to privacy.[45] He instead found a complicated interrelationship among four separate torts: (1) intrusion upon a plaintiff's seclusion or solitude or into the person's private affairs; (2) public disclosure of embarrassing private facts; (3) publicity that places a plaintiff in a false light; and (4) appropriation of a plaintiff's name or likeness for a defendant's advantage. This classification has since been widely accepted. Despite valiant attempts to integrate the law within a comprehensive and clearly limited definition of privacy, it is apparent that it is impossible to find an objective and immutable formulation that is not so hopelessly broad as to be synonymous with other elusive values, such as autonomy, liberty, or intimacy.

The conceptual confusion was only compounded when privacy was granted the status of a constitutional right in 1965. In *Griswold v. Connecticut* the Supreme Court struck down a state law that had made it illegal for even married couples to use contraceptive devices.[46] The Court reasoned that various constitutional guarantees (specifically the First, Third, Fourth, Fifth, and Ninth Amendments) create "zones of privacy." Thus implicit within the "penumbra" of the Constitution is a clear belief that without privacy these other rights are less secure, perhaps meaningless. The Court held, in one of the most

43. Warren and Brandeis, "The Right to Privacy."
44. Cooley, *A Treatise on the Law of Torts*, p. 29.
45. Prosser, "Privacy."
46. 381 U.S. 479 (1965).

striking and controversial examples of judicial activism in American history, that this "penumbral right" should prevent the "long arm of the government reaching into the marital chamber." Since *Griswold* the same logic has been held to protect the right of a woman to decide whether to terminate her pregnancy,[47] as well as to safeguard other activities relating to marriage, procreation, and intimate family relationships.

The origins and development of the right to privacy in American thought and law have been discussed to emphasize its importance in American political debate.[48] Privacy law, therefore, is not limited to the 1974 Privacy Act but has sources in the Constitution and in common law. The concerns about computerization that arose in the 1960s should be seen in the light of this wider discussion about the span and application of a powerful concept with deep roots in the American political culture and which finds expression in a complex variety of sources.

Yet the common law of privacy, and its more recent constitutional branch, have proven virtually irrelevant in the separate attempts to fashion a public policy to deal with the dangers of information technology. Indeed, David O'Brien argues that the issue of information privacy rose to the agenda precisely because of the failure of judicial and constitutional interpretation to provide effective safeguards through case law.[49] The widespread development and application of computers (particularly to government) had presented new relationships and different policy problems, one that the courts were unable to resolve. "The judicial process, in short, seems functionally ill-suited to initiating development of general common law rules relating to record-keeping practices," concluded the Advisory Committee on Automated Personal Data Systems of the Secretary of Health, Education, and Welfare.[50] The paucity of relevant case law in a context of rapid technological change raised the need to devise a more synoptic policy solution to protect the

47. *Roe v. Wade*, 410 U.S. 113 (1973).
48. The salience of privacy in the American political culture was seen most vividly in the failed nomination of Judge Robert Bork to the Supreme Court in 1987. His rejection by the Senate was due, in large part, to his refusal to recognize the right to privacy as formulated in *Griswold*. The successful nominees, Anthony Kennedy and David Soutar, were subjected to rigorous questioning along similar lines by the Senate Judiciary Committee.
49. David M. O'Brien, *Privacy, Law, and Public Policy* (New York: Praeger, 1979), p. 203.
50. U.S. HEW, *Records, Computers, and the Rights of Citizens*, p. 37.

relationship between the individual and the record-keeping organization. It also meant that, despite the long-standing concern for privacy issues in the United States, American policy-makers were essentially looking for new solutions to new problems. They were working with as blank a slate as were their counterparts in Western Europe.

Policy Analysis and Advocacy

As noted above, the factors that led to the enactment of the Privacy Act in the United States were broadly the same as those in Western Europe—principally, the propagation and centralization of personal record-keeping systems using the latest information technology. The 1965 proposal from the Social Science Research Council to establish a Federal Data Center of all basic statistical data originating in federal agencies prompted investigation by both the Senate Judiciary Committee's Subcommittee on Administrative Practice and Procedure and the House Committee on Government Operations's Special Subcommittee on Invasion of Privacy. These initial hearings precipitated a more general survey of government record-keeping practices by the Senate Judiciary Committee. It concluded that agencies had amassed a large amount of inessential personal information and that the safeguards were inadequate. The committee advised the federal agencies to reexamine their procedures and standards "in order to determine that the maximum protection is being afforded the individual with respect to the personal data which he has surrendered."[51]

Moreover, the climate of tension surrounding American politics (the 1968 Democratic Convention, the assassination of Robert Kennedy and Martin Luther King, Jr., the Vietnam War, etc.) produced an increase both in official surveillance and in congressional investigation into that surveillance. Between the beginning of 1965 and the end of 1974 (when the Privacy Act was passed), there were forty-seven separate sets of congressional hearings and reports on a variety of privacy-related issues. Aside from the National Data Center, subjects of particular concern were: the activities of consumer-credit and insurance-reporting enterprises; political intelligence; criminal arrest records;

---

51. U.S. Senate, *Government Dossier*, Report from the Subcommittee on Administrative Practice and Procedure of the Committee on the Judiciary, Senate, 90th Cong., 1st sess. (Washington, D.C.: Government Printing Office, 1967), p. 8.

polygraph screenings and other psychological tests; wiretapping; the procedures and safeguards surrounding the 1970 census; and unsolicited mail.[52] Moreover, in the 89th, 90th, 91st, and 92d Congresses (1965-72), there were introduced respectively 15, 19, 150, and 87 different legislative bills relating to privacy.[53] But throughout this whole period, only two laws were enacted which directly addressed the issue: the Omnibus Crime Control and Safe Streets Act of 1968 (limiting the use of wiretaps),[54] and the Fair Credit Reporting Act of 1970 (regulating credit-reporting agencies).[55]

Of critical importance for the later passage and content of the Privacy Act was the work done by the Senate Judiciary Committee's Subcommittee on Constitutional Rights, chaired by Senator Sam J. Ervin, Jr., from 1970 to 1974. Ervin's subcommittee provided the coordinated investigative analysis of the general problem of federal databanks. Diligent probing into agency record-keeping practices exposed many inconsistencies, much carelessness, and some very intrusive procedures.[56] These efforts culminated in an influential report issued in 1974 entitled *Federal Data Banks and Constitutional Rights.* The subcommittee concluded that "there are immense numbers of government data banks, littered with diverse information on just about every citizen in the country." It recommended that the existence, creation, and operation of data banks should be put on a statutory basis with full and accurate reporting requirements, inherent privacy safeguards, subject notification, constraints on interagency exchange, and strict security precautions—in other words, "continued legislative control over the purposes, contents and uses of government data banks."[57]

52. Rule et al., *The Politics of Privacy*, pp. 190–97.
53. U.S. Senate, *Federal Data Banks and Constitutional Rights*, Report from the Subcommittee on Constitutional Rights of the Committee on the Judiciary, Senate, 93d Cong., 2d sess. (Washington, D.C.: Government Printing Office, 1974), p. 7.
54. *The Omnibus Crime Control and Safe Streets Act of 1968*, 18 U.S.C. 2510–2520. The basic provision subjects to criminal liability "any person" who without a warrant "willfully intercepts" any "wire or oral communication."
55. *Fair Credit Reporting Act*, 15 U.S.C. 1681 et seq. Consumer reports maintained by consumer reporting agencies may be disclosed to government agencies only in response to a court order or to an agency that requires a consumer report for legitimate business purposes.
56. U.S. Senate, *Federal Data Banks, Computers, and the Bill of Rights*, Hearings before the Subcommittee on Constitutional Rights of the Committee on the Judiciary, Senate, 92d Cong., 1st sess. (Washington, D.C.: Government Printing Office, 1971).
57. U.S. Senate, *Federal Data Banks and Constitutional Rights*, pp. iv–v.

Congressional investigations were complemented by a wealth of scholarly analysis from a number of official and unofficial bodies. The works of Westin and Miller have already been cited for their impact on the framing of the privacy problem as a policy issue. Both books made a critical distinction between "information privacy" and other behavioral aspects of privacy such as intrusion and surveillance. For both authors, information privacy meant giving individuals "the ability to control the circulation of information"[58] relating to them, or "to determine for themselves when, how and to what extent information about them is communicated to others."[59] Westin followed up his earlier work (coauthored by Michael Baker) with a project for the National Academy of Sciences entitled *Databanks in a Free Society*, an empirical study of the computerized record-keeping practices of over fifty public and private organizations. The aim was to discover the actual implications of record keeping, both manual and computerized, for the constitutional rights of privacy and due process. The findings were surprising and somewhat contentious. Central-databank developments were not as advanced as the more alarmist commentary had assumed; organizations were a long way from the total consolidation of personal information. There was little evidence, the report concluded, that the computer itself was having an adverse effect on privacy.[60]

The third and final source of policy analysis was the executive branch. The first real signal of executive branch interest was the appointment in 1972 by the then Secretary of the Department of Health, Education, and Welfare, Eliot Richardson, of an Advisory Committee on Automated Personal Data Systems. The committee's membership encompassed a diverse range of expertise and viewpoints, and the early meetings were conflictual. Most outsiders viewed the committee as a palliative, more designed to mollify the growing concern than to formulate viable policy recommendations. The 1973 report *Records, Computers, and the Rights of Citizens*, however, was surprisingly coherent and influential. The report noted the growth in automated record keeping and accepted the need for safeguards. It proposed "fair information practices" that "assure the individual a right to partici-

---

58. Miller, *The Assault on Privacy*, p. 40.
59. Westin, *Privacy and Freedom*, p. 7.
60. Westin and Baker, *Databanks in a Free Society*, part 5.

pate in a meaningful way in decisions about what goes in records about him and how that information shall be used."[61] This codification served as a model for the Privacy Act and will be discussed more fully in Chapter 3.

The Legislative Process

How were all these concerns and ideas combined to produce a law? John Kingdon contends that policy is made in America when "the separate streams of problem, policies and politics come together at certain critical times. Solutions become joined to problems, and both of them are joined to favorable political forces."[62] In this case, the "solution" of fair information practices became linked to the "problem" of information privacy. But policy formulation not only requires a problem and an available solution but also two other critical conditions according to Kingdon.

The first is an "open policy window" when the climate of public and political opinion is propitious for action. For the present discussion that climate was provided by the Watergate crisis. The many and various cases of political bribery, corruption, malpractice, intrusiveness, and abuse of personal data that are captured by the emotive term "Watergate" gave the privacy advocates the perfect horror story. But, more generally, Watergate pushed the whole problem of the executive abuse of power, vis-à-vis the Congress, the courts, and the citizen, to the forefront of press and public attention. No greater indication of the salience of privacy is available than the national radio address by President Nixon, "American Right to Privacy" during which he announced the establishment of a "top priority Domestic Council Committee on the Right to Privacy" to be chaired by Vice President Ford.[63] This example demonstrates that when an issue is at the forefront of public attention, there is a strong incentive for policy makers to utilize the opportunity. There may never be another such occasion when the

---

61. U.S. HEW, *Records, Computers, and the Rights of Citizens*, p. 41.
62. Kingdon, *Agendas, Alternatives, and Public Policies*, p. 204.
63. U.S. Congress, *Legislative History of the Privacy Act of 1974*, Source Book on Privacy from the Committee on Government Operations, Senate, and the Committee on Government Operations, House of Representatives, 94th Cong., 2d sess. (Washington, D.C.: Government Printing Office, 1976), pp. 1005–8.

various legislative and executive actors have the same incentive to investigate an issue and cooperate in a joint legislative effort.

The Privacy Act would not have been passed in 1974 had it not been for Watergate. Its enactment was seen as part of a wider effort to open up the executive establishment and cleanse the government of the murky and conspiratorial influences of the Nixon White House. The same period saw the strengthening of the 1967 Freedom of Information Act, the passage of the Government in the Sunshine Act (which opened up certain governmental committees to public scrutiny), and, perhaps most importantly, the enactment of the Congressional Budget and Impoundment Control Act (designed to reassert Congress's authority over public expenditures).[64]

"Policy entrepreneurs" are the second factor that Kingdon suggests will facilitate the "coupling of the streams"; these are "advocates who are willing to invest their resources . . . to promote a position in return for anticipated future gain in the form of material, purposive or solidary benefits."[65] In the case of information privacy, the policy entrepreneur was Senator Ervin, who had staunchly campaigned for protective legislation since the late 1960s. Ervin's central role as the chair of the Senate investigative committee that held televised hearings on the Watergate affair enhanced his stature and motivated both the House and the Senate to provide a policy response. It was also Ervin's last term in the Congress, and there was a general sense that he deserved a retirement present in the form of a piece of pet legislation.

For these propitious reasons the consideration and passage of the Privacy Act in the summer and fall of 1974 were astoundingly quick by American standards. The primary Senate bill (S. 3418), cosponsored by Senators Ervin, Percy, Muskie, and Ribicoff, was introduced on 1 May 1974; it provided for a Federal Privacy Board to oversee the collection, use, and disclosure of information concerning individuals.[66] Hearings were held in June by the Senate Committee on Government Operations's ad hoc Subcommittee on Privacy and Information Systems. The bill was "marked up"—a procedure where the

64. *Freedom of Information Act* (FOIA), 5 U.S.C. 552; *Government in the Sunshine Act*, 5 U.S.C. 552b; *Congressional Budget and Impoundment Control Act of 1974*, 31 U.S.C. 1301.
65. Kingdon, *Agendas, Alternatives, and Public Policies*, p. 188.
66. U.S. Senate, *A Bill to Establish a Federal Privacy Board*, S. 3418, 93d Cong., 2d sess. (Washington, D.C.: Government Printing Office, 1974).

detailed wording is negotiated—on 20 August. It was reported unanimously out of committee on 26 September. It was considered and passed by the full Senate on 21 November 1974, by a vote of seventy-four to nine.[67]

House action centered on H. R. 16373, introduced on 12 August 1974; its principal sponsor was Congressman Moorhead.[68] This bill was reported out of the House Government Operations Committee on 2 October 1974 after hearings similar to those held in the Senate. But the bill did not recommend a privacy board or any other separate mechanism to enforce privacy principles. Ten members of the committee dissented from the report; they also promised to offer an amendment on the floor of the House to establish an administrative body to oversee the implementation of the legislation. On 1 November the House of Representatives considered and passed H. R. 16373 without provision for a separate privacy board; the vote was 353 for, one against.

When both the House and the Senate pass different versions of the same bill, a conference committee is normally convened to negotiate a compromise and to agree on a text. Because of pressures on congressional time—the Ninety-third Congress was in its last hours—and because of the general desire to get legislation passed while the climate was favorable, an ad hoc meeting was arranged late one night in Senator Ervin's private office. The four principal sponsors—Senators Ervin and Percy and Congressmen Moorhead and Ehrlenborn—were present as were their counsels. All knew that any one of them could veto the whole idea; all knew that the President endorsed the House version. This meeting resulted in two compromises: the Federal Privacy Board, which Ervin had insisted on, was transformed to a Privacy Protection Study Commission, a temporary body with advisory and analytical responsibilities only;[69] and the oversight responsibility was given to the Office of Management and Budget on the grounds that

67. See U.S. Congress, *Legislative History of the Privacy Act of 1974*, for full documentation of the law's passage.

68. U.S. House of Representatives, *A Bill to Safeguard Individual Privacy from the Misuse of Federal Records*, H. R. 16373, 93d Cong., 2d sess. (Washington, D.C.: Government Printing Office, 1974).

69. Three years later the Privacy Protection Study Commission produced the report *Personal Privacy in an Information Society* containing over 160 recommendations for reform to information practices in both public and private sectors.

this duty was better-placed within the Executive Office of the President than in a cabinet department (such as the Justice Department). Hence, the way was clear for enactment. The text of H. R. 16373 was substituted for S. 3418, and after a further round of minor amendments, the bill passed both Houses on 18 December 1974. On 1 January 1975, President Ford signed the Privacy Act of 1974, just five months after Richard Nixon had resigned from office.

The passage of the Privacy Act in the final days of the Ninety-third Congress was quick, but it was hardly smooth. The battles over the nature of enforcement were typical of the American legislative process, as we shall see more completely in Chapter 5. Nevertheless, the act's final passage constituted a perceived solution to a long-standing problem, a legislative response to the presidential abuse of power, and a personal tribute to Senator Ervin in his final term.[70] The relative speed of the enactment of the 1974 Privacy Act is evidence that the American system is very good at responding to issues when those issues are unequivocally a matter of wide political concern.

The Construction of the West German Data Protection Act

The factors that led to the enactment of the federal German Data Protection Act in 1977 were broadly the same as those in other countries—proposals for the establishment of large integrated databanks as well as for unique PINs for administrative purposes. Anxieties about such developments should be seen against a background of higher rates of participation and a more acute sense of citizen efficacy within the German political culture. There was also a growing sense of awareness about the dangers of nuclear power and environmental pollution during this same period. A new generation, unaffected by memories of the World War II, had reached political maturity. A more deferential culture had given way to a rising con-

70. David H. Flaherty, "The Need for an American Privacy Protection Commission," *Government Information Quarterly* 1 (1984): 240. For other discussions of the legislative history, see Priscilla M. Regan, "Personal Information Policies in the United States and Britain: The Dilemma of Implementation Considerations," *Journal of Public Policy* 4 (1984): 19–38, and David F. Linowes and Colin J. Bennett, "Privacy: Its Role in Federal Government Information Policy," *Library Trends* 31 (1986): 19–42.

sciousness of nonmaterialistic issues (the environment, civil liberties, nuclear power) and to a willingness to challenge authority through such movements as the Greens.[71]

A 1980 Federal Government press bulletin reflects this change in public consciousness:

> Frequently the dangers in an automated processing of information are compared with those of nuclear power or of polluting the environment. In all three spheres, the issue is the right use of technical developments. . . . In all these areas the citizen is dominated by the feeling that, do as he may, he cannot grasp all the interconnected issues—and accordingly is at the mercy of the technical experts. To be sure, the conflict about the computer is not likely to escalate to the same intensity as that which concerns the atomic-power plants. . . . Nonetheless, data protection today has become a matter of major political and social significance.[72]

Despite the relative novelty of data protection as an issue of technology, the right to privacy has played a part in West German law since the nineteenth century. There being no equivalent German word for "privacy," this area of law is based on different "rights of the personality" (*Persönlichkeitsrechte*). As the Germans were sensitive to their tyrannical past, two related rights were included in the Basic Law of 1949: Article 1 (1) declares that "a person's dignity is inviolable" and that "the state is obligated to respect and protect it"; and Article 2(1) declares that "each person has the right to freely develop his personality, insofar as he does not injure the rights . . . of others and does not violate the constitutional order and moral law."[73] These two articles allowed the courts to protect a variety of privacy-related concerns and thus increasingly enhance the protection of "spheres of privacy" (*Privatsphäre*). The basic German formulation of the right to privacy is similar in its scope and vagueness to the American notion of the "right to be let alone," although it is nowhere near as developed.

---

71. David P. Conradt, "West Germany: A Remade Political Culture," *Comparative Political Studies* 7 (1974): 222–38.

72. Federal Republic of Germany, Press and Information Office, *Data Protection in the Federal Republic of Germany*, 11 January 1980 (Bonn: Deutscher Bundesverlag, 1980).

73. Eckhart K. Gouras, "The Reform of West German Data Protection Law as a Necessary Correlate to Improving Domestic Security," *Columbia Journal of Transnational Law* 24 (1986): 605–6.

By the early 1970s, the Constitutional Court (*Bundesver-fassungsgericht*) had held that the free development of one's personality was of "highest constitutional value" and that there should always be an "untouchable sphere of private life withdrawn from the influence of state power."[74] Data protection achieved constitutional protection in 1983 when the Constitutional Court articulated a "right to informational self-determination": henceforth, the individual, and not the government, should control the circulation and use of his or her information. This decision was prompted by the controversial census of 1983 and has had profound implications for the scope and application of German data protection policy.

Until 1983, however, the protections afforded by disparate strands of constitutional and civil law were too imprecise to deal with the special problems posed by information technology. Hence, the word "Datenschutz" (literally, data protection) was coined and entered current usage, first that of technical and legal experts and later that of the general public. Hans Peter Bull, the first Federal Data Protection Commissioner, blames the drafters of the Hessian law for the term's creation.[75] A misnomer from the start, it tends to connote data security or secrecy rather than the rights of the individual to the fair and appropriate collection and circulation of information. Moreover, it has been considered an unfortunate label "because it is not so much data, but people, that must be protected."[76] It also brings an unnecessary technical and esoteric air to the issue. Nevertheless, the word fairly rapidly became the rallying call for those seeking the regulation of information technology, not only in Germany, but in other countries as well.

Data Protection Law in the Länder

Given that the bulk of administrative activities in the Federal Republic are conducted at the Land level, it is natural that here is where the problems should first surface. The decentralized data processing

---

74. J. Lee Riccardi, "The German Federal Data Protection Act of 1977: Protecting the Right of Privacy?" *Boston College International and Comparative Law Review* 6 (1983): 245.

75. Bull, *Datenschutz oder die Angst vor dem Computer*, p. 84.

76. Otto Mallmann, "Computers and Civil Liberties: The Situation in the Federal Republic of Germany," *Law and Computer Technology* 7 (1974): 3.

facilities established in the late 1960s for planning purposes had their terms of reference laid down by law. As part of the legitimating process, clauses and regulations were introduced to protect the rights of citizens. The state of Hesse, however, resolved that the rules on data protection should be included in a separate legal instrument. Thus, in 1970, was born the world's first data protection act, a piece of legislation that had an international impact far exceeding its intrinsic scope and importance.

The Hessian Data Protection Act applies to official files of the Hessian government and is limited to automatic data processing. Its most significant feature is the establishment of an independent data protection commissioner, appointed by and responsible to the Land Parliament. This person is responsible for ensuring the security of state files, for advising on the impact of new data processing techniques, and for checking as to whether computerization leads to any change in the distribution of powers among governmental bodies. Since 1971 the office has been held by Spiros Simitis, one of the most respected and effective advocates for data protection in the world. Early experience with the Hessian Act was considered of "immense value to other countries . . . considering options for data protection legislation."[77] It has since been amended twice: in 1978, to take account of the provisions of the Federal Data Protection Act; and in 1986, in response to the ruling of the Federal Constitutional Court on the Census Act of December 1983.[78]

Four years later a second Land, Rheinland-Pfalz, acted. Its data protection law of January 1974 also made provision for institutionalized outside control but went about it in a different way. The responsibility for supervision was given to a committee composed of three Landtag members and two officials or judges. As in Hesse, the law was restricted to the regulation of the automatic processing of personal data within the framework of the Land administration.[79] The other Länder subsequently followed with similar laws.

For reasons concerning the preservation of cross-national equivalence, I am only focusing on the protections provided at the central

77. Hondius, *Emerging Data Protection*, p. 36.

78. Hessian Data Protection Commissioner, *The Hessian Data Protection Act* (Hessisches Datenschutzgesetz) of 11 November 1986 (Wiesbaden: Hessian Data Protection Commissioner, 1987).

79. Simitis et al., *Kommentar*, p. 67.

level of administration. It is important to bear in mind, however, that given the federal structure of West Germany, most of the important data processing concerning individuals takes place at the Land level. Moreover, a basic tenet of West German federalism is that the Länder regulate the powers of their agencies independently of the federal government. The Federal Data Protection Act (*Bundesdatenschutzgesetz* [BDSG]) is, therefore, at the apex of a complex and integrated network of legal instruments that in concert comprise the system of regulation in Germany. Developments in the Länder had profound implications for federal policy makers and administrators. Those who developed the federal law were very conscious of evolving state legislation, they recognized that a wholly effective system of data protection would have to be an integrated and consistent one.

Passage of the Federal Data Protection Act of 1977

The story of the passage of the Federal Data Protection Act of 1977 is a complicated one. It is also very much an inside story. There was no official study commission that held open hearings and published a series of recommendations. There was very little pressure from civil libertarians. Rather, the genesis of the BDSG is to be found within more elite circles: within the legal profession, whose National Conference of Lawyers (*Deutsche Juristentag*) instituted a data protection commission in 1972 that set forth a series of principles for computer regulation;[80] and most importantly, within the corridors and committee rooms of the Bundestag and the Ministry of the Interior.

Developments at the federal level properly begin with a 1969 resolution of the Bundestag that demanded general regulation of data processing as soon as possible. This resolution led to intensive discussion amongst an interparliamentary working group and a proposal in January 1970 for a "preliminary plan for the protection of privacy against the misuse of automatically processed personal data."[81] After further discussions, this plan became the first draft of the data protec-

---

80. Ibid.
81. Bull, *Datenschutz oder die Angst vor dem Computer*, p. 104.

tion bill and was tabled in the Bundestag in December 1971.[82] The bill was modeled after the Hessian law but contained a more specific regulatory framework. It was intended as a basis for discussion and as a means to prompt the government into producing a bill of its own. The proposals were endorsed by representatives of all three major parties including three subsequent federal ministers.[83] It fell from consideration, however, when the Sixth Legislative Session ended in 1972.

Throughout the Seventh Bundestag, data protection was one of the most controversial and time-consuming issues. In July 1972, a report was prepared for the Ministry of the Interior by Wilhelm Steinmuller. In August a draft plan was circulated within the federal bureaucracy by the ministry; this plan formed the basis for the first public hearings on federal data protection in November 1972. It was at these hearings that the first major opposition to data protection was aired by industry representatives and members of the federal administration.[84] This opposition was not confined just to minor details but to the very principle of data protection legislation, which was considered an intolerable intervention into the affairs of public, and especially private, organizations. These hearings were a signal as to how drawn out and complicated the legislative process would be.[85]

The first government draft was presented to the Bundestag for an initial reading on 29 November 1973.[86] It was then reviewed by a series of legislative committees. The government clearly expected a quick and smooth passage of its legislation, but such was not the case. In an untypical assertion of legislative independence, representatives from all parties declared themselves to be opposed to the government draft and intent on making radical changes. The central issue was, as in the United States, one of enforcement. The government draft was based on a theory of data protection in direct contrast to that applied in Hesse. It had very specific and strict regulations of subject matter but a very weak control mechanism, whereas the Hessian law combined a flexible regulation of information with a powerful control

---

82. Federal Republic of Germany, Bundestag, *Drucksache 6/2885*, December 1971.
83. Bull, *Datenschutz oder die Angst vor dem Computer*, p. 105.
84. Ibid.
85. Simitis et al., *Kommentar*, p. 67.
86. Federal Republic of Germany, Bundestag, *Drucksache 7/1027*, November 1973.

mechanism. Many experts and legislators, led by certain respected backbenchers in the Social Democratic Party (SPD) and the Free Democratic Party (FDP), declared support for implementation through a supervisory authority on the Hessian model.[87]

Thus began a drawn-out process of bargaining within the committee rooms of the Bundestag. Somewhat unusually, two public hearings before the main Interior Committee were inserted into the process; these took place on 6 May 1974 and 31 March 1976. By the time of the later hearing, a noticeable change in mood was visible. Radical opposition to data protection had disappeared, and criticism centered more on the details of the law, especially as it related to the private sector. The constant and expert advice and testimony given by advocates such as Spiros Simitis who favored an independent control authority, also convinced many skeptics that self-surveillance would not suffice.[88]

During this period the Ministry of the Interior had also placed before the Bundestag a population registration bill (*Bundesmeldgesetz*), the main objective of which was to put upcoming computerized information systems on a full statutory basis.[89] A controversial component of the bill was the assignment of a twelve-digit personal identification number to all persons (not only citizens) living within the Federal Republic. The proposal led the Bundestag to decide that it would not pass this bill until data protection safeguards had been enacted.[90] In the end, the population registration bill was declared unconstitutional by the Legal Affairs Committee of the Bundestag, and attention focused thenceforth entirely on data protection.

Two and a half years after its first reading in June 1976, the bill was ready for second and third readings. The Interior Committee, however, had a split opinion about the final version; the lack of unity was seen in the opposition of the Christian Democratic Union (CDU) and Christian Social Union (CSU) parties to these second and third readings. This somewhat sudden about-face was prompted by the belief

---

87. Simitis et al., *Kommentar*, p. 68.
88. Spiros Simitis, "Establishing Institutional Structures to Monitor and Enforce Data Protection," in OECD, *Policy Issues in Data Protection and Privacy*, OECD Informatics Studies No. 10 (Paris: OECD, 1976), pp. 83–94.
89. Federal Republic of Germany, Bundestag, *Drucksache* 7/1059, May 1973.
90. Mallmann, "Computers and Civil Liberties," p. 6.

that the control authority should work from within the Federal Audit Office rather than as an independent body. What followed, as it did in the United States, was a dramatic race against the clock, for the legislative period was to end in the fall.[91] Approval of the bill by the Bundesrat—the next step, which in nine out of ten cases is usually a formality—was not forthcoming, however. The draft approved by the Bundestag was considered to be an unacceptable encroachment on the rights of the Länder to organize and control their public agencies. By insisting on an independent control authority at the federal level, the Bundestag had raised a thorny set of issues about federal and state relations, issues that the Bundesrat—the upper house, which represents the states' interests—naturally wanted settled.

A Joint Conference Committee (*Vermittlungsauschuss*) was duly appointed to hammer out a compromise—there were no informal midnight meetings as in the United States. A compromise recommendation, made on 2 July 1976, did little to assuage the concerns of a number of Länder; they asked the committee to reconsider the recommendation, but it refused. On 10 November 1976, the Bundestag endorsed the bill as rewritten, again with the opposition of the CDU and CSU parties. The Bundesrat passed the bill two days later with the opposition of Bavaria, Baden-Württemburg, Rheinland-Pfalz, and Schleswig-Holstein. The law was finally signed by Bundespresident Scheel on 27 January 1977 after a further tense delay during which the constitutionality of the law was affirmed. It was promulgated on 1 February 1977, and its main provisions took effect on 1 January 1978.[92]

The length and complication of the legislative history of the Federal Data Protection Act are somewhat untypical. It has even been suggested that "in the history of the Federal Republic, there could have been few laws that have had such a complicated legislative history."[93] There are also parallels between the German process and that in the United States: the battles over the type of enforcement mechanism, the intense pressures of legislative time, the intransigent bureaucracy, and

91. Bull, *Datenschutz oder die Angst vor dem Computer*, p. 106.
92. *Bundesdatenschutzgesetz* (BDSG) of 27 January 1977 (BGB1. IS. 201). English translation from Dammann et al., *Data Protection Legislation*, pp. 70–107.
93. Simitis et al., *Kommentar*, p. 69 (translation mine).

the final compromise that everyone accepted reluctantly. The German law was passed amid serious controversy and much skepticism. And as soon as it was enacted, both critics and advocates of data protection spoke of its possible amendment. Yet for thirteen years amendments have been proposed and have failed. Thus at the beginning of the 1990s, with the fall of the Berlin Wall and the rapid reunification of Germany, the Federal Data Protection Act remained just as it was in 1977.

The Evolution of the British Data Protection Act

Great Britain, the last of our four countries, is also the one in our sample that most recently legislated on data protection. Concerns about the privacy implications of information technology were aired in Britain in the 1960s, just as they were in other countries. The delay in legislating was not caused by the lack of a recognition of a problem but rather by procrastination and controversy that were not seen to the same extent elsewhere.

The first disadvantage that British advocates of privacy legislation faced was the absence of a written constitution. In Sweden, the United States and West Germany, data protection principles could be derived, to some extent at least, from constitutional doctrine. The problem was everywhere a new one, and one that required new solutions. But the existence of even tangentially related rights in constitutional law (the Fourth Amendment in the U.S. Constitution, the *Persönlichkeitsrechte* in the West German Basic Law) allowed advocates to argue that data protection was not a radical departure from previous practice but was firmly grounded in constitutional tradition.

In Britain there is no written constitution, nor is there thought to exist in the "unwritten" constitutional law a distinct right to privacy. English legal journals contain very little on the subject. Though the United Kingdom is a party to the European Convention on Human Rights, the convention has not been incorporated into English law and is not able to be adjudicated, therefore, in British courts. Certain areas of the common law (most notably, the laws of confidence, trespass, and defamation) are tangentially related. Some statutes (such as the infamous and now-reformed Section 2 of the 1911 Official Secrets

Act)[94] may apply in narrow instances. Overall, however, we can agree with Sieghart's conclusion that "the law of England extends only patchy and imperfect protection for the privacy of information, and what protection there is takes the form of costly therapy rather than cheap prophylaxis."[95]

British policy makers were therefore working with even more of a tabula rasa than were their overseas counterparts. The inadequacy of English law was graphically exposed when the 1960s arrived. At first the issue centered on the activities of the popular press. Bugging devices, miniature cameras, telephoto lenses, and other new technologies had raised British exposé journalism to new levels of tastelessness. Many become convinced that the Royal Family, film personalities, and other celebrities deserved more privacy.

This concern with "behavioral" rather than "information" privacy is reflected in the first two private members' bills on this issue to be introduced in Parliament. In February 1961, Lord Mancroft introduced a bill designed "to protect a person from any unjustifiable publication relating to his private affairs and to give him rights at law in the event of such publication." It was admitted that the bill was "purely an extension of our age-old protection against eavesdropping, 'Peeping Toms' and 'Paul Prys.' "[96] A similar Right of Privacy Bill was introduced in the House of Commons under the Ten-Minute Rule on 8 February 1967 by Alex Lyon. Bills introduced in this way, however, rarely succeed in becoming law unless given the blessing of the government and the necessary parliamentary time. They all tend to have the

---

94. Section 2 of the 1911 Official Secrets Act forbade the unauthorized disclosure of any official information however inconsequential. Attempts to revise this discredited law go back at least twenty years. In 1989 the government was successful in passing a new Official Information Act, which specified a set of sensitive categories to which criminal penalties apply. Many reformers, hoping for an access to information statute, argued that the government had produced a law even more dangerous than Section 2. For an analysis of the whole debate, see Colin J. Bennett, "From the Dark to the Light: The Open Government Debate in Britain," *Journal of Public Policy* 5 (1985): 187–213.

95. Sieghart, *Privacy and Computers*, p. 31.

96. Lord Mancroft, HL Debs., 5s., 13 March 1961, col. 607. The British obsession with press intrusiveness into the private lives of public figures continues into the 1990s. Private members' bills from Tory M.P.s in 1988/89 led to the appointment of a committee to investigate whether individuals needed greater protections against the more tasteless and scurrilous activities of the British press. The Calcutt Committee recommended in 1990 a number of changes to the criminal law and to the procedures for complaints against the press. Great Britain, Home Office, *Report of the Committee on Privacy and Related Matters*, Chairman: David Calcutt (London: HMSO, 1990).

same purpose as that stated by Alex Lyon, who introduced his bill "not because I expected that piece of legislation to be enacted, but simply to begin a campaign to introduce into our law, a law of privacy which would be an effective protection for . . . the freedom to keep one's private life to oneself."[97]

By the end of the decade, however, the question of record-keeping systems and databanks had emerged as a more prominent concern. A bill that dealt exclusively with computerized personal information was tabled in 1969 by Kenneth Baker in the Commons and by Lord Windlesham in the Lords. This Data Surveillance Bill made no headway at the time. In calling for registration of and a code of conduct for computerized personal databanks, however, it presaged later developments in an extraordinary way.[98] The bill that clearly pushed the issue onto the institutional agenda was that of Brian Walden. Introduced in late 1969, this bill was drafted by "Justice," whose influential report *Privacy and the Law*[99] did much to advance the debate above polemics. Walden was successful in the annual ballot for private members' bills and was thus assured a full second-reading debate for his Right of Privacy Bill.

This debate, on 23 January 1970, was the first time that the issue received a full and public airing in Britain, and it generated much goodwill on all sides of the House toward a statute on privacy protection. Borrowing from American rhetoric, Walden declared that "the right to be left alone may not sound a very exciting freedom, but it is the one about which the British people care most." The diversity, complexity, and rapid development of new intrusive technologies persuaded both "Justice" and Walden that the correct approach was to create a completely new statutory tort of "infringement of privacy" in which all "substantial and unreasonable infringements would be actionable." Because the intrusion itself was the wrong, rather than the means of intrusion, the solution was to provide the "general right, and then, give definitions and defences."[100]

This broad scope covered the actions of many organizations and aroused considerable disquiet. The press, for instance, was far from

97. Alexander Lyon, HC Debs., 5s., 8 February 1967, col. 1565.
98. Warner and Stone, *The Data Bank Society*, p. 117.
99. Justice, *Privacy and the Law*.
100. Brian Walden, HC Debs., 5s., 23 January 1970, cols. 862–68.

enthusiastic about the legislation and saw damaging implications in it for the freedom of speech. The reaction of the government (then Labour) was also ambivalent. Home Secretary James Callaghan was generally "satisfied that certain actions by business organizations, reputable and disreputable, certain actions by the press, and certain actions by individuals have constituted serious infringements to personal privacy." But he also added that while "it seems likely that legislation should be introduced, it is far from clear that the range of discretion provided by the Bill should be given to the courts at this stage."[101]

In reality, the government's intention, and certainly that of the Home Office, was to block Walden's bill at any cost. Accordingly, a deal was struck. In return for relieving the government of the embarrassment of voting down the bill after its second reading and thus appearing to oppose privacy, Walden was promised the establishment of a study committee to analyze the issue and report back to Parliament. Walden had no choice. There was indeed a widespread feeling that more consideration was necessary. Therefore, in May 1970 (one month before the Labour government fell in the general election) an interdepartmental committee was appointed under the chairmanship of Sir Kenneth Younger. And so began the next phase of the privacy debate in Britain.

Committee Analysis and Recommendation

It was a pity that Younger's terms of reference were not also discussed at the time of the agreement. For, when announced, they appeared far more restrictive than many had anticipated: "To consider whether legislation is needed to give further protection to the individual citizen and to commercial and industrial interests against intrusions into privacy by private persons and organizations, or by companies, and to make recommendations."[102] The committee asked both James Callaghan and new Conservative home secretary, Reginald Maudling, whether its terms of reference could be extended to cover the public as well as the private sector. This group argued that "many of the anxieties which had led to a demand for a legal right of privacy concerned the activities of Government Departments and other public

101. James Callaghan, HC Debs., 5s., 23 January 1970, col. 943.
102. Great Britain, *Report of the Committee on Privacy* (1972), p. 1.

agencies" and that "the demarcation between public and private sectors might prove difficult."[103] In response, the government allowed the committee to enquire into the workings of the British Broadcasting Corporation and the Independent Television Authority. It also promised to set up an internal working party to examine the extent and nature of government personal record-keeping systems. But the public sector was generally excluded from the Younger Committee's charge, and report of the internal investigation was never published. Complaints were also heard about the composition of the committee and the fact that there was no mention of computers in its terms of reference.[104]

The Younger Committee submitted its report in July 1972. The committee opted for a piecemeal approach rather than a general right to privacy as in the Walden bill. Thus the report had a fragmented appearance with a diversity of recommendations relating to the different instances of intrusion that had been brought to its attention. The most interesting conclusions, and those that had a strong influence on the later debate, pertained to computerized information: "Of all the forms of invasion of privacy which have been cited in evidence to us, that involving the use or misuse of computers has been the least supported in concrete terms. . . . Put quite simply, the computer problem as it affects privacy in Great Britain is one of apprehensions and fears and not so far one of facts and figures."[105]

The committee was influenced, however, by the evidence given by Alan Westin that the actual abuses which had already occurred in the United States (described in *Privacy and Freedom*) would almost certainly also occur eventually in Europe. Despite its inability to conclude that the computer was a present danger, the committee did concede that there was a possibility of such a threat becoming a reality in the future. Consequently, in order to anticipate and combat potential abuses, the committee proposed ten fair information principles for personal information as described in Chapter 3.[106] It also suggested that the government set up a standing commission to keep the situation under review.

103. Ibid., p. 2.
104. Madgwick and Smythe, *The Invasion of Privacy*, p. 15.
105. Great Britain, *Report of the Committee on Privacy*(1972), p. 179.
106. Ibid., pp. 183–84.

Some of Younger's recommendations were adopted in the Consumer Credit Act of 1974, which gives individuals the right to access and to correct credit reports.[107] Other committee recommendations were embodied in a professional code of conduct by the British Computer Society.[108] The official response, however, was affected more by the cautionary and equivocal tone set by Younger. In answer to a written question, Home Secretary Maudling stated the Conservative government's wish to consult and deliberate:

> It is our intention to take public reaction and the views of those interested in this matter into account before announcing a conclusion. Meanwhile, as the House knows, the Government have been reviewing the categories of personal information held in Government computers and rules governing its storage and use, and in due course we shall be publishing a White Paper setting out our own conclusions both on the Younger Committee Report and our own review.[109]

Nothing further was done until the Conservative government left office in 1974.

The incoming Labour administration, and its more enthusiastic Home Secretary, Roy Jenkins, promised an early White Paper on privacy. That document, *Computers and Privacy,* was eventually published in December 1975[110] along with a supplementary report on central-government computers.[111] That these White Papers were published at all owes much to the persistence of the Home Secretary and of his junior minister, Alex Lyon, who was a member of the Younger Committee. They also reflect an important change in official thinking. Recognizing that a general right to privacy would alienate many seg-

---

107. *Consumer Credit Act of 1974.* This act regulates the activities of firms in the consumer credit industry by licensing all companies in the field, by requiring the credit grantor to supply the consumer on request with the name and address of any credit reference agency that has supplied information about him or her, and by providing a right of access to personal credit information.

108. British Computer Society, *Steps to Practicality* (London: British Computer Society, 1972).

109. Reginald Maudling, HC Debs., 5s., 12 July 1972, col. 383 (written answers).

110. Great Britain, Home Office, *Computers and Privacy,* Cmnd. 6353 (London: HMSO, 1975).

111. Great Britain, Home Office, *Computers: Safeguards for Privacy,* Cmnd. 6354 (London: HMSO, 1975).

ments of the press, Jenkins decided to deal first with the issue around which a broader coalition could be built. Thenceforth, the issue be-, came one of computers and privacy (or more accurately, computers *versus* privacy), and the discourse centered on the European concept of "data protection." *Computers and Privacy* also owes much to Paul Sieghart, barrister and chair of the executive committee of "Justice," who was brought in to assist in its drafting and to overcome the intransigence of Home Office civil servants.[112]

The document reflects a certain ambivalence in British thinking on this subject. Paralleling the Younger Committee's conclusions about the private sector, the government found that there was "no evidence to suggest that fears about the improper use of computers in the public sector are justified by present practice. These systems are operated in accordance with administrative rules and procedures which provide substantial safeguards against the realisation of any such fears." The findings were based on a survey of official computer practice that was published in the supplementary report. It contended that these assurances "should go a long way towards reassuring the public about the past, the present and the immediate future."[113]

On the other hand, the risk of computers and the obvious fear of the general public were a cause for concern. It was therefore admitted that "the time has come when those who use computers to handle personal information, however responsible they are, can no longer remain the sole judges of whether their own systems adequately safeguard privacy." The White Paper thus contained a specific commitment to legislation that would set up machinery, not only to keep the situation under review, but also to ensure that all existing and future computer systems would operate with appropriate safeguards. The function of the perceived legislation was to define standards and criteria and to establish a permanent statutory agency "to oversee the use of computers, in both the public and private sectors, to ensure that they are operated with proper regard for privacy and with necessary safeguards for the personal information they contain."[114]

According to one reading of the White Paper, then, there would be a statute in the current Parliament; there would be an independent Data Protection Authority; the law would apply to all computer systems in

112. Campbell and Connor, *On the Record*, p. 25.
113. Great Britain, *Computers and Privacy*, p. 3.
114. Ibid., pp. 8–9.

both the public and the private sector; and there would be a statutory code. Others, however, were more skeptical. Their doubts arose from the decision to appoint another committee to prepare the way for the legislation, "a sort of St. John the Baptist for the computing industry."[115] The Committee on Data Protection was appointed and was to be headed again by Sir Kenneth Younger; however, Younger's untimely death led to his replacement at the last minute by Sir Norman Lindop. The Lindop Committee began its work in July 1976, and it reported two years later. Six months after that, in December 1978, the government published its report.[116]

More focused than those for the Younger Committee, Lindop's terms of reference were confined to the protection of computerized personal data. Evidence was gathered on the implications of and the actions taken overseas on information technology. It recommended that legislation should be enacted to set up a data protection authority that would prepare codes of practice, defining in detail the rules applicable to any system used for collecting, processing, or storing personal data on computers. The codes of practice would be drawn up according to a central set of fair information principles, that would be very similar to those of the Younger Committee but would also be tailored to specific institutional needs and contexts. The new authority would require the registration of every application involving personal data handled by corporate entities, including government departments. The operations of registered organizations would be inspected periodically to ensure their observation of required standards.

In general, the report was well received, even though the timing of its publication was terrible. Six months later a successful (and unusual) vote of no confidence forced the Labour government from office. With the advent of Mrs. Thatcher's Conservative administration in May 1979, the data protection issue entered a new phase.

The Passage of the British Data Protection Act

After the publication of the Lindop Report, the only stated commitment by the Labour Home Secretary was that "the Government will

115. Sieghart, "Background to the Issue," p. 13.
116. Great Britain, Home Office, *Report of the Committee on Data Protection*, Cmnd. 7341 (Chairman: Sir Norman Lindop) (London: HMSO, 1978).

wish to have the views of computer users and others who would be affected by the recommendations."[117] The government subsequently published in *Hansard* a list of over 250 organizations with which consultations were being conducted. The Thatcher government continued this process on taking office.

The new administration also was more skeptical about the necessity for data protection law. The government initially saw the Lindop Committee as a Labour-inspired group and was distrustful of its recommendations. Some, such as *The Times*, for instance, questioned the inherent sense of data protection:

> Does the notion of trying to control computer data by legislation make sense at all? A growing body of opinion both inside and outside the computer industry thinks not. There is a shortage of hard evidence that computers are causing an invasion of privacy. . . . It usually turns out that the computer is not the real culprit, and that such wrongs as there are can be dealt with under existing laws.[118]

In the meantime, other groups were growing increasingly impatient. The civil liberties lobby in the form of the NCCL published a report and draft scheme for legislation in August 1980.[119] The Labour party, too, pressed for prompt action along the lines of the Lindop Committee's proposals in a discussion document of July 1981.[120] But the government was in no mood to hurry. Indeed, the first indications from the Home Secretary in 1981 were that the government would *not* seek to establish an independent data protection authority along the lines of the Lindop recommendations in any legislation that it might introduce.[121]

British Conservative governments, especially ones with parliamentary majorities of 140 members, do not normally feel compelled to listen to the arguments of the civil liberties lobby or the Labour party. The computer industry's concerns, however, are a different matter.

---

117. Merlyn Rees, HC Debs., 5s., 5 December 1978, cols. 556–57 (written answers).
118. *The Times*, 26 March 1980.
119. NCCL, *Legislating for Information Privacy* (London: NCCL, 1980).
120. Labour Party, *Personal Information and Privacy* (London: Labour Party, 1981).
121. James Cornford, "The Prospects for Privacy," *The Political Quarterly* 52 (1981): 295.

When the government was faced with the argument that British hardware and software manufacturers, as well as many others in the service sector, would be adversely affected unless Britain had data protection legislation, it was forced to respond. In the final analysis, the British Data Protection Act of 1984 was passed for economic rather than for civil libertarian reasons.

The first arguments of this nature are to be found in a report from the Advisory Council for Applied Research and Development, published by the Cabinet Office in September 1980.[122] The principal impetus behind this report was the promulgation in January 1981 of the international convention on data protection by the Council of Europe,[123] which will be discussed in more depth in Chapter 4. In brief, the agreement now allows data protection authorities to refuse the transmission of personal data to countries that do not have adequate safeguards. Some in Britain feared that the country's computers would stand idle because of a new nontariff trade barrier imposed by her European partners. Personal data protection could become a legal pretext for trade protectionism, leading to the isolation of the British data processing industry and of other service sectors of the economy that rely on unimpeded communications. These were pressing concerns, especially for the Department of Trade and Industry.

The government actually signed this convention in May 1981, which indicated a desire to ratify it fully as soon as a British data protection act reached the statute book. At the same time, the government was pursuing various courses of action to stimulate the British information technology industry: 1982 was declared "Information Technology Year," and a minister for information technology and Information Technology Advisory Panel (ITAP) were appointed. The ITAP was intimately involved in the internal discussions within the Home Office about the government's data protection bill.

The first official commitment to data protection came in September 1981 from Timothy Raison, Minister of State at the Home Office. In a speech to the British Medical Association, he affirmed the government's intention to give statutory protection to automatically record-

---

122. Great Britain, Cabinet Office, Advisory Committee for Applied Research and Development, *Information Technology* (London: HMSO, 1980).
123. Council of Europe, *Convention for the Protection of Individuals with Regard to Automatic Processing of Personal Data* (Strasbourg: Council of Europe, 1981).

ed personal information. The central enforcement scheme was to be a public register of databanks which was to be located in the Home Office. Lindop's codes of practice and independent data protection authority were rejected out of hand. These same ideas were floated at the "Info 82" Conference in February 1982.

The public announcement of the specific timetable for legislation actually resulted from a bizarre and totally unrelated incident involving the medical files of Michael Meacher, M.P. Meacher had introduced a private member's data protection bill in early 1982. In response the *Sun* newspaper engaged several private detectives to pry into Meacher's personal life. They came up with some medical files, which were published all over the *Sun*'s front page. When Meacher raised this matter during Prime Minister's question time in February 1982, Mrs. Thatcher commiserated with him and pronounced the government's intention to legislate on data protection in the next parliamentary session. It is widely believed that "this was the first that stunned and dismayed Home Office officials had heard of it."[124] This exercise in prime-ministerial power was fairly typical of Mrs. Thatcher's style.

Thus the Home Office had to produce a White Paper in a hurry, and this paper was duly published in April 1982.[125] It proposed a data registrar who would be independent of the government and responsible for establishing and overseeing a public register of computer systems that process personal, name-linked data. Through the registration process, personal data users would have to comply with a general set of principles consistent with those of the Council of Europe Convention. The White Paper gives the appearance of being put together in a hurry. It certainly received widespread criticism. Nevertheless, a bill with features similar to those in this paper was accordingly introduced in the House of Lords in December 1982. There it was given an unopposed second reading on 20 January 1983, and it was given a second reading in the Commons on 11 April. It did not complete its final stages, however, before the dissolution of Parliament in May.

Having taken account of additional commentary and simplified some of the registration provisions, the government reintroduced the

---

124. Campbell and Connor, *On the Record*, p. 29.
125. Great Britain, Home Office, *Data Protection: The Government's Proposals for Legislation*, Cmnd. 8539 (London: HMSO, 1982).

bill in the Lords on 23 June 1983; it received a second reading on 5 July. In the Commons it was read a second time on 30 January 1984 and was passed by a vote of 226 to 104. The government was supported by the Liberals and the Social Democrats but was opposed by the Labour party on the grounds that the bill did not go far enough. The bill was read a third time on 5 June and then duly enacted on 12 July 1984. Given the large parliamentary majority in favor of the legislation the bill was expected to be enacted in more or less the same form as that in which it was introduced. It nevertheless experienced a controversial passage. The Labour Opposition was conscious that the Conservatives were not wholeheartedly in support of the libertatian objectives of the bill. On second reading, the Labour spokesman, Gerald Kaufman, said that the bill contained "the absolute minimum the government can get away with" to enable it to sign the Council of Europe Convention.[126]

Critics were particularly concerned that the bill did not apply to manual records and thus opened the possibility of transferring computerized data to manual form, or not computerizing the data in the first place, in order to escape the requirements of the law. Civil liberties groups argued that the bill was in some respects the reverse of the progressive step intended, because it legitimized transfers of data which before had been impossible.[127] Critics also pointed to the highly restrictive access rights. Doctors worried about the confidentiality of medical records held by area and regional health authorities. Educators were concerned that students might gain access to confidential school and exam records. Some even doubted whether the bill would meet its aim of allowing Britain to ratify the European convention.[128] For many the bill was an ill-conceived compromise; for others it was a "Big Brother" measure.

So ends the long and complicated story of how Britain finally achieved its Data Protection Act. The legislation passed in "Orwell's year," twenty-three years after the first privacy bill was introduced in Parliament. It is a story that contrasts in interesting ways with those in Sweden, the United States, and West Germany. It is a far more frus-

126. Gerald Kaufman, HC Debs., 6s., 30 January 1984, col. 43.
127. NCCL, *Data Protection Bill 1983: NCCL Briefing* (London: NCCL, 1983), and Roger Cornwell and Marie Staunton, *Data Protection: Putting the Record Straight* (London: NCCL, 1985).
128. See, Bourn and Benyon, eds., *Data Protection*, p. 35.

trating story (for civil libertarians at least) than that told elsewhere. The bill's passage took longer and involved more public and private actors than did similar legislation elsewhere. But as in the United States and West Germany, the process was a conflictual rather than a consensual one, as in Sweden.

The juxtaposition of these four accounts allows us to compare and contrast the policy-making styles of these four countries, and these comparisons are the subject of Chapter 7. It is now time, however, to write more fully about the content of these laws. How is data protection achieved in these four states? From this analysis we can begin to investigate whether a convergence has occurred despite the different paths along which these four countries traveled.

3

Evidence of Policy Convergence

Many participants in, and observers of, the data protection movement have remarked on the similar content of the laws passed from country to country. Two figures with important responsibilities within international organizations had a central view of this convergence. Frits Hondius, the Secretary to the Council of Europe's Committee of Experts on Data Protection, for instance, states: "In spite of the great variety of methods and styles, the various European laws exhibit a basic harmony. They share a common philosophy in purpose and objective."[1] Justice Michael Kirby, the chair of the OECD's committee of government experts on data protection, has a similar impression: "Given the different languages, legal traditions, and cultural and social values, fundamental disagreements might have been expected. Surprisingly, in all of the major international efforts that have so far addressed this problem, there has been a broad measure of agreement on the 'basic rules' around which domestic privacy legislation should cluster."[2] As early as 1974, an OECD survey found that "there is a striking similarity to the independent yet correlative actions in data protection and privacy" conducted by OECD governments.[3]

Outside commentators have made remarks in a similar vein. Oswald and Gladys Ganley are impressed that "the various national laws

1. Hondius, "Data Law in Europe," p. 94.
2. Michael D. Kirby, "Transborder Data Flows and the 'Basic Rules' of Data Privacy," *Stanford Journal of International Law* 16 (1980): 29.
3. OECD, *Developments in Data Protection and Privacy by OECD Countries,* Unpublished Survey from the OECD's Computer Utilization Group (Paris: OECD, Directorate for Scientific Affairs, 1975), p. 2.

on privacy, including those of the United States, are remarkably uniform regarding the principles of protection."[4] They make the general observation that "although the advanced countries may differ on details, they subscribe to the same basic communications and information philosophies."[5] And Flaherty has concluded from a long-term analysis of this issue that "the resemblances among the various data protection laws are strong."[6]

These impressions rest mainly on the detection of a common set of principles for the treatment of personal data. Names range from "principles for privacy safeguards" to "principles for handling personal information" to the "principles of fair information practice" to "data protection principles" to the most commonly used "fair information principles."[7] I will show that, while the nomenclature and codification may vary from country to country, the substance and purpose of these principles are basically the same. I shall also demonstrate that these similar tenets are contained in the laws of all four countries.

Statements of Fair Information Policy

Tracking the genesis of ideas is an inherently difficult enterprise. Reliance on the word and memory of participants, some of whom may have an exaggerated perception of their role in history, exacerbates the task of discovering the origins of the fair information principles. Nevertheless, one line of development can certainly be traced to the debates in the United States in the late 1960s and early 1970s among the small number of data protection experts.

One source of fair information policy is American labor and trade law and the notion of fair and unfair labor or trade practices. More directly, the conceptualization of information privacy that Westin and Miller advocated led naturally to a set of procedural guarantees to assist individuals to determine for themselves when, how and to what

4. Ganley and Ganley, *To Inform or to Control*, p. 89.
5. Ibid., p. 175.
6. Flaherty, "Governmental Surveillance and Bureaucratic Accountability," p. 8.
7. Sieghart, *Privacy and Computers*, p. 109; Great Britain, *Report of the Committee on Privacy* (1972), p. 182; U.S. HEW, *Records, Computers, and the Rights of Citizens*, p. 41; Flaherty, *Protecting Privacy in Surveillance Societies*, p. 380.

extent information about them is communicated to others. The first manifestation of this kind of thinking is in the 1970 Fair Credit Reporting Act. A more explicit discussion of the policy options is found in Westin and Baker's report for the National Academy of Sciences. The final chapter discusses public policy priority areas, among which are citizen access, rules for confidentiality and data-sharing, and the limiting of unnecessary data collection.[8]

Therefore, when the Advisory Committee to the Secretary for Health, Education and Welfare deliberated these issues, they had a sound foundation of research and analysis upon which to build. "Personal privacy as it relates to personal-data record keeping," the 1973 report states, "must be understood in terms of a concept of mutuality."[9] Echoing Westin, they offered the following formulation:

> An individual's personal privacy is directly affected by the kind of disclosure and use made of identifiable information about him in a record. A record containing information about an individual in identifiable form must, therefore, be governed by procedures that afford the individual a right to participate in deciding what the content of the record will be, and what disclosure and use will be made of the identifiable information. Any recording, disclosure, and use of identifiable personal information not governed by such procedures must be proscribed as an unfair information practice unless such recording, disclosure or use is specifically authorized by law.[10]

These assumptions lead logically to the first explicit enumeration of "certain fundamental principles of fair information practice":

> There must be no personal-data record-keeping systems whose very existence is secret.
> There must be a way for an individual to find out what information about him is in a record and how it is used.
> There must be a way for an individual to prevent information about him obtained for one purpose from being used or made available for other purposes without his consent.

8. Westin and Baker, *Databanks in a Free Society*, pp. 355–92.
9. U.S. HEW, *Records, Computers, and the Rights of Citizens*, p. 40.
10. Ibid., pp. 40–41.

There must be a way for an individual to correct or amend a record of identifiable information about him.

Any organization creating, maintaining, using or disseminating records of identifiable personal data must assure the reliability of the data for their intended use and must take reasonable precautions to prevent misuse of the data.[11]

The committee points out that "this formulation does not provide the basis for determining *a priori* which data should or may be recorded and used, or why, and when."[12] These are *procedural* safeguards, consistent with the American emphasis on "due process" rights. Together, the National Academy of Sciences and HEW reports granted the privacy issue a status it did not have before and provided a ready-made solution if policy makers ever wanted to tackle the problem. The addition of the label "fair" to the solution also granted a certain legitimacy: if you want to legislate fairness, who can be against you?

The United States, therefore, is one possible source of the fair information principles. The other source was Britain. For at virtually the same time, the Younger Committee was devising a very similar formulation. Ten principles were stated:

1. Information should be regarded as held for a specific purpose and not to be used, without appropriate authorization, for other purposes.
2. Access to information should be confined to those authorized to have it for the purposes for which it was supplied.
3. The amount of information collected and held should be the minimum necessary for the achievement of a specified purpose.
4. In computerized systems handling information for statistical purposes, adequate provision should be made in their design and programs for separating identities from the rest of the data.
5. There should be arrangements whereby the subject could be told about the information held concerning him.
6. The level of security to be achieved by a system should be specified in advance by the user and should include precautions against the deliberate abuse or misuse of information.
7. A monitoring system should be provided to facilitate the detection of any violation of the security system.

11. Ibid.
12. Ibid.

8. In the design of information systems, periods should be specified beyond which the information should not be retained.
9. Data held should be accurate. There should be machinery for the correction of inaccuracy and the updating of information.
10. Care should be taken in coding value judgements.[13]

With the exception of the last item, these, too, are procedural principles, suggesting nothing about the substance of the personal information collected. The Younger principles, however, were directed only toward computerized information; they had their origin in a 1971 Code of Conduct from the British Computer Society.[14] The American policy, by contrast, was formed more to protect the individual (regardless of how the information was stored). Nevertheless, in their assumptions and substance, the two formulations are very similar, though it is impossible to judge which came first or how one influenced the other.

Subsequent statements of fair information principles follow similar lines. The Younger principles are broadly accepted in the Lindop Committee report of 1978, the 1982 White Paper, and the 1984 legislation. The HEW formulation finds later expression in the 1974 Privacy Act, in a report from the Federal Council of Science and Technology (COSATI),[15] and in the subsequent report by the Privacy Protection Study Commission. This latter body concluded that an effective data protection policy should have three objectives: to minimize intrusiveness; to maximize fairness; and to create legitimate, enforceable expectations of confidentiality.[16]

In Germany, similar statements of principle can be found. The Hessian Data Protection Commissioner published ten principles in March 1975 for the proper use of electronic data processing; these are strikingly similar to those of Younger.[17] Flaherty suggests that in Germany as a whole the "detailed principles of both federal and state laws for the control of surveillance incorporate the fair information practices common in such legislation in other countries."[18] In Sweden, too, he

13. Great Britain, *Report of the Committee on Privacy* (1972), pp. 183–84.
14. British Computer Society, *Steps to Practicality.*
15. Committee on Scientific and Technical Information of the Federal Council of Science and Technology (COSATI), "Legal Aspects of Computerized Information Systems," *The Honeywell Computer Journal* 7 (January 1973).
16. PPSC, *Personal Privacy in an Information Society*, pp. 14–15.
17. Quoted in Sieghart, *Privacy and Computers*, p. 156.
18. Flaherty, *Protecting Privacy in Surveillance Societies*, p. 21.

notes that "the Data Act also contains the customary code of fair information practices."[19] The Commission on Informatics and Freedom, which provided the basis for the French law, is organized according to similar precepts.[20] One of the earliest study commissions, the Canadian Task Force on Privacy and Computers, which reported in December 1972, contains like principles.[21]

By far the most influential expression of fair information principles, however, has been the two resolutions of the Council of Europe (September 1973 and September 1974) and the subsequent Council of Europe Convention promulgated in 1981.[22] The development and impact of this convention is discussed more fully in Chapter 4. For the moment, we can note that it stipulates that personal data undergoing automatic data processing should be: (1) obtained and processed fairly and lawfully; (2) stored for specified and legitimate purposes and not used in a way incompatible with those purposes; (3) adequate, relevant, and not excessive in relation to the purposes for which they are stored; (4) accurate and, where necessary, kept up-to-date; and (5) preserved in a form that permits identification of the data subjects for which these records are stored. It also confirms the rights of individuals to establish the existence of an automated personal data file and determine its main purposes, to be informed of whether personal data relating to them are stored in such a file, to rectify or erase false or out-of-date information, and to have a remedy for noncompliance. A companion set of guidelines issued by the OECD in 1981 defines eight basic principles: collection limitation, data quality, purpose specification, use limitation, security safeguards, openness, individual participation, and accountability. Again, the OECD guidelines will be more fully discussed below.[23]

A finding of policy convergence should rest on more than an obser-

19. Ibid., p. 107.
20. *Rapport de la Commission Informatique et Libertés.*
21. Department of Communications and Department of Justice, *Privacy and Computers: A Report of the Task Force* (Ottawa: Information Canada, 1972); see also Colin J. Bennett, "The Formation of a Canadian Privacy Policy: The Art and Craft of Lesson-Drawing," *Canadian Public Administration* 33 (1990): 551–70.
22. Council of Europe, Resolution (73) 22 on the *Protection of the Privacy of Individuals vis-à-vis Electronic Data Banks in the Public Sector* (Strasbourg: Council of Europe, 20 September 1974); Council of Europe, *Convention for the Protection of Individuals.*
23. OECD, *Guidelines on the Protection of Privacy and Transborder Flows of Personal Data* (Paris: OECD, 1981).

vation that different international and national bodies have articulated similar expectations. One must also demonstrate that the laws enacted reflect a substantial uniformity. The next task, therefore, is to present how each fair information principle is embodied in the four laws under consideration. For analytical purposes, I condensed these different formulations into six essential tenets. Having established a convergence around these core statutory principles, I can then examine the more tangential questions that produced controversy and national variations.

The Core Fair Information Principles

The Principle of Openness

The first prerequisite for any system of control for personal data is openness or transparency. The very existence of record-keeping systems, registers, or databanks should be publicly known. "Public" may mean everyone or just those on whom the data are stored. "Known" may mean a variety of things: published in a register, available for online access, or open for inspection at a records office or library. The prevailing assumption is that no organization may conceal the existence of any personal record-keeping system, the kinds of information in it, and the way in which it may be used.

Under the U.S. Privacy Act, for example, agencies are required to publish in the *Federal Register* at least once a year a notice of the existence and nature of each system of records. This notice must detail the categories of individuals maintained in the system, the type of information stored, and the practices of the agency regarding storage, retrievability, access, retention, and disposal. These systems notices are also sent to the Office of Management and Budget (OMB) and Congress for review.[24]

In Britain, the entire regulatory system is based on the requirement that "all users of data systems which process automatically information relating to identifiable individuals should register."[25] Registration requires applying to the office of the Data Protection Registrar

---

24. *The Privacy Act of 1974*, PL 93-579, 5 U.S.C. 552a, Sec. 3(e) (4). Hereafter cited as "Privacy Act."

25. Great Britain, *Data Protection: The Government's Proposals for Legislation*, p. 4.

and providing: a notification of the type of and purposes for which data are held; a description of the sources and recipients of these data; and an address to which individuals may write for access to their data. The register is available for perusal on microfiche in many public libraries. The assumption was that "a public register should go a long way to meet the objective that the existence and purpose of computerized personal information systems should be publicly known."[26]

The Swedish licensing system under the 1973 Data Act stipulates that "a personal register may not be started or kept without permission by the Data Inspection Board."[27] This choice of a comprehensive regulatory system owes much to the assumption that such a system would open up the mysterious world of data processing. The Swedes talk much of "transparency." In keeping with the spirit of the publicity principle mandated by the Freedom of the Press Act, registration of personal record-keeping systems was seen as the first essential step toward protecting privacy.

The German Federal Data Protection Act of 1978 (BDSG) is also explicit about openness. Section 12 requires that "immediately following the initial storage public authorities and other official establishments shall announce in the relevant official bulletin for their sector: 1. the type of personal data stored by them or on their behalf; 2. the tasks for which knowledge of these data is required; 3. the persons concerned; 4. the establishments to which they regularly communicate personal data; and 5. the type of data to be communicated."[28] The BDSG, however, has jurisdictional limitations. It applies to all branches of the federal government—legislative, executive, and judicial. It covers the actions of public authorities in the Länder, however, only to the extent that they administer federal law. So this public notice provision yields far fewer record systems than do others.

There are also some extensive exemptions to this provision for the defense and intelligence services, the Federal Criminal Investigation

---

26. Ibid.
27. *Swedish Data Act*, Sec. 2. The 1973 version of the act is found in the Swedish Code of Statutes (SFS) 1973: 289. The amended version is at SFS 1982: 446. The English translation is from Dammann et al., *Data Protection Legislation*. Hereafter cited as "Data Act."
28. *Bundesdatenschutzgesetz* (BDSG), Sec. 12 (1). The German text is found in *Bundesgesetzblatt* 1: s. 201, 27 January 1977. Hereafter cited as "BDSG." The English translation is taken from Dammann et al., *Data Protection Legislation*.

Office (*Bundeskriminalamt*), and certain tax authorities.[29] Similar exemptions are provided in the British law for files relating to national security and the prevention of crime, for the collection of tax or duty, and for health and social work purposes.[30] The American law only allows the exemption of whole systems of very sensitive security and intelligence files.[31] The Swedish law exempts, for constitutional reasons, registers compiled by the King-in-Council and the Riksdag.[32] But no form of personal record is exempted by content or purpose. Only very routine uses of personal data (for mundane clerical functions) are allowed a simpler, and less bureaucratic, process of registration under the 1982 amendments to the Data Act. The British law, too, exempts data held for payroll or accounting purposes, for preparing the text of documents, for mailing lists, or for purely domestic or recreational purposes.[33]

Experience shows that lists of personal record-keeping systems are rarely consulted. In the more comprehensive registration systems in Sweden and Britain, only a proportion of computer users even register. Nevertheless, underlying this first principle is the belief that the complexities and dangers of the information-processing environment can be mitigated if exposed, that no harm can be done if the nature and purpose of automatic data processing is in the public arena. Publicity and transparency mean propriety; secrecy facilitates malfeasance.

The Principle of Individual Access and Correction

The openness principle is also a prerequisite for what some have regarded as the most important privacy protection safeguard; individual access to personal files.[34] A concomitant principle is the right to correct any portion of the data that is not accurate, timely, or complete. This right is provided only to the individual to whom the record

29. BDSG, Sec. 12 (2) 1.
30. United Kingdom, *Data Protection Act*, c. 35. Sec. 26–29. Hereafter cited as "Data Protection Act."
31. Privacy Act, Sec. 3 (1).
32. Data Act, Sec. 2.
33. Data Protection Act, Sec. 32.
34. OECD, *Guidelines*, p. 31.

pertains, the "data subject." The expectation is that individuals themselves can do much to mitigate any problems arising from the wrong people using the wrong data for the wrong purposes. The principle is sometimes termed "the right to print-out."[35] Although data protection experts contest its importance, all data protection law reflects this principle.

The American Privacy Act requires agencies to allow the individual access to "information pertaining to him" that is contained in a "system of records." A very similar right had existed since 1967 in the more widely drawn Freedom of Information Act (FOIA). Unlike FOIA, however, the Privacy Act grants the individual the concomitant right to correct any portion of the record that is not "accurate, relevant, timely or complete."[36] The right of access in the Swedish law also supplements an existing freedom of information provision, in this case the publicity principle in the Freedom of the Press Act. Section 10 stipulates: "At the request of an individual registered the responsible keeper of the register shall as soon as possible inform him of the personal information concerning him in the register."[37]

In Britain and West Germany, the respective data protection laws grant an access right in the context of a presumption of secrecy; few, if any, freedom of information provisions exist.[38] In both countries, moreover, the right is much qualified. In the British act, data subjects are entitled only to a copy of their personal data from a system that is itself registered—and many are not.[39] Furthermore, the "data user" may refuse access if it would prejudice the prevention or detection of crime, the apprehension or prosecution of offenders, or the assessment or collection of any tax or duty. Certain legal data concerning judicial appointments and the lawyer/client privilege are exempted as are data held solely for statistical or research purposes. The Secretary of State

35. Sieghart, *Privacy and Computers*, p. 117.
36. Privacy Act, Sec. 3(d).
37. Data Act, Sec. 10.
38. In Britain, the long-term attempt to reform Section 2 of the 1911 Official Secrets Act did not culminate in a freedom of information act but in the Official Information Act of 1989, which some regard as a more draconian statute than was the original Section 2. The only access provisions that exist relate to specific categories of environmental, health and safety, medical, and local government records. In Germany, the campaign for freedom of information has been far more recent and is associated with the rise of the Greens.
39. Data Protection Act, Sec. 21.

is also empowered to exempt certain data concerning physical or mental health or relating to social work.

The German law is even more restrictive, the presumption of secrecy being even stronger in the Federal Republic than in Britain. Section 13 states that "the person concerned shall, at his request, be provided with information or stored data concerning him."[40] There are, however, some vague exemptions: the person must be able to describe "in detail" the type of personal data required and where it is stored; the organization is allowed to exercise "due discretion" in the provision of information; and access can be properly refused if it would be "prejudicial to the legitimate accomplishment" of organizational tasks, to "public security or order, or otherwise to the disadvantage of the federal republic or of a Land."[41] The BDSG is consistent with other information law in Germany: the burden of proving that disclosure outweighs confidentiality lies squarely with the individual.

A right of access is superfluous unless the individual is also allowed to correct data found to be inaccurate, obsolete, or incomplete. In Germany, data processing centers are required to remedy incorrect personal data and to block its transmittal if its accuracy is in question.[42] The American Privacy Act permits individuals to request amendment of a record pertaining to them and requires the agency to "make any correction of any portion thereof which the individual believes is not accurate, relevant, timely or complete."[43] The Swedish Data Act tries to achieve the same result by stipulating that correction is a duty of the responsible keeper of the register rather than a right of the individual.[44] Schedule 1 to the British law states that "an individual shall be entitled . . . where appropriate, to have such data corrected or erased."[45] This is not a direct right, however; inaccurate data can be corrected or erased only by taking legal action or by complaining to the Registrar.

The accuracy, completeness, and relevance of data may be achieved

40. BDSG, Sec. 13 (1).
41. BDSG, Sec. 13 (3).
42. BDSG, Sec. 14.
43. Privacy Act, Sec. 3(d) (2).
44. Data Act, Sec. 8.
45. Data Protection Act, Sch. 1, Part I (7).

in a number of other ways: by inspection of data processing facilities, for example, or by providing compensation to data subjects harmed through the processing or transmittal of wrong information. In the vast majority of cases, of course, correct information is also to the advantage of the organization concerned. Thus the inconvenience and expense of providing subject access and correction may be offset by the advantages provided by another source of "quality control."

There is, then, a cross-national consensus around the principles of access and correction. Disagreements tend to focus on the details of implementation: should a fee be charged by the data user, and if so, how much of a fee? Should a time limit be set within which an organization has to respond to an access request, and if so, how long a time? To what extent should a data subject be made to describe the information requested and to prove his or her own identity? These minor but tricky issues also apply to broader access statutes.

More generally, and in light of the low use of access rights, some have questioned whether this principle is an essential one or merely a means to ensure that the right data are used by the right people for the right purposes. Is it, according to our framework in Chapter 1, a basic human right to know what others know about you, or a functional means to improve administrative decision making? Whatever the motive, the principle of access and correction may allay the feeling of powerlessness that many experience in the face of big bureaucracy and complex technology. For these symbolic reasons, if for no other, the principle is a central component of the data protection schemes of every country that has legislated data protection so far.

The Principle of Collection Limitation

The third principle addresses the collection of personal data, and it is the first of the OECD's principles: "There should be limits to the collection of personal data and any such data should be obtained by lawful and fair means and, where appropriate, with the knowledge or consent of the data subject."[46] This principle is also reflected, in different ways and with different emphasis, in the four laws.

Under the United States Privacy Act, agencies should only maintain

---

46. OECD, *Guidelines,* p. 10.

those records that are "relevant and necessary to accomplish the purpose of the agency." Records should be comprised of information gleaned "to the greatest extent practicable directly from the subject individual." Data subjects should be informed of the authority for collection, the agencies to which the information may be transmitted, and the "routine uses" to which the information may be put.[47] Individuals are provided a Privacy Act statement when identifiable information is requested on government forms.

The German law discusses the storage of data (*Datenspeicherung*) rather than its collection. This too, however, is "permissible where necessary for the legitimate accomplishments of the tasks for which the storage unit is competent." The BDSG adds, however, that "where data are collected from a person on the basis of a legal provision, his attention shall be drawn thereto, and in all other cases he shall be informed that he is not obliged to provide the data."[48] This emphasis on the proper statutory authority for collection is also seen in the British law: "The information to be contained in personal data shall be obtained, and personal data shall be processed, fairly and lawfully. Personal data shall be held only for one or more specified and lawful purposes."[49] It is basically up to the Registrar to interpret this statement.

The Swedish law also leaves room for interpretation. The Data Inspection Board will grant permission to start and keep a personal register unless "undue encroachment on the privacy of individuals will arise."[50] The DIB is then authorized to issue regulations concerning the "obtaining of information on the personal register."[51] The Swedish law also specifies certain especially sensitive categories of data that may not be collected except by the authority with statutory responsibility. This information includes data on criminal conviction or suspicion and on the individual's physical or psychiatric condition. The act also requires special reasons for establishing a register that contains information on "anybody's political or religious views."[52] The British law likewise provides additional safeguards for information about

---

47. Privacy Act, Sec. 3(e).
48. BDSG, Sec. 9.
49. Data Protection Act, Sch. 1, Part I (2).
50. Data Act, Sec. 3.
51. Ibid., Sec. 6.
52. Ibid., Sec. 4.

racial origin, political and religious opinions, physical and mental health, sex life, and criminal convictions.[53]

The collection limitation principle is designed to prevent "fishing expeditions." Personal data should be collected only to fulfill a clearly specified function. With the exception of the British and Swedish definitions of these especially sensitive categories, the draftees of data protection law have shunned the codification of precise limits on collection. The OECD also found that it was not possible "to define any set of data that are universally regarded as sensitive."[54] The process of collection, then, cannot be separated a priori from the question of use and disclosure.

The Principle of Use Limitation

This principle asserts that, once personal data are collected, there are limits to the internal uses to which an agency may put them. The basis for both this and the fifth principle is the notion of *relevance*: data may be used only for purposes that were specified at the time of collection. Data collected for one purpose may not be used for an unrelated purpose. For example, data provided for the assessment of income tax liability may not be used for an evaluation of eligibility for social assistance or for the determination of criminal wrongdoing. The practice of this principle is invariably very different; nevertheless, we see it articulated in each of the four laws.

The U.S. Privacy Act establishes the general rule that communication of personal data to any person is not permissible "except pursuant to a written request by, or with the prior consent of, the individual to whom the record pertains."[55] There are a number of controversial exemptions to this rule. Disclosure is permitted without consent to those within an agency who have a "need for the record in the performance of their duties," or to agencies in connection with "routine uses," in other words, for purposes "compatible with the purposes for which it was collected."[56] Agencies have found some creative ways to define "compatible," with the result that the routine

53. Data Protection Act, Sec. 2 (3).
54. OECD, *Guidelines*, p. 29.
55. Privacy Act, Sec. 3(b).
56. Ibid., Sec. 3(a) (7).

use exemption is the most flexible and controversial provision in the law.[57]

The German law uses some very similar language. Section 5 states that "persons engaged in data processing . . . shall not, without authorization, process, communicate, grant access to or otherwise use protected personal data for any purpose other than that of the legitimate accomplishment of their task."[58] Agency officials are expected to sign an undertaking to abide by this rule when taking up their duties. The British law says the same thing in more convoluted language: "personal data in respect of which services are provided by a person carrying on a computer bureau shall not be disclosed by him without the prior authority of the person for whom these services are provided."[59] Use limitation is enforced in the Swedish Data Act through the process of obtaining permission from the Data Inspection Board. The DIB then issues regulations as to the purpose of the register and the uses to which personal information may be put.

In conclusion, it is very difficult for either the individual or any supervisory authority to enforce this principle. The relevance criterion is susceptible to a variety of interpretations, and the internal use of data is very difficult to monitor on a regular basis. The same problem exists with the fifth, and related, principle—disclosure limitation.

The Principle of Disclosure Limitation

Intimately associated with use limitation both in principle and in the language of legislation is disclosure limitation: personal data shall not be communicated externally (to another agency) without the consent of the data subject or legal authority. This principle also relies on an understanding of purpose specification and relevance.

The American restrictions are subsumed under the same section

57. For instance, in 1980 the Office of Personnel Management (OPM) released some of its records to help the Veterans Administration check the accreditation of its hospital employees. The OPM claimed that the disclosure constituted a "routine use" of its data because the agency believed "that an integral part of the reason that these records are maintained is to protect the legitimate interests of government and, therefore, such a disclosure is compatible with the purposes for maintaining these records." The OPM statement is quoted in Jake Kirchner, "Privacy: A History of Computer Matching in the Federal Government," *Computerworld* 14 December 1981, 15. The Canadian Privacy Act has a similar exemption for "consistent uses."

58. BDSG, Sec. 5 (1).

59. Data Protection Act, Sec. 15 (1).

that covers use limitation: "No agency shall disclose any record which is contained in a system of records by any means of communication to any person, or to another agency, except pursuant to a written request by, or with the prior consent of, the individual to whom the record pertains." Exceptions are provided for "routine uses," for agencies engaged in "civil or criminal law enforcement activity," for information that might affect the health and safety of the individual, and for the National Archives, the comptroller general, and both houses of Congress.[60]

The German data protection law also provides for "routine uses" in its own way: "the communication of personal data to public authorities and other public establishments shall be permissible where it is necessary for the legitimate accomplishment of the tasks for which the communicating unit or the recipient is competent."[61] The principle as stated in the British Data Protection Act reads: "personal data held for any purpose or purposes shall not be used or disclosed in any manner incompatible with that purpose or those purposes."[62] The act makes a distinction between the deliberate passing of data to a third party not declared in the registration and disclosure through carelessness or poor discipline. The Swedish law is also explicit: "Personal information in a personal register may not be issued if there is reason to assume that the information will be used for ADP contrary to this act." The Data Act also empowers the DIB to regulate the transmission of personal data to another country.[63] As we shall see, it was this type of provision that made others (particularly the British and the Americans) worry that data protection would become a form of trade protectionism.

The Security Principle

This final principle covers a number of different sins. The OECD guidelines state a "security safeguards principle": "personal data should be protected by reasonable security safeguards against such risks as loss or unauthorised access, destruction, use, modification or disclosure of data."[64] They have in mind a variety of physical (e.g.,

---

60. Privacy Act, Sec. 3 (b).
61. BDSG, Sec. 10 (1).
62. Data Protection Act, Sch. 1, Part I (3).
63. Data Act, Sec. 11.
64. OECD, *Guidelines*, p. 10.

locked doors and ID cards), organizational (e.g., clearances for access), and informational (e.g., encryption) measures to reinforce the other principles. Privacy and security are not identical values. Adequate security measures in the personal data processing environment, however, may go a long way toward advancing the privacy value.

In some laws this principle is quite explicit; in others it is more implicit. In the American Privacy Act, each agency is enjoined to "establish appropriate administrative, technical and physical safeguards to insure the security and confidentiality of records and to protect against any anticipated threats or hazards to their security or integrity which could result in substantial harm, embarrassment, inconvenience, or unfairness to any individual on whom information is maintained."[65] The responsibility of monitoring the contents of personal records is placed with the organization, thus reducing the burden on the individual.

One of the stated purposes of the British Data Protection Act is to "ensure good practice in the use, processing and protection of personal data in computing systems."[66] Accordingly, the last principle in the British law stipulates that "appropriate security measures shall be taken against unauthorized access to, or alteration, disclosure or destruction of, personal data and against accidental loss or destruction of personal data."[67] The German statute is a little less explicit: "persons processing personal data . . . shall take the technical and organizational measures necessary to ensure the implementation of the provisions of this Act."[68] The Swedish Data Act merely says that the DIB shall issue regulations concerning "the carrying out of the ADP" and "control and security."[69]

The Convergence and the Variations

Convergence means more than "similarity." It denotes a pattern over time, a dynamic process rather than a static condition. The counterfactual, therefore, is not only variance among national policies but also a state of divergence or variability at some former stage.

65. Privacy Act, Sec. 3(e) (10).
66. Data Protection Registrar, *First Report* (London: HMSO, 1985), p. 1.
67. Data Protection Act, Sch. 1, Part I (8).
68. BDSG, Sec. 6 (1).
69. Data Act, Sec. 6.

Thus, from a position in which these states had no, or little, data protection and therefore varied significantly in their approach to the treatment of personal data, a consensus emerged during the 1970s around these fair information principles. We can conclude, then, that a convergence has occurred.

Six principles have been distilled from the language of these four laws. Any other combination of countries could have been chosen, and virtually the same principles would have appeared. That these six should appear is not necessarily surprising; many of them might be considered self-evident. They are, however, based on a set of assumptions that have rarely been explicitly stated or questioned within the data protection movement. Fair information principles are squarely within the tradition of Anglo-American procedural justice. Nowhere is there given a substantive definition of privacy. And, nowhere do we find any attempt to define those data that may be inherently more sensitive to an individual or those organizations that might be more prone to intrusiveness. Any privacy problem that arises in any organization can be alleviated through the fair and consistent application of these principles. This reluctance to second-guess what privacy interests are important to an individual is understandable. Privacy, as has been demonstrated, is a subjective notion; the personal information about which one individual might be anxious, may not necessarily be of concern to another. The fair information principles therefore reflect the insurmountable problems of regulating a diversity of institutions in order to protect an elusive resource that individuals may value in widely different ways.

Furthermore, these principles are based on a common faith in the ability of humans to control technology. The computer is a human creation and can be controlled by a set of rational precepts. There is nothing inherently new about this technology that cannot be understood and incorporated into existing systems of legal rules. The computer has created a temporary imbalance between the individual and the modern complex organization. The fair information practices rest on a theoretical assumption that privacy can be maintained, tyranny averted, and decision making improved by the successful application of these rationally conceived principles to the public and private organizations of the late twentieth century.

One might question, however, whether these principles represent a

112

statement of the solution or merely a statement of the problem. Their comprehensive quality may be characterized more as a symbolic attempt to grant rights that will rarely be exercised and procedures that will rarely be adhered to. The answer to the question obviously depends on the motivation and resources of the various implementing agents; this subject is discussed in Chapters 5 and 6. Nevertheless, what should not be overlooked is the clear symbolic quality of these attempts to legislate "fairness." In this context, solutions and problems are probably the two sides of the same coin; the principles raise as many questions about the protection of privacy as they answer. So these different states have either agreed on a solution, or they have agreed on the definition of the problem. Either way there has been a convergence.

The central point about convergence, however, should not be allowed to obscure some important differences in these laws; most of these dissimilarities are irrelevant to this study, but one is critical. First, there are some interesting differences in style and expression. The American Privacy Act, for instance, is very much couched in individualistic terms: fair information practice bolsters the right to privacy, which, as the Privacy Act states, is a "personal and fundamental right protected by the Constitution of the United States."[70] The German act, by contrast, has a more negative thrust; it provides blanket prohibition against the processing of personal data unless it is specifically permitted by the BDSG, by any other legal regulation, or by the consent of the data subject. This legal approach necessitated a very detailed law with more precise stipulations of the specific conditions under which personal data could be stored, utilized, and disseminated. The BDSG is thus consistent with the Roman or civil law approach of codifying precise expectations of behavior. The Swedish Data Act is far more vague. Personal data may not be processed automatically if it would cause an "undue encroachment of privacy"; the DIB is given wide discretion to interpret this wording as it sees fit. The British law is more of a hybrid, containing statements of individual rights, the duties of the data processing institutions, and wide grants of discretionary authority to the Registrar.

The varying scope of these laws also deserves attention. Most coun-

---

70. Privacy Act, Sec. 2(a) (4).

tries apply these same principles to both the public and private sectors. Canada, the United States and Australia are the only countries so far to have restricted their data protection laws mainly to government bodies. The United States Privacy Act of 1974 contained a provision establishing the Privacy Protection Study Commission (PPSC) to investigate whether the fair information practices should be extended to the private sector. The PPSC recommended in 1977 that different methods of implementation should apply to the very different record-keeping relationships that exist in the private sector.[71] This "sectoral" approach to the problem was at the time in stark contrast to the "omnibus" legislation in force in Europe.

The federal structure of the United States also precludes the application of the Privacy Act to the records of state and local authorities, which by and large have similar safeguards.[72] Federalism complicates the picture in West Germany too. Public and private data users must comply with the same general principles (with some exceptions), but they are answerable to different authorities. The Federal Data Protection Commissioner has jurisdiction over the federal public sector. Private data users are regulated at the Land level. These complications should not obscure our interest in the central relationship between the individual and the state. From the point of view of democratic theory and comparative politics, it is the regulation of the public sector that is of primary interest. All laws cover the personal data policies of central government, because *government* data use was considered the principal threat at the time of enactment, and, therefore, the main focus of the research.

Whether the laws should apply just to computers or also to manual (paper) record-keeping systems as well comprises a second difference in scope (and one that caused considerable controversy). Some have argued that the problem is the computer (or automated record-keeping systems) and that the computer should be the target of regulation. Others have contended that manual record-keeping systems can pose just as much of a threat. There is a dilemma: if one regulates just the computer, many data subjects remain unprotected, and users can evade data protection by transferring to a manually recorded system

71. PPSC, *Personal Privacy in an Information Society.*
72. See Robert Ellis Smith, *Compilation of State and Federal Privacy Laws* (Washington, D.C.: Privacy Journal, 1988).

or by refusing to automate in the first place. On the other hand, the comprehensive approach catches many harmless data handlers in its net. How, moreover, does one draw a clear distinction between computerized and manual records? Of the countries that have so far legislated, only Sweden, Austria, Luxembourg, and the United Kingdom concentrate solely on automated record-keeping systems.

The final difference in scope concerns the application of the fair information practices to corporate bodies or associations. The question of whether collective entities can (or should) have privacy rights is a matter of philosophical debate and some political controversy. So far, only the laws of Norway, Denmark, Austria, and Luxembourg apply to data about corporate bodies as well as data about individuals.

These, as well as enormous problems of definition, consumed much time and effort for the men and women who first grappled with data protection. As some of these differences concern countries that are outside of our four-nation sample, however, they do not affect the validity of the investigation or the theoretical framework on which it is based. The one critical variation is the method of implementation. That comparison is the subject of Chapters 5 and 6. Until then, we may proceed under the assumption that the "first generation" of data protection statutes is founded on a very similar set of principles.[73] European and North American countries with diverse cultures, institutions, and legal traditions have resolved to tackle the dangers to privacy from the computer in virtually the same way. Why? Chapter 4 explores the reasons.

73. The current terminology among data protection experts distinguishes between the "first-generation" statutes of the 1970s, the "second-generation" statutes of the early 1980s, and the "third-generation" laws of the late 1980s. Besides the difference in timing, I cannot see that these categories are especially helpful. There is, however, an emerging conventional wisdom that upcoming regulations should be more sensitive to the different relationships and transactions that exist within different sectors. See Spiros Simitis, "Reviewing Privacy in an Information Society," *University of Pennsylvania Law Review* 135 (1987): 742. This recognition is also reflected in the Council of Europe's recent attempts to issue guidelines for specific types of information. See, for example, *Protection of Personal Data Used for the Purposes of Direct Marketing*, Recommendation No. R(85) 20 of 25 October 1985 (Strasbourg: Council of Europe, 1986); and *Protection of Personal Data Used for Social Security Purposes*, Recommendation No. R(86) 1 of 23 January 1986 (Strasbourg: Council of Europe, 1986). There are other recommendations on scientific research and statistics, medical data, police information, and employment data. See Peter J. Hustinx, "COE and Data Protection: What Has Been Achieved?" *Transnational Data and Communications Report* 12 (November 1989): 21–22.

4

Explaining the Convergence

The term "policy convergence" has entered the language of political scientists in a pragmatic way, as a range of studies from diverse methodological and ideological perspectives has concluded that advanced industrial states tend to face similar problems and tend to solve them in similar ways.[1] While the concept is very important, there are several possible pitfalls that have to be avoided in trying to explain why a convergence might have occurred. First, we must be quite explicit about what aspect of public policy is supposed to be converging; we saw in the last chapter that the convergence in data protection is manifested in a strikingly similar set of statutory principles. Second, convergence should be defined in dynamic terms, as a process rather than as a condition; thus time becomes a central variable in the analysis. Finally, we must resist the logic of the so-called convergence thesis—that similar conditions produce similar problems which produce similar policies. This overly deterministic logic may obscure no less important political mechanisms and processes that may be just as instrumental.

We need a framework, therefore, that specifies alternative propositions which operate at different levels of analysis. Five explanations for convergence are examined: these are technological determinism; the emulation of the pioneers in the field; the close interaction of a transnational elite of experts; the harmonization efforts of interna-

1. See Bennett, "Review Article: What Is Policy Convergence," for a review of recent literature, and "Different Processes, One Result: The Convergence of Data Protection Policy in Europe and the United States," *Governance* 1 (1988): 415–41.

tional organizations; and penetration, where states are forced to make their policies conform to those of others. The application of this open framework helps us to avoid the deterministic argument and also to assess whether different explanations prevail at different stages for different states. These arguments should not be seen as mutually exclusive. Is it more plausible that one all-embracing argument explains all, or that different countries have converged at different times for different reasons?

The explanations for convergence are transnational in scope and character; convergence has occurred because of forces which transcend the level of domestic politics and which hypothetically affect different states in similar ways. Yet it is by no means implausible that the same results could occur through the fortuitous coincidence of similar, but disconnected, domestic factors. Convergence could be the result of a number of compensating circumstances that effectively neutralize those domestic forces which might cause variation.[2] A crucial part of the analytical task, therefore, is to reject the influence of certain domestic factors before concluding that transnational processes are at work.

The purpose of this chapter is to investigate the explanatory power of each argument for convergence and then to demonstrate that constitutional, group, partisan, and bureaucratic factors played no significant part in shaping the choice of fair information principles in each country. We cannot engage in a systematic evaluation of these propositions by ascribing precise weights to each. The evidence is not going to be tidy, and it should not be forced into these preconceived categories if, in so doing, the complexity and richness of the story is sacrificed. We will interrogate the data, or like Peter Gourevitch, we will "clarify the nature of different arguments, their logic, and their internal characteristics. Then, having gathered the sorts of evidence appropriate to each explanation . . . [we will] examine events from the argument's point of view."[3] Together, the five arguments serve to guide the

2. This argument can be found in a recent comparative study of chemical regulation; see Ronald Brickman, Sheila Jasanoff, and Thomas Ilgen, *Controlling Chemicals: The Politics of Regulation in Europe and the United States* (Ithaca: Cornell University Press, 1985), p. 303. See also George Hoberg, Jr., "Technology, Political Structure, and Social Regulation: A Cross-National Analysis," *Comparative Politics* 18 (1986): 357–76.

3. Peter Gourevitch, *Politics in Hard Times: Comparative Responses to International Economic Crises* (Ithaca: Cornell University Press, 1986).

choice and presentation of empirical evidence and to shape the interpretation of events.

Convergence Because of the Technology

We first examine the proposition that the solution of fair information principles was predetermined by the problem. Policy preferences were guided inevitably by the common perception of common difficulties. Flaherty, having examined the formulation and implementation of data protection policy over twenty years, came to this conclusion: "The uniformities in the development of data protection are a tribute to the common problems of protecting personal privacy that the laws are trying to deal with."[4] Similarly, a United States Senate report entitled *Privacy and Protection of Personal Information in Europe* asserted that "it is the similarity of perceived threats rather than any convergence of cultural and traditional patterns which has internationalized the privacy issue."[5]

The policy problem was generated by the confluence of two characteristics of postindustrial society—bureaucracy and information technology. Before the computer arrived, there was no data protection movement, though there was bureaucracy and a privacy issue (confined to questions of surveillance and physical intrusiveness). Information technology was the catalyst that generated the policy problem. But why is it also a cause of policy convergence? The argument presupposes that policy makers are constrained by certain imperatives, in that external forces guide human choice, in the form of elite preferences, to a common solution. For the problem to determine the solution, two further conditions must be met. First, we must be able to identify the intrinsic properties of *this* technology that would force policy makers to treat the dangers in a similar manner. But second, these qualities must be recognized by the key policy makers in different states. In other words, it is not enough that the technology is the same; the perception of the technology must also be the same. Three

4. David H. Flaherty, "On Making Data Protection Effective," *Transnational Data Report* 9 (April 1986): 15.

5. U.S. Senate, *Privacy and Protection of Personal Information in Europe*, Report from the Committee on Government Operations, Senate, 93d Cong., 2d sess. (Washington, D.C.: Government Printing Office, 1975), p. 5.

characteristics of the technology can been noted: its pervasiveness, its rapid development, and its mystical or closed quality.

The Pervasiveness of Information Technology

Technology is a major independent variable in some theories of social and political change. Industrialization, it has been argued, was principally a product of technological invention. The policy problems associated with industrialization (urban poverty, communications, transportation, water quality, and so on) are indirectly the product of industrial technology. In a corresponding way, information technology is one of the driving forces behind the transformation from an industrial to a postindustrial society. As was noted in Chapter 1, the essential theme in this wide and varied literature on postindustrialism is that knowledge and information are replacing work and capital as the criteria for economic worth and national wealth. While writers differ on the extent and effects of this transformation, there is common agreement that an information society is upon us. To the extent that these changes are affecting all advanced industrial societies, the social, political, and legal problems will be similar.

The technology may force convergence in one further sense. The policy problems of the industrial age were conditioned by obvious national and cultural characteristics. The resources on which the industrial economy was based (capital, labor, natural resources) were variable: raw materials and human skills are inevitably shaped by social and environmental conditions. Consequently, the resulting social, economic, and environmental policy problems (and the solutions framed to deal with them) have been more dependent on country-specific criteria. Being more pervasive and malleable, information has fewer national or cultural attachments. This currency of the postindustrial economy is a commodity that is far easier to collect, store, and transmit than are work or capital. The resource upon which wealth in the postindustrial society is based is a more pervasive one. As information technology facilitates the more rapid and efficient communication of vast quantities of this resource, the contingent changes should also have a more common impact, forcing states to respond in increasingly similar ways.

The recognition of pervasiveness is found in many authoritative sources. The PPSC in the United States began its report by discussing the "information-dependent" society, in which "records mediate relationships between individuals and organizations and thus affect an individual more easily, more broadly, and often more unfairly than in the past."[6] The Lindop Committee in Britain recognized that "computing is becoming far more ubiquitous and less remote."[7] The pervasiveness of the computer, and of the information resource that it stores and disseminates, is a feature of the policy problem stressed everywhere by respondents to my project.

The Rapid Development and Application of Information Technology

The rapid pace of development in the information technology environment is also a powerful force for convergence and one that has clearly influenced policy makers in all countries. A new generation of hardware and software has appeared about every five years; new items have increased computational speed and reliability while physical size and relative cost have been reduced. These swift changes have demanded an anticipatory and prescient attitude toward future technological advances and social dangers. Simitis sees the problem as follows: "All legislators face, however, the same dilemma: their reaction is not so much meant to master problems already well-known and therefore easily discernible but it attempts to anticipate possible future developments. Legislators do not move, in other words, on a ground nearly as stable as for instance in the case of automobile accidents or product liability."[8] Hondius adds that "it was feared by many that if legal measures were not enacted at an early date, one would finally run up against the same kind of difficulty as in the field of environment protection: a future generation would have to pay the price for today's indifference." He characterizes the effort as "fighting against windmills which have not yet been built."[9]

In framing policy in anticipation of largely unknown events and

6. PPSC, *Personal Privacy in an Information Society*, p. 3.
7. Great Britain, *Report of the Committee on Data Protection*, p. 14.
8. Spiros Simitis, "Data Protection: A Few Critical Remarks," *Transnational Data Report* 6 (March 1983): 95.
9. Hondius, *Emerging Data Protection*, p. 8.

dangers, there is clearly a strong incentive to formulate laws with enough latitude to embrace future eventualities. The cross-national uniformity of the fair information practices is in one sense a reflection of the need for a set of basic rules of sufficient breadth and adaptability. The generality of these principles has overridden the specificity of national laws. The broader the language, the wider the possibilities of different applications. Hence in their generality and similarity the first generation of data protection laws also reflects an admission of ignorance. If the technological context becomes more settled, it is likely that more specific and sensitive regulations will be adopted and that national differences will then surface. At the moment, the fight against the "windmills," while not quixotic, is of a general and insensitive nature. Consensus on these basic fair information principles may not be so surprising when so much has been left to future interpretation and implementation.

The "Demonology" of Information Technology

One last feature of the technology helps our understanding of convergence. There is always a certain amount of fear of technology, but computers have a particularly enigmatic quality. They are complex black boxes that are difficult for the average person to understand. People fear that these strange, impersonal machines are coming to dominate our public and private institutions. One guiding assumption behind policy making, therefore, is the need to "take the lid off" the data processing environment. Openness and transparency about how personal information is collected, stored, used, and disseminated can theoretically allay these concerns.

Basing legislative action on the assumption that the "lid must be taken off" leads data protection policy to some inevitable conclusions. If the data processing environment has to be opened up, then citizens must be given certain knowledge about the processing of data about them, for example, about the existence of record-keeping systems, the nature of the information collected and stored, the uses and disclosures of the data, and so on. These assumptions lead to a set of principles that are logically bound to be similar. Sieghart has spoken about a "learning curve" that every data protection commission, working party, and committee followed before arriving at these principles. Speaking about the process that the British Conservative government went through to produce its data protection bill, he states:

> There are some general principles which come out of the woodwork, as one moves up this learning curve. There is a sort of inherent logic to data protection, and perhaps the best demonstration of that is the recent Bill. . . . If one looks at the structure of the Bill, it follows precisely the structure of thought and of the recommendations of the Lindop Committee. That is not surprising, because that is also the structure of the European Data Protection Convention, and it is the structure of all the European data protection laws. This has to be because the logic of the subject requires it. And this alone excludes doctrinaire, ideological or party-political considerations from this entire subject.[10]

Thus we can paint a picture of policy makers in different countries independently investigating how to solve the same puzzle and necessarily, because of the intrinsic nature of that puzzle, coming to very similar conclusions. This argument is persuasive, particularly in the early years. The Commission on Publicity and Secrecy (1972) in Sweden, the HEW report (1973) in the United States, and the Younger Report (1972) in Britain all came to similar conclusions in a largely independent manner. This situation occurred because it is very difficult to conceive how the policy problem (as defined) could lead to any other solution.

On the other hand, not all countries had to accept the same definition of the problem and the same assumptions about that problem. Once one accepts that the problem is one posed by the technology, then the characteristics of that technology force policy makers to some common conclusions. But we should qualify the word "deterministic." While the technology frames the context of policy choice, authoritative decisions are made only by political actors who undoubtedly develop a variety of interesting views about that technology. To say that each country was forced independently and inexorably to a common solution ignores other processes that might play an intermediary role between the understanding of the technological context and the choice of policy.

10. Sieghart, "Information Privacy and the Data Protection Bill," pp. 30–31.

This position is supported by policy analysis in other sectors. Eliot Feldman and Jerome Milch, for instance, explore the politics of international airport development and stress that one should not jump too quickly to the deterministic conclusion: "there are alternative explanations for common strategies which do not require metaphysical interpretations of human behavior."[11] With respect to telecommunications policy, Frederick Williams has argued that "communications technologies are more a catalyst or intensifier of change than they are a sole cause of anything."[12] Ithiel de Sola Pool concludes his analysis of free speech in the electronic age with the statement that technology "shapes the structure of the battle, but not every outcome."[13]

In short, the argument for technological determinism excludes *politics*. In pure analytical terms it has some attractions, but it does not tell the whole story. This argument views the political process as simply an exercise in problem solving. Policy making undoubtedly is problem solving, but it is other things too. For example, it is also about communication, which underpins the second and third arguments for convergence.

Convergence through Emulation

Other studies have noted a striking similarity in a variety of policy areas and have concluded that the process of problem solving is highly imitative. In the first place, the range of possible solutions to a problem is often not that great. There is not a universe of alternatives but a very limited range of practical ways to deal with public issues. In this world of bounded rationality, imperfect information about the causes and consequences of public policy, and limited human resources, the motivation to draw lessons from abroad is likely to be strong. It can be expected, especially in cases of new policy problems where a high

11. Eliot J. Feldman and Jerome Milch, *Technology versus Democracy: The Comparative Politics of International Airports* (Boston: Auburn, 1982), p. 56.
12. Frederick Williams, *The Communications Revolution* (Beverly Hills: Sage, 1982), p. 11.
13. Ithiel de Sola Pool, *Technologies of Freedom* (Cambridge: Harvard University Press, 1983), p. 251.

degree of innovation is required and no readily apparent model exists within the present repertoire of policy techniques.

Yet emulation is a slippery concept, one that can mean at least two things. First, it can denote a process of lesson drawing,[14] in which the policy of one country is used as a model or blueprint that is then adapted and perhaps improved upon. Thus we must be able to identify a clear *exemplar*, a state that has both passed the legislative finish line first and is also clearly recognized elsewhere as a pioneer. Moreover, we require evidence of awareness of the exemplar through textual citations and personal contacts with policy makers from the pioneering state. But emulation can also mean the copying or imitation of policy content. To confirm emulation in this case requires some evidence of plagiarism—proof of a political and practical motivation for imitation.[15]

An obvious candidate for an exemplar would be the world's first data protection statute in Hesse. Spiros Simitis was instrumental in publicizing this law and translating it into other languages. The law was discussed extensively during the preparation of the Swedish Data Act, as it was the only provision in effect at the time. But few people in Britain or the United States were aware of the Hessian statute. It receives no mention in the contemporaneous Justice Report in Britain, even though other aspects of German information law are discussed,[16] and only two sentences of description in the Younger Report.[17] In the American HEW report, the statute is discussed in two paragraphs and dismissed, erroneously as a matter of fact, because it seemed "designed more to protect the integrity of State data and State government than to protect the interests of the people of the state."[18] The

14. Richard Rose has suggested this concept. See his "Comparative Policy Analysis: The Program Approach," in *Comparing Pluralist Democracies*, ed. Mattei Dogan (Boulder: Westview Press, 1988), pp. 219–41, and his *Lesson-Drawing across Time and Space* (Tuscaloosa: University of Alabama Press, forthcoming). Lesson drawing is defined by Rose as the process of deriving practical conclusions about the effectiveness of a program elsewhere and about its transferability to one's own political system. It is a more precise concept than the "learning" approach advocated in Heclo, *Modern Social Politics*. See also the special issue of the *Journal of Public Policy* titled *Lesson-Drawing across Nations*, vol. 11 (January–March 1991).

15. The dictionary definition of "emulation" also indicates two connotations: on the one hand, the desire to "rival" or "excel," and on the other, the desire to "imitate zealously." *The Concise Oxford Dictionary* seventh ed. (Oxford: Clarendon Press, 1982).

16. Justice, *Privacy and the Law*, pp. 21–25.

17. Great Britain, *Report of the Committee on Privacy*, p. 313.

18. U.S. HEW, *Records, Computers, and the Rights of Citizens*, p. 169.

1970 Hessian statute did provide the model for subsequent legislation in Germany. It evoked curiosity abroad because of its pioneering quality rather than serious attention because of its potential usefulness as an exemplar.

The 1973 Swedish Data Act had a more widespread impact because of the efforts of a single person, Jan Freese, the Chair of the DIB from 1974 until 1986, who ensured that the Swedish approach was widely known. Other countries were naturally eager to learn of the early Swedish experiences of implementation. The Swedish Data Act was translated into English, French, and German. Delegations of British, German, French, and other European officials visited Stockholm in the first years of the act's existence. Even though its enactment came too late to influence the deliberations of the Younger and HEW committees, it aroused keen interest as the first national attempt to regulate data processing. The Swedish Data Act was regarded as far less relevant in the United States, however. For many experts its concentration on the technology rather than on the information as well as its comprehensive licensing approach to both the public and private sectors rendered the Swedish approach inapplicable to American conditions.

With the exception of the United States, however, in each country there was an immediate awareness of overseas legislation and a keen desire to learn from the experience of others. These states were confronted with the same policy problem at the same time and with a problem that is of enormous complexity. The uncertainty about the technology and the nature of the danger generated a widely recognized need to share experience. As Herbert Burkert concludes: "The history of data protection in Western Europe is a good example of legislators helping each other."[19] Cross-national learning may also have a salutary effect. As Justice Michael Kirby writes: "For all this, it is reassuring that there is consensus in the adoption of the 'basic rules.' It suggests that there is sense in the basic endeavor."[20] Thus, the cause of convergence in this interpretation is insecurity.

Evidence of a desire to draw lessons from others' experience is easy to find. Most study commission reports, for instance, contain sections

19. Herbert Burkert, "Institutions of Data Protection: An Attempt at a Functional Explanation of European Data Protection Laws," *Computer Law Journal* 3 (1982): 182.
20. Kirby, "Transborder Data Flows," p. 65.

on "foreign approaches."[21] We find frequent examples of experts such as Westin, Simitis, and Freese giving testimony before the commissions of other countries. There was also a plethora of more informal conferences, colloquia, and symposia, under the auspices of a range of national and international organizations, through which views and information could be exchanged. Therefore, the first two conditions seem to have been confirmed: the Swedish law acted as an exemplar, and there existed an awareness and utilization of foreign reports, laws, and experience. There was a natural tendency for countries, with the exception of the United States, to learn from abroad, to see how other states had responded, and to bring foreign evidence to bear on the domestic policy-making process.

But the evidence of cross-national learning does not constitute an explanation for convergence in and of itself. There is little proof that the utilization of foreign experience motivated a crude exercise in imitation. Nowhere does one find convincing and instrumental arguments to the effect that fair information principles had to be legislated in a certain manner because "that was the way the Swedes or the Americans or the Germans did it." Moreover, there is no reason for countries to copy from one another just to "get a policy." All countries devoted their time and resources to studying the questions themselves. There is no logical or empirical reason to believe that they would wish to blindly follow the lead of another, especially when there was such little evidence of policy impact. And policy makers have admitted that, despite their awareness of other laws, they were still working with a relatively blank slate in their respective countries. In 1983, Lindop spoke about the decision making of his committee: "It was an interesting exercise in self education, because we had to start from scratch. We did not start with pre-conceived ideas, and we had to learn as we went along."[22]

So although there was emulation in the sense of "lesson drawing," there was very little in the sense of "imitation." Awareness and utilization of overseas policy are common enough occurrences, though evidence may be utilized in a number of different ways in response to

21. Sweden, *Computers and Privacy*, pp. 43–45; Great Britain, *Report of the Committee on Privacy* (1972), pp. 308–19; U.S. HEW, *Records, Computers, and the Rights of Citizens*, pp. 167–77; Great Britain, *Report of the Committee on Data Protection*, pp. 411–21.
22. Norman Lindop, "Data Protection: The Background" in *Data Protection*, ed. Bourn and Benyon, p. 19.

various motives.[23] But the awareness of overseas legislation, the utilization of that evidence, and the action based on that evidence are three very distinct forms of behavior. There are only rare examples in the comparative policy literature where the adoption of a program in one country can be clearly attributed to outright copying. We might hypothesize that imitation is more likely to occur when there is some urgency to innovate in order to solve a common problem. Here, there was time to analyze and debate the issue in every country.

Convergence through an International Policy Community

The third explanation for policy convergence also rests on an assumption of interaction between key policy actors. It suggests that the primary cause is not a technological constraint or a sense of collective insecurity but is a consensus among a relatively coherent transnational elite. The notion of a "policy community," "issue network," or "subgovernment" is a familiar one within national, and particularly American, policy studies.[24] As a concept in comparative public policy, however, the notion is more recent. In this interpretation, convergence results from the interaction within a policy community which is bound by a shared expertise and motivation and which operates initially above the fray of domestic politics. A consensus of motivation and concern crystallizes at the transnational level. Members of this elite then convince their respective national governments of the extent of the problem and of the need for a solution in the form of fair information practices. We therefore need to identify a transnational policy community, show that there was a consonance of motivation and outlook among its members, and demonstrate that each member had sufficient influence at the domestic level to advance the cause of data protection.

The first test is easy. Many commentators have noted the existence

23. Colin J. Bennett, "How States Utilize Foreign Evidence," *Journal of Public Policy* 11 (1991): 31–54.

24. See Hugh Heclo, "Issue Networks and the Executive Establishment," in *The New American Political System*, ed. Anthony King (Washington, D.C.: American Enterprise Institute, 1978), and Randall B. Ripley and Grace A. Franklin, *Congress, the Bureaucracy, and Public Policy*, 4th ed. (Chicago: Dorsey Press, 1987).

of a network of data protection experts. Moreover, as Carmody indicates, the data protection movement worldwide "owes much to the constant exchange of ideas between national experts who are called upon to advise governments and formulate legislative proposals."[25] Identifying a transnational policy community is most effectively achieved through interviews. Experts in each country were asked to name the key figures in the data protection movement worldwide. While the results of this line of inquiry are not systematic, not surprisingly the same names were mentioned repeatedly by different respondents.

The following names were most frequently cited as members of the policy community: Spiros Simitis (Germany), Jan Freese (Sweden), Louis Joinet (France), Peter Seipel (Sweden), Paul Sieghart (United Kingdom), Michael Kirby (Australia), Hans Peter Gassmann (OECD), Frits Hondius (Council of Europe), and Stefano Rodota (Italy). No Americans were considered permanent members of this group, although several were on the fringes. Also, each of these individuals had a legal background rather than the technical expertise in computer and communications technologies that one might expect. This background differs from that found in the more technocratic policy communities detected in other recent comparative studies; as a result, these communities tend to reduce policy making to the pursuit of techniques rather than values.[26] There can be no question that the debate within this network has been rich in philosophical understanding and deeply conscious of the human rights implications.[27] As more laws were enacted, the number of experts obviously expanded to the extent that collaboration became more regular with the Annual Conference of Data Protection Commissioners.[28] But the number who

25. Carmody, "Background to Data Protection in Europe," p. 27.
26. See Steven Kelman, *Regulating America, Regulating Sweden: A Comparative Study of Occupational Safety and Health Policy*, (Cambridge: MIT Press, 1981), and Feldman and Milch, *Technology versus Democracy*.
27. See, for example, the variety of papers presented at the OECD's symposium in Vienna in *Transborder Data Flows and the Protection of Privacy*, Proceedings of the Symposium held in Vienna, 20–23 September 1977 (Paris: OECD, 1979).
28. This meeting in Bonn in May 1979 began as an informal gathering of data protection officials from six countries. It is now a larger and more institutionalized affair at which participants from some twenty different countries share their expertise and opinions and reach resolutions on issues of common concern. For a report of the 1989 meeting, see *Transnational Data and Communications Report* 13 (November 1989): 5–37.

have been consistently engaged in the subject since the late sixties is confined principally to those mentioned. Their participation and influence can be traced to a multitude of international and national forums over almost twenty years.

The technical and legal complexity of the issue, the consonance of concern, and the strong sense of innovation seem to have produced a "consensually integrated elite," to use the language of elite theory.[29] The network is bound by expertise in the data protection problem and by a shared concern for its resolution. The first two strands of the argument—that there is a transnational policy community whose members have similar motivations and outlooks—appear to be supported. As with much elite theory, however, such a finding raises the central question, so what? Has this consensus forged at the transnational level been translated into domestic politics? And if so, how? Is this consensus really the "cause" of the convergence?

It is at this point that this explanation for convergence becomes less convincing. Each participant did "spread the word"—about the data protection problem and the need for fair information practices—in both formal and informal institutional arenas. Simitis played a central role in the construction of the BDSG, Sieghart helped draft the 1975 White Paper in Britain, Freese became the first chair of the DIB, and so on. But the explanation goes too far. It ignores the role played by study commissions as well as the legislative debates that took place. It also accords an exaggerated influence to a group of men with little if any formal institutional authority, whose voices tended to be one, albeit influential, voice among many in the cut and thrust of domestic politics. Finally, this explanation defines the issue in technocratic and elitist terms, ignoring the issue's roots in the concerns of the mass public. The American HEW report rejected the argument for similar reasons: "Concern about the effects of computer-based record keeping appears to have deep roots in the public opinion of each country, deeper roots than could exist if the issues were manufactured and merchandised by a coterie of specialists, or reflected only the views of a self-sustaining group of professional Cassandras."[30]

29. John Higley and Gwen Moore, "Elite Integration in the United States and Australia," *American Political Science Review* 75 (1981): 581–97.
30. U.S. HEW, *Records, Computers, and the Rights of Citizens*, p. 168.

Convergence through Harmonization by International Organizations

The fourth model of convergence places the political arena, not within national governments, but at the international level. Perhaps our policy community of "professional Cassandras" had more influence on this level than they had on their respective governments. The willingness of governments to surrender to the harmonization efforts of the international organization or "regime" will depend on the extent to which they recognize *interdependence*, where policies by one state have effects (positive or negative) on the policies of another.[31] If the nature of the problem is such that a full solution cannot be framed and applied without the cooperation of others, then governments may be convinced that they have to collaborate to avoid unnecessary discrepancies. To what extent is data protection a "transnational" problem?

There is no doubt that by the mid-1970s the increased sophistication of computer and communications technologies had created transnational data protection problems to some extent. Though the amount of personal data transferred across borders has been estimated to be a minuscule proportion of all transborder data communication, the growing volume of that traffic has meant a proportionate, though indeterminate, increase in data protection problems. As it was gradually recognized that the international dimension of the problem could severely weaken domestic data protection efforts, three broad concerns surfaced.

First, many feared that data processing industries would prefer to install their systems in countries where the regulatory structure was relatively weak. The creation of "data havens" would provoke those countries with higher privacy standards to erect protectionist barriers, thus forbidding the export of data and disrupting free information flow and trade. Second, discrepancies among laws could create severe jurisdictional conflicts when an increasing amount of data can be efficiently and perhaps more cheaply stored somewhere other than the data's country of origin. If data about an Englishman are sent via an

---

31. Robert O. Keohane and Joseph S. Nye, *Power and Interdependence: World Politics in Transition* (Boston: Little, Brown, 1977), pp. 8–9.

American multinational company to the government of France, which country's laws apply and at what stage? At first it seemed reasonable to protect the "data subject" (the Englishman in the example above) under the laws of his country. Hondius explains the difficulty with this position: "But what if a computer center in country A violates the rights of data subjects in 33 different countries, some of which have no data protection laws? Moreover, what power does a supervisory authority in B have to regulate a data user in A, particularly if the data user in A is a public authority?"[32] Finally, even if the laws of two countries are equivalent, any data subject abused by the actions of a data user operating abroad faces considerable practical difficulties in recovering damages from an overseas user—problems of language, expense, unfamiliarity with laws and procedures, and the like.

Two basic models of protection surfaced. The first was based on the principle of reciprocity, whereby country A would not permit the data processing of information about a citizen from country B if that activity would be prohibited in country B; within Europe this principle is now termed "mutual recognition." It was soon realized, however, that such arrangements could not have any long-term validity given the increasingly extensive and complicated nature of international data relations. Hence, the policy community tended toward use of the second model, that of harmonization, or the "gradual construction of a common legal order."[33] International organizations have subsequently proceeded to act on this theory.

Early International Cooperation

We have already noted the importance of ad hoc visits to foreign countries by data protection experts and national commission members. Without regular and institutionalized contact, however, learning about data production took place in a pragmatic manner. The more regularized contact was provided by certain international organizations that played a critical role as forums for debate, disseminators of ideas and research, and catalysts for policy harmonization.

The very first efforts to discuss privacy in an international frame-

32. Hondius, "Data Law in Europe," p. 104.
33. Ibid, p. 105.

work took place in Scandinavia. In May 1967 a conference of distinguished jurists from many countries met in Stockholm under the auspices of the International Commission of Jurists to discuss the right to privacy. The conference recognized that "the right to privacy, being of paramount importance to human happiness, should be recognized as a fundamental right of mankind"; it recommended that "all countries take appropriate measures to protect by legislation or other means the right to privacy in all its different aspects."[34] The Nordic Council, a periodic forum for discussion among executive and parliamentary representatives from Denmark, Iceland, Norway, Sweden, and Finland, also took an early interest. This effort culminated in a 1971 recommendation that all Nordic governments establish uniform data protection measures.[35]

More general international cooperation, however, properly begins in Tehran in 1968 with the International Conference on Human Rights, which was called on the twentieth anniversary of the Universal Declaration of Human Rights. The broad issue was the protection of human values in the context of rapid technological progress. United Nations General Assembly Resolution 2450 (XXIII) expressed the general concern and intent of the conference, namely, that "recent scientific discoveries and technological advances, although they open up vast prospects for economic, social and cultural progress, may nevertheless endanger the rights and freedoms of individuals and peoples and consequently call for constant attention." The resolution specifically drew attention to the "respect for the privacy of individuals and the integrity and sovereignty of nations in the light of advances in recording and other techniques."[36]

Scores of international groups have been involved in some way with data protection since the 1970s. A full treatment of the subject would include a range of organizations that deal with a complex array of legal, human rights, telecommunications, computer, and economic issues. An incomplete list of involved intergovernmental bodies would include the International Telecommunications Union, the Intergovernmental Bureau of Informatics, the United Nations Center on Transna-

34. Quoted in Justice, *Privacy and the Law*, p. 1; see also Stig Stromholm, *Right of Privacy and Rights of the Personality: A Comparative Survey* (Stockholm: Norstedt, 1967).
35. Hondius, *Emerging Data Protection*, p. 75.
36. United Nations, Doc. A/7218, (1968), p. 54.

tional Corporations, and the European Community. A range of non-governmental organizations exists as well: the International Federation for Information Processing, the European Computer Manufacturers Association, the International Institute of Administrative Sciences, and so on.[37] Given our interest in efforts at harmonization, however, only two international organizations have had a substantial impact in this area so far: the Council of Europe and the Organization for Economic Cooperation and Development. As the issue grew in transnational importance, these two bodies were not only meeting places for the exchange of views but also were centers for the writing and dissemination of more authoritative international agreements. We now explore the development of these agreements through the international data protection policy community.

The Council of Europe

The Council of Europe was established in 1949 to achieve a greater degree of collaboration among the democratic states of Europe. With its particular obligation being to promote cooperation in the area of law and human rights, the Council of Europe is a natural forum for the discussion of data protection. Its two statutory institutions, the Parliamentary (formerly Consultative) Assembly and the Committee of Ministers, have been engaged since the late 1960s in a whole range of activities on the question. It began extensive consideration of the broad impact of technology on human rights in 1968. In January of that year the Consultative Assembly adopted a recommendation asking the Committee of Ministers (the Council's intergovernmental ruling body) to commission a study on human rights and technology. They specifically wanted to know whether the protection offered by the European Human Rights Convention was equal to the possible violations to privacy caused by modern scientific devices.[38] The Committee of Ministers duly asked a Committee of Experts to look into the question.

This group of experts answered the question in the negative in a 1970 interim report. The particular focus for concern was the computer, and a consensus emerged that the Council of Europe should con-

37. See Hondius, *Emerging Data Protection*, pp. 73–79.
38. Council of Europe, Consultative Assembly, Recommendation No. 509 (1968).

centrate for the time being on that question and leave other aspects of privacy aside. The work of the committee therefore paralleled the work being done by study commissions in the member countries. As Hondius, the secretary to the committee, remarked: "The Committee pronounced itself in favour of an early concertation between the Council of Europe's member states in order to avoid that unnecessary divergencies would arise between their laws on the subject. It was felt that common European norms were highly desirable both because human rights were involved and because the computer medium was itself international in character."[39] The Committee of Experts divided its activities into two phases: the first phase (1971–73) was devoted to electronic data processing in the private sector, and the second phase (1973–74) dealt with the public sector.

Their work found expression in two resolutions, which member states were advised to incorporate into their own domestic law. The first ([73]22 of September 1973) advised that information recorded on private sector databanks should be accurate, up-to-date, and relevant; that information should be used only for the purpose for which it was collected; that electronic security systems should be installed; and that individuals should have a general right to know the information recorded against them. Resolution (74)29 of September 1974 applied the same principles to the public sector.[40] The Committee of Experts, therefore, served in the critical role of disseminator of fair information policy. Indeed, the members of this committee were both the core of the European policy community and the key actors in the domestic data protection efforts. Every subsequent national commission report, proposal, or bill has made reference to these two resolutions.

By the time of the second resolution, only one nation (Sweden) and two German states had legislated. Consequently, the committee believed that a full European convention having the force of law would be premature. Two years later, however, the growing sophistication of information technology and the increasingly transnational character of the data processing industry caused many to realize that a more substantial instrument of protection would be required. Accordingly, in 1976 the Committee of Ministers instructed the Committee of

39. Hondius, *Emerging Data Protection*, p. 66.
40. Council of Europe, Resolution (73) 22 and Resolution (74) 29.

Experts to prepare such an instrument. From 1976 to 1979, in close cooperation with officials from national governments, the OECD, and the EEC, the Committee of Experts prepared the "Convention for the Protection of Individuals with Regard to Automatic Processing of Personal Data," which was duly adopted by the Parliamentary Assembly of the Council of Europe in February 1980 and by the Committee of Ministers in September 1980. It was opened for ratification in January 1981, but only to those countries with national data protection laws. As of March 1988, eighteen member countries had signed the convention; they indicated their intention to adopt domestic data protection law so as to be able to ratify the agreement. The convention received its requisite five ratifications on 1 October 1985.

Essentially, the convention elaborates on and reaffirms as being binding rules of international law those data protection principles that the council had already ratified in 1973-74. It states that personal data undergoing automatic data processing should be: (1) obtained and processed fairly and lawfully; (2) stored for specified and legitimate purposes and used in a way compatible with those purposes; (3) adequate, relevant, and not excessive in relation to the purposes for which they are stored; (4) accurate and, where necessary, kept up-to-date; and (5) preserved in a form which permits identification of the data subjects for whom these data are stored. It also confirms the right of individuals to establish the existence of an automated personal data file and to determine its main purposes; to be informed of whether personal data relating to them are stored in such a file; to rectify or erase false or out-of-date information; and to have a remedy against a noncompliant organization.

The convention also addresses the important issue of international data communications (transborder data flow). It contains the general rule that "a party shall not, for the sole purpose of the protection of privacy, prohibit or subject to special authorization transborder data flows of personal data to the territory of another party." This party may, however, control such flow if "its legislation includes specific regulations for certain categories of personal data or of automated personal data files" and the other party does not offer equivalent protection.[41] Prohibitions are also permissible for data going to or

41. Council of Europe, *Convention for the Protection of Individuals*, Article 12.

through noncontracting states. The recognition that the growing volume of international data traffic could jeopardize national attempts to protect privacy pushed the whole issue onto a new dimension where implications transcended the civil liberties concerns. The OECD was the organization primarily responsible for resolving these further issues.

The Organization for Economic Cooperation and Development

The OECD, which includes not only European nations but also Japan and the important data processing countries of North America and Australasia, took an early interest in computerization, information processing, and data communications. This interest was justified in terms of its dedication to the economic development of its member countries. From the 1960s onward, the OECD has considered data (both personal and otherwise) to be an increasingly important commodity that can be traded nationally and internationally. In 1968 the OECD Committee for Science Policy established the Group on Computer Utilization to investigate technological, economic, and legal questions relating to computers and telecommunications. The efforts of this group are reflected in a widely disseminated series of "OECD Informatics Studies."

For some time, however, the issue of privacy was tangential rather than central to the OECD's efforts. The organization took a direct interest in privacy per se only as a result of the work being done in the Council of Europe and only after the international ramifications of data protection had been realized. In 1974 the Computer Utilization Group appointed the Data Bank Panel to study specific policy issues arising from the widespread use of computerized databanks. The immediate product of their work was a seminar in June 1974 during which information specialists from most OECD countries exchanged views on a number of data protection issues, namely, the personal identifier, citizen access, the regulatory structure, and transborder data flow.[42] This meeting was followed in 1977 by a fuller and more lavish symposium—titled "Transborder Data Flows and the Protec-

42. OECD, *Policy Issues in Data Protection and Privacy.*

tion of Privacy"—held in Vienna. Eighteen nations were represented by their various information specialists.[43]

The Vienna symposium also afforded the first formal opportunity for American representatives to confront those from Europe, a confrontation that pointed up several sharp contrasts between American and European approaches to international data protection. To many Europeans, the American espousal of free flow was a veiled attempt to protect the dominance of its own data processing industry. As a result of the incremental and sectoral approach to data protection in America, many Europeans viewed the standard of privacy protection in the United States as unacceptably low. They were unwilling to allow a completely unregulated flow of personal data to a country with such a mammoth data processing industry and seemingly inadequate safeguards. On the other side, Americans considered privacy to be a less important value than were freedom of speech and of information, values that (in the history of constitutional interpretation) can only be compromised in narrow and defined circumstances. Some American commentators saw ulterior trade protectionist motives behind the data protection label.[44] As Congressman Barry Goldwater, Jr., warned the House Committee on Government Operations in 1980: "I think we are now seeing the emergence of national privacy legislation which is actually aimed at creating new trade barriers. . . . They have discovered the simple fact that to block data flow in the 1980s is to block trade."[45]

Despite these transatlantic suspicions, the atmosphere at the Vienna symposium was sufficiently uncontentious to enable a group of government experts to begin work in 1978 on draft guidelines on the protection of privacy in the transborder flow of personal data. The group worked in close cooperation with the Council of Europe, and "every effort was made to avoid unnecessary differences between the texts produced by the two organizations."[46] Agreement was reached

43. OECD, *Transborder Data Flows and the Protection of Privacy.*
44. John M. Eger, "Emerging Restrictions on Transnational Data Flow: Privacy Protection or Non-Tariff Trade Barriers?" *Law and Policy in International Business* 10 (1978): 1055–1103; Robert Bigelow, "Transborder Data Flow Barriers," *Jurimetrics* 20 (1979–80): 8–17.
45. U.S. Congress, House of Representatives, *International Data Flow*, Hearings before a Subcommittee of the Committee on Government Operations, House of Representatives, 96th Cong., 2d sess. (Washington, D.C.: Government Printing Office, 1980), p. 1.
46. OECD, *Guidelines*, p. 21.

in June 1979, and the recommendation was adopted in September 1980.

These guidelines (the essential principles of which were explained in Chapter 3) constitute a parallel effort to that of the Council of Europe toward the harmonization of privacy protection rights and requirements. They are voluntary in nature and in some respects were intended to provide an interim standard of conduct until the Council of Europe Convention took effect. There are subtle but important distinctions between the two documents that should not concern us here.[47] In order to reach an agreement, the Committee of Experts clearly had to gloss over some philosophical differences over the issue of free flow versus privacy. And there is still some distrust in the United States of the underlying European motives as well as a marked lack of enthusiasm for the monitoring of the compliance of the data processing and communications industries.[48] Nevertheless, the OECD's guidelines represent a fundamental statement of international consensus on communications policy. The cooperative instinct and the desire to learn clearly outweighed national and cultural differences. The OECD forum provided a unique opportunity for both Americans and Europeans to debate the safeguarding of human rights in the computer age.

The international process of study visits, seminars, conferences, and conventions during the 1970s in itself constitutes a fascinating study in international relations. The intense activity of such a variety of international bodies provided an opportunity for constant learning about different views and experiences. If policy making is conceived as a process of lesson drawing, we can infer that the transnational nature of the search for solutions had a direct impact on policy choice in advanced democratic countries. Kirby, for instance, contends that "the nature of information technology and geographical proximity of

47. According to the OECD's *Guidelines*, the major differences stem from the fact that these are not legally binding, whereas the Council of Europe's convention is, for those countries that ratify it. There is also a difference in scope: the Council of Europe convention applies primarily to automatic data processing; the guidelines apply to personal data irrespective of the methods and machinery used in their handling. The terminology also differs in some respects. See Craig T. Beling, "Transborder Data Flows: International Privacy Protection and the Free Flow of Information," *Boston College International and Comparative Law Review* 6 (1983): 591–624.

48. United States, General Accounting Office (GAO), *Privacy Policy Activities of the National Telecommunications and Information Administration* (Washington, D.C.: GAO, 1984).

the nations of Europe, as well as shared cultural, political, telecommunications and trade interests, made the effort to secure harmony in legislation natural—and indeed inevitable."[49]

But are these more authoritative international agreements, the OECD guidelines and particularly the Council of Europe Convention, the main causes of policy convergence? As we shall see, they had a direct impact on the states that did not take action on data protection until the late 1970s. What is less clear, however, is the effect of international harmonization efforts on those countries that legislated earlier. For example, the United States, which was not party to the discussions in the Council of Europe, had developed a model similar to that in the convention in the HEW Report of 1973 and in the Privacy Act of 1974. While there is plenty of evidence that American officials were aware of developments in Europe, there is no proof that they felt pressured to conform to any European model. They felt a need for mutual understanding, yes—but for conformity, no. The Swedes had also reached their conclusions about the basic principles of protection *before* the Council of Europe and OECD became vigorously involved.

Moreover, it is clear from debates in the early 1970s that the international dimensions of the problem had only just been realized and that they were not considered sufficiently serious to warrant an international treaty. Thus the OECD seminar held in June 1974 apparently reached a consensus "that the evidence so far available did not indicate that these were serious problems yet, but it was felt that in the not too distant future difficulties might indeed develop."[50] More convincing evidence is presented in a 1974 survey of data protection developments in OECD countries by the Data Bank Panel of the OECD's Computer Utilization Group. The panel concluded that "there is a striking similarity to the *independent yet correlative* actions in data protection and privacy conducted by the fourteen governments responding to this questionnaire."[51] They also found that, up until 1975, minimal attention had been given to transborder data flow issues: "Except for Sweden, the focus of central governments has been to formulate policy without special attention to extra-territorial movement of data. . . . It must be recognized that until governments

49. Kirby, "Transborder Data Flows," p. 40.
50. OECD, *Policy Issues in Data Protection and Privacy*, p. 27.
51. OECD, *Developments in Data Protection*, p. 2 (italics mine).

formulate their own policies over personal information, approaching international transfers is problematic."[52]

Hence, up until 1975–76, it can be concluded that governments acted under little pressure to conform to international guidelines because of a common perception of interdependence. Debates were already underway in most states by this time. By 1981, when the OECD and Council of Europe guidelines were promulgated, the first generation of statutes was already being implemented in about a dozen countries. The harmonization efforts both informed and were informed by these ongoing policy debates. The whole process of mutual influence is fueled by the continual interaction among a small technocratic elite of lawyers operating on both international and domestic levels and constantly moving between them. The countries that were most influenced by these harmonization efforts, however, were those that delayed legislating. This brings us to our final determinant of convergence, penetration.

Convergence through Penetration

In the final process, which contrasts with the more cooperative relations under harmonization, states may be forced to conform to the actions taken elsewhere. The penetration process assumes that policy making by one country often entails implications and costs for others. In an interdependent world, many policy efforts carry externalities that force other countries to conform or to suffer the adverse consequences of maintaining a different legal framework. This process is one under which state officials have the least independence from external forces, as outsiders will engage in their policy-making processes and wield sufficient influence to force conformity.

One proposition that comes to mind is that policy convergence may be due to American influence in Western Europe, and that along with the technology the idea of fair information practice was more or less exported across the Atlantic through U.S.-based multinational companies. Computerization generally occurred earlier in the United States than it did in Europe, and several commentators have stressed

52. Ibid., p. 4.

how the problems also tended to surface earlier in the United States than they did elsewhere. Hondius, for example, observes that "almost every issue that arose in Europe was also an issue in the United States, but at an earlier time and on a more dramatic scale."[53] This impression helps explain the attention paid by Europe to the early works of Alan Westin and Arthur Miller.

It seems, however, that the influence stops there. For little evidence exists that American political or economic interests had any direct influence on policy choice in Europe. We can dismiss the theory of American penetration simply by pointing to the fact that the very first data protection law in the world was in the German state of Hesse. The first national law in Sweden preceded that of the United States by over a year. The idea that such policy is another example of the "Americanization" of Western Europe can be rejected.

The penetrative process of convergence does apply, however, to Britain, the country that legislated last. The Council of Europe Convention allows data protection authorities to refuse the transborder flow of data to countries that do not have adequate data protection legislation; it thus had a direct impact on those nations that legislated late. It was generally assumed in Britain that the final passage of the 1984 Data Protection Act took place for economic rather than libertarian reasons. Britain feared that personal data protection could become a legal pretext for trade protectionism, and would lead to the isolation of the country's data processing industry as well as other service sectors of the economy that rely on unimpeded communications. The Conservative government admitted as much in its white paper of April 1982:

> Without legislation, firms operating in the United Kingdom may be at a disadvantage compared with those based in countries which have data protection legislation. When the Council of Europe Data Protection Convention comes into force it will confirm the right of countries with data protection legislation to refuse to allow personal information to be sent to other countries which do not have comparable safeguards. This could threaten firms with international interests operating in this country and the activities of computer bureaus which increasingly process data for customers in many

53. Hondius, *Emerging Data Protection*, p. 6.

different countries. Accordingly, in order to conform with international standards of privacy protection and to avoid possible barriers to trade, the Government has decided to introduce legislation which will apply throughout the United Kingdom and will enable the United Kingdom to ratify the Convention.[54]

This justification appears to accord equal weight to both civil libertarian and economic motives. Evidence from other sources, however, strongly suggests that the economic motive was predominant and that Britain would still be without data protection legislation had it not been for the Council of Europe Convention. David Waddington, the Minister of State at the Home Office and the man responsible for shepherding the bill through the House, provided these insights:

> In my view the case for legislation on privacy, on privacy grounds alone, was a very finely balanced one. The number of serious cases of misuse of information brought to our attention was very small, and I don't believe that it's right to introduce legislation without . . . there being a prospect of real benefits flowing from it. But when the commercial considerations prompted by the convention were added to the plain privacy dimension, and when added also was the importance of calming public fears about the new technology in order to remove barriers to the introduction of computers, then to my mind the case for legislation was proven.[55]

In the Standing Committee debates, the same Minister chided the Opposition for suggesting that there was "something wrong in the Government wishing to ratify the European Convention and in the British Government safeguarding the jobs of people engaged in the computer industry." This goal was a "highly laudable object," he claimed.[56]

Mr. Waddington fails to say, however, that the government had little choice in the matter. Pressured by the British computing industry and its administrative advocate, the Department of Trade and Industry, the government recognized that information technology was one of the few areas of the economy offering growth prospects; thus it was forced to protect Britain's perceived position at the "crossroads in the inter-

---

54. Great Britain, *Data Protection: The Government's Proposals for Legislation*, p. 48.
55. David Waddington, speech to Ontario Bar Association, Toronto, 1984.
56. David Waddington, HC Debs., 6s., 7 February 1984, col. 10 (Standing Committee H).

national data highway."[57] The real or imagined dangers of trans-border data flow influenced the British debate, as nowhere else.

The government was under pressure from another source. European data protection officials played a direct role in ensuring that the British law contained all the principles of fair information practice and that its enforcement mechanism was "credible." Both Jan Freese and Spiros Simitis were brought in to say loudly and clearly that if the law did not contain all these elements, they would advise their governments that it was not in compliance with the Convention and that European data protection authorities would therefore be justified in refusing requests for the international flow of personal data from their countries to the United Kingdom. At the Annual Conference of Data Protection Commissioners held in London in 1982, the commissioners "discreetly prodded their British hosts to enact strong, comprehensive legislation."[58] By 1984 the international pressures had become so inexorable that the government had absolutely no option but to enact legislation based on the Council of Europe Convention.

So we can conclude that the only country (in our sample) where a penetrative process was clearly at work was Britain, although it also presumably applies to other states that have legislated since then (the Netherlands, Australia, and Japan are the most important examples). In this case, the government had very little autonomy. It was forced to react and conform to decisions made in international arenas largely without any British input. This conclusion contrasts in an ironic way with the heady aspirations expressed by the British Computer Society in 1972, a time of idealism about European cooperation: "If workable legislation in relation to data banks and privacy can be developed in the U.K., it could, therefore, set the pattern for the whole of Europe."[59]

The Insignificance of Domestic Factors

Before summarizing the foregoing arguments and reaching some conclusion as to their relative merits, it is necessary to provide con-

57. Colin Mellors and David Pollitt, "The Data Protection Bill: Protecting Privacy or Promoting Commerce?" *The Political Quarterly* 55 (1984): 311.
58. Tom Riley, "Data Commissioners Meeting Spotlights Lack of UK Law," *Transnational Data and Communications Report* 5 (December 1982): 369.
59. British Computer Society, *Steps to Practicality*, p. 26.

vincing evidence that the convergence has not resulted simply from the fortuitous coincidence of similar national events or characteristics. This problem is avoided in part by my choice of cases, which vary on a range of institutional, ideological, and structural variables. Before concluding that one, some, or all of the transnational forces for convergence are valid, I must demonstrate that different constitutional, political, ideological, bureaucratic, and economic differences have indeed been transcended.

First, policy convergence in the data protection area has obscured differences in formal institutional arrangements, in constitutional frameworks, and particularly in legal philosophy. Both West Germany and the United States have had to adapt the policy to a federal system, thus establishing a more decentralized system of enforcement. But at the level of statutory principle, convergence has been relatively unaffected by constitutional differences. Most basically, the fair information principles have bridged the legal systems of countries based on the common law tradition (the United States and United Kingdom) and those based on the continental civil-law (or Roman law) approach. The common-law countries regard legislation as a last resort, "as an *ultima ratio* to be used only if a demonstrable mischief exists which customary law or judicial case law cannot remedy."[60] Hence, it is not typical in such countries for there to be a clear articulation of principles before legislation is proposed or for these principles then to be defined in and incorporated into the final statute. The civil (Roman) law tradition prefers anticipatory enactment before any mischief can manifest itself, broad principles of expected behavior, and a detailed codification of exceptions for particular problems and situations.

It can be argued, however, that the Americans, and to a greater extent the British, have formulated data protection policy with some disregard for their respective common law legal traditions. It has already been argued that policy action everywhere has an uncommonly anticipatory flavor. The concern has been to set out a legal framework to guide the development of technology rather than to wait for the courts' definition of identifiable abuses to shape the nature of the law. In the United States in the 1960s, privacy invasions

60. Hondius, "Data Law in Europe," p. 97.

and policy responses were very loosely related. Moreover, because of the rapidity of technological change, there was a paucity of case law and thus a need to devise a more synoptic public-policy solution. This effort began with the 1972 HEW Report, which provided the "analytical framework" for the 1974 Privacy Act, in which a refined set of principles is easily discerned from the language of the law.[61] The HEW report does represent a relatively rare example of the prelegislative conceptualization of a set of principles to guide public policy. In most other areas of civil liberties, the rights of the individual are stated, assumed, or interpreted from the Constitution. Here, the pressure of evolving technology rendered the Constitution inadequate and prompted the articulation of a more specific and relevant set of supplementary statutory principles to protect this new and more complicated relationship between the citizen and the state.

The British case presents a more interesting dilemma. While a common law country, the United Kingdom was clearly caught between the evolutionary nature of its legal and constitutional system and its close economic relationship with continental Europe. Some have argued that the British would have preferred a code of practice with a voluntary implementation framework,[62] which would certainly have been more consistent with its common law traditions. The pressure for harmonization from its trading partners on the continent, however, generated the comprehensive Data Protection Act, which is of the continental European mold.

Second, we must reject that argument that the convergence is created by comparable pressure from similar dominant social groups. One might quite plausibly hypothesize that the same policy output merely reflects the same constellation of group forces in each country, forces that were marshaled by politicians in the same way to produce

---

61. PPSC, *Personal Privacy in an Information Society*, p. 501. Congress refined the five HEW principles into an eightfold framework, which influenced the drafting of the law: the Openness Principle, the Individual Access Principle, the Individual Participation Principle, the Collection Limitation Principle, the Use Limitation Principle, the Disclosure Limitation Principle, the Information Management Principle, and the Accountability Principle. The PPSC subsequently used this framework for its own evaluation of the Privacy Act's effectiveness. PPSC, *The Privacy Act of 1974: An Assessment*, Appendix 4 to the Report of the Privacy Protection Study Commission (Washington, D.C.: Government Printing Office, 1977).

62. Regan, "Personal Information Policies in the United States and Britain"; Hondius, "Data Law in Europe," p. 97.

data protection law. In all countries, however, the newness and complexity of the problem demanded analysis rather than the negotiation of different group demands. Hence, with respect to statutory principles, group interaction had little influence on policy choice. The only possible exception was the pressure by certain professional groups (such as doctors and educators) for exemptions from the public access and disclosure provisions. Civil libertarian groups were also active, of course, but again, their influence was very marginal.

The policy-making process in every country was predominantly elitist in nature. Public concern for the loss of privacy has been relatively high everywhere, as we saw in Chapter 1. But this concern has not translated into anything more than intermittent and sporadic political action. Westin argues that privacy even in its wider aspects is an inherently elitist issue:

> For the most part, demands for legal protection of a right to personal privacy have traditionally been made by elite groups in modern democracies: by political and cultural dissenters, by celebrities seeking some respite from intrusive cameramen and reporters, and by intellectual elements. For the poor, privacy was generally not available as a social condition nor was it a primary social objective.[63]

The problem has been defined by a tightly knit group of Western-educated technocrats with constant contacts at the international level. The question that is central to other policy studies, namely, the different vectors of social pressure and their reflection in group forces, is virtually irrelevant here. In this context, group pressure had only a marginal impact on the concerted search for a rational legal solution to this commonly perceived problem.

Third, we must examine whether data protection has been a Left/Right issue; the commonality in policy choice may be caused by the same ideological current that swept through these states at the same time. Several commentators have noted that pressure for privacy and data protection comes principally from the civil liberties groups to the left of the political spectrum; they have inferred that the issue is basically a liberal one.[64] It is more probable, however, that data pro-

63. Alan Westin, "Entering the Era of Databank Regulation and How We Got There," in OECD, *Policy Issues in Data Protection and Privacy,* p. 95.
64. Flaherty, "The Need for an American Privacy Protection Commission," p. 245.

tection is one of those "motherhood-and-apple-pie issues"; as Westin concludes, "concern over unlimited governmental or private surveillance runs the ideological spectrum from the Daughters of the American Revolution to the New Student Left, and from the National Review to the Nation."[65]

The issue is so sufficiently broad that it can encompass a variety of different positions, from the civil libertarian who demands constraints on overzealous law enforcement to the conservative business group that wants tax data to be kept confidential. The issue tends to pose a dilemma for democratic socialist parties in particular; it exposes a tension between the welfare statism of the old Left, which relies on a sacrifice of individual privacy for the collective benefit, and the more antistatist individualism of the new Left. Thus below the broad liberal democratic concern for individualism and human dignity lies a complex and often contradictory set of positions. As Rule argues, in reply to Westin: "No one is likely to come out against privacy. But a close look at the clamor for more of it suggests that its proponents do not all have the same thing in mind. . . . People do protest what they consider unfair surveillance—often in the same breath with which they demand surveillance for more vigorous purposes which they support."[66]

The ideological foundations of the issue are inherently ambiguous because privacy and data protection do not stir partisan emotion until the debate centers on particular information in specific contexts. We then find a complexity of crosscutting concerns. But at the abstract level of fair information practice—the level of transnational policy convergence—consensus has embraced all positions on the ideological spectrum with the possible exception of the far Left and far Right. Arguments over particulars were not sufficiently divisive to alter the inherent logic of data protection or to obstruct the passage of these similar principles into law.

An examination of the partisan orientation of those governments that introduced data protection laws supports this view. Table 3 gives results from sixteen countries, ranging the dates of enactment against the ideological complexion of the government. It can be readily seen

65. Westin, *Privacy and Freedom*, p. 378.
66. Rule et al., *The Politics of Privacy*, p. 135.

Table 3. Partisanship and the formation of personal data protection policy

Country	Date of legislation	Partisan Orientation of government in power
Sweden	July 1973	Social Democratic
United States	January 1975	Republican President/ Democratic Congress
West Germany	January 1977	Social Democratic/Free Democratic Coalition
Canada	October 1977	Liberal
France	January 1978	Independent Republican/Gaullist
Norway	June 1978	Labour
Denmark	June 1978	Social Democratic
Austria	October 1978	Socialist
Luxembourg	March 1979	Democrat/Socialist Worker
New Zealand	December 1982	National
United Kingdom	July 1984	Conservative
Finland	April 1987	Social Democratic/National
Ireland	July 1988	Fianna Fail (Republican)
Australia	December 1988	Labour
Japan	December 1988	Liberal Democratic
The Netherlands	December 1988	Christian Democratic

Sources: Compiled from Alan J. Day and Henry W. Degenhardt, *Political Parties of the World* (Detroit: Gale Research, 1980), and Francis Jacobs, ed., *Western European Political Parties: A Comprehensive Guide* (London: Longman, 1989).

that data protection laws have been introduced by governments of varying persuasions, from the cohesive center right government of Mrs. Thatcher in Britain in 1984 to the social democratic governments of Scandinavia. It will also be recalled that the final bills were passed with enormous legislative majorities in both Sweden and the United States. Britain's Labour party opposed the Data Protection Act on final reading because it was not sufficiently progressive. The opposition of the CDU/CSU parties in West Germany to the BDSG was prompted by the nature and function of the Federal Data Protection Commissioner rather than by the goals and principles of the legislation.

To conclude, however, that political contention has been confined to questions of detail rather than to matters of principle, is not to say that the occurrence of elections has not affected the final outcome of the legislative process. In particular, the calling of elections in Britain in February 1974, May 1979, and June 1984 interrupted the process, and this was certainly one cause of the long delay in legislating. One

148

might also speculate whether the Data Protection Act would have been motivated more by civil libertarian rather than by economic reasons had the Labour party won the 1979 election. The federal election in 1972 was also a probable cause of some delay in West Germany's response. Therefore, while data protection can be regarded as a nonpartisan issue, it is not true that electoral politics have been entirely irrelevant. Elections affect the timing of legislation in interesting, if unpredictable, ways. They raise a number of intractable "what if" questions that should make us pause before concluding that the formation of data protection policy has been totally unaffected by the democratic process.

Finally, consider the argument that bureaucratic politics influenced the content of the fair information principles. For a number of structural and behavioral reasons, we would expect national bureaucracies to offer resistance to data protection policy. Bureaucracies have special incentives to engage in the political arena when their own control of information is at stake. Information is a vital resource for both the organization's internal decision-making processes and its relations with the external environment. Under data protection policy, bureaucracies are expected to surrender their exclusive control of a vital resource. Because they face limitations on the collection, storage, retrieval, and transmittal of that resource, one might expect a certain resistance. And resistance there was, as will be fully demonstrated in Chapter 6. But that opposition was largely directed toward the method by which the principles were to be enforced rather than toward the principles themselves. The forces for convergence also overwhelmed bureaucratic interests, which would be expected to vary from nation to nation in relation to the ability and propensity of different bureaucratic agencies to engage in the political arena.

The only qualification to this general conclusion relates to the principle of individual access and correction. Exemptions to public access differ, particularly for "national security" or "law enforcement" purposes. Some of the expansive exemptions in the British, German, and American laws had much to do with civil service resistance. The "routine use" exemption in the United States Privacy Act for interagency disclosures can also be attributed to similar forces. At a wider level, however, bureaucratic resistance was clearly not sufficient to cause major variation in the legal principles enacted. When it appeared inevitable that data protection was an "idea whose time had come" (and this realization occurred at different times), the national bureaucracies accepted the principles as a fait accompli and shifted their attention and resources to the question of implementation and enforcement.

Conclusion: Explaining Convergence

The full causes of public policy are ultimately elusive. The generalizations presented here, then, are not definitive causal statements but are more provisional accounts of likely trends and relationships. We cannot ascribe precise weights to each of these arguments. All we can do is investigate their plausibility in the light of the empirical evidence. We have "interrogated" the data. It is now time to summarize the results of that interrogation by painting a composite picture of the reasons for the similar choices of policy.

No one explanation of convergence is fully adequate for all cases and all stages of the process; all have some weakness or blind spot. But a combination of these explanations can improve our understanding of why the laws are so similar. One will recall that the application of a more deductive theoretical framework was justified for three reasons: it helps us avoid an overly deterministic conclusion; it allows us to observe convergence over time and thus to assess whether different determinants prevail at different points in the process; and it allows us to compare the relative validity of different arguments for different states. Seemingly mutually exclusive arguments can in fact be reconciled if we bear in mind both their spatial and temporal dimensions. Very different countries have converged at different times for different reasons.

The process of policy making in the data protection area is clearly one where broad transnational forces for convergence have transcended variations in national characteristics. The background to the legislation is the rapid technological progress that is commonly recognized to be restructuring individual, social, economic, and political relationships. On one level, convergence has occurred within this common technological context. Information technology and its proliferation through the transnational economic structure, its pervasiveness, and its closed and enigmatic nature have obviously set limits on policy choice. These characteristics have forced policy makers to structure the legal safeguards with close regard for the transnational nature of the resource being regulated, with sufficient latitude to anticipate future developments in a fluid technological and social context, and with a compelling desire to demystify the data processing environment. For Sweden and the United States, the pioneers, the fair information principles emerged from mainly indigenous analysis and recognition of this inherent logic within the data protection problem.

The technology, however, should not be regarded as an independent force that "causes" anything. The crucial variable is the common set of attitudes that developed about the technology. In the mid-1970s, these attitudes coalesced within an international policy community. The environment of technological uncertainty produced a strong motivation not so much for imitation as for cross-national lesson drawing, which stimulated frequent interaction among a tightly knit community of mainly legal specialists. For the countries that legislated in the middle to late 1970s, including West Germany, convergence is primarily a result of this constant communication among members of a policy community from nations sharing the same technological problems and the same concerns for privacy. The international forums provided by the OECD and the Council of Europe afforded regular opportunities for this community to meet and to frame this common viewpoint.

The problems associated with the transborder flow of personal data have probably been exaggerated. Nevertheless, the common perception of the transnational nature of the technology and of the data protection problem convinced many that the concept of national data protection was obsolete and unworkable. The subsequent harmonization efforts by the Council of Europe and the OECD were both a consolidation of efforts already taken by the pioneer states, and a stimulus to the laggards. Thus the actions of international organizations were not the cause of the similar choices made by Sweden, the United States, and West Germany. They were the primary cause of convergence for Britain and for the other states that have adopted a slower and more reactive posture. The penetrative theory of convergence, therefore, applies to these countries.

In this context, the salience of national factors as independent variables has been reduced. The partisan orientation of governments has been insignificant. The reason is not because the issue is nonideological but rather because it has its roots in more broadly construed liberal democratic thought. It is not, therefore, a technocratic issue that supports an "end of ideology" thesis but one which is deeply embedded in the belief systems of advanced democratic societies. These beliefs have evolved over centuries toward ever more sophisticated conceptions and codifications of contractual obligations and duties. Fair information practice exposes the commonalities among the closely interlinked historical, cultural, and political developments of these societies.

Furthermore, the common international legal framework has been incorporated into national laws with little regard to the essential distinction between the common law traditions of the United States and the United Kingdom and the civil law approach of continental Europe. There are, of course, marginal differences in style and emphasis. Nevertheless, data protection does not appear to support the contention of legal scholars that each country is constrained by constitutional and legal imperatives. The similarities in the purpose and principles of data protection from country to country far outweigh any differences imposed by the need to conform to preordained schemes and legacies. We have also noted the elitist nature of the policy process, a quality that has prevailed with only slight and intermittent pressure from the mass public. Opinion polls show widespread and significant concern for the myriad issues to which the computerization of personal data gives rise. But this anxiety has generally *not* been translated into political pressure. The activity of interest groups has been confined to the civil liberties lobby and to the most directly affected professional groups. Bureaucratic constraints also had little impact on the content of fair information policy.

At the level of policy goals and statutory principles, countries have converged. This convergence should not be regarded as either surprising or inevitable. It is an empirical finding that is explained by the combination of factors discussed above. As we shall see, however, countries have diverged significantly on the question of how these principles should be implemented. The task now is to describe that divergence in Chapter 5 and to attempt to understand its causes in Chapter 6.

5

The Choice of Policy Instruments

We now move from questions of principle to questions of method—from the broad cross-national agreement on statutory goals to the sharp divergence on the means chosen to meet those goals. In this chapter I describe and compare the instruments selected by each country and discuss how they were chosen. From here on I focus completely on the four-nation sample of Sweden, the United States, West Germany, and the United Kingdom, the countries that have selected the widest range of methods for implementing the fair information principles.

I proceed by setting out the seemingly available choices, the "international repertoire" of possible solutions. These are the options that appear intuitively to be possible if one knew nothing about the social and political contexts involved. They are stated first as models or abstractions that point to the possible methods of implementation. I then move to the less neat level of empirical reality, discussing each country case in turn and focusing on: (1) the options that reached the policy agenda, (2) the way the final choice was made, and (3) the policy instrument established in each country.

The Repertoire of Policy Instruments

Personal data protection policy in all countries is characterized by its attempt to grant individuals a right to control the nature, content, and circulation of information relating to them. As we saw in Chapter

153

3, this right entails a number of principles of fair information practice. The general presumption had previously been that information was the property of an organization and that, with only minor exceptions, it was the prerogative of the organization to decide its own information practices. Personal data protection policy shifts this presumption in some major and radical ways. This policy asserts that personal data should only be collected by lawful means and with the knowledge or consent of the individual concerned; that data should be relevant for the purposes for which they are used, and these purposes should be made explicit to the individual at the time of collection; and that data should only be used and disclosed for these stated purposes. Organizations now have a responsibility to maintain reasonable security safeguards. But at the same time, they must ensure that the existence and nature of record-keeping systems are public knowledge and that data subjects can obtain and correct any information pertaining to them which is not timely, accurate, or complete.

In practice, of course, these relationships are still highly ambiguous in most record-keeping activities. Personal data protection policy does, however, reflect a significant change in emphasis with profound and widespread implications. As these principles represent a potentially major departure from previous practice, the question then becomes how they can, or should, be translated into reality. In most countries, it was this issue that dominated debate and aroused the most political controversy. Disagreements over this question, both within and between nations, centered on a number of methods of implementation. In common with recent contemporary usage in political science, I call these methods of implementation "policy instruments."[1] Five models can be identified as the international repertoire of potential policy instruments: voluntary control, subject control, licensing, a data commissioner, and registration.

These five "models" are just that—models. They are ideal types, and as such they are not empirically observed in their pure form in any

1. For a general discussion, see Hood, *The Tools of Government*; Stephen H. Linder and B. Guy Peters, "Instruments of Government: Perceptions and Contexts," *Journal of Public Policy* 9 (1989): 35–58; and Kenneth Woodside, "Policy Instruments and the Study of Public Policy," *Canadian Journal of Political Science* 19 (1986): 775–93. For a prior analysis of instruments of data protection, see Colin J. Bennett, "Regulating the Computer: Comparing Policy Instruments in Europe and the United States," *European Journal of Political Research* 16 (1988): 437–66.

one context. They provide an abstraction or representation of the options rather than an explanation thereof. The presentation of these models, however, does allow us to easily clarify and contrast the choices made according to a clear, comparative framework. The remainder of the chapter is devoted to identifying how the choice was defined in each country, which options reached the policy agenda, and how the chosen method of implementation reflects these different models of control. We shall see that all data protection law contains a combination of approaches. We will also see that one approach dominates the theory and practice of implementation in each country.

The Voluntary Control Model

The first scheme is one of self-regulation, where fair information practice is implemented internally with minimal intervention from external bodies. The assumption is that personal data protection can be guaranteed through a modification of the existing professional rules within an organization. The record keeper is expected to take the necessary organizational and technical steps to protect against abuse, to provide rights of access, to publish the nature of each system, and to control the use and disclosure of personal data. These expectations correspond to what Hondius terms "self-surveillance."[2]

The role of the law under this model is twofold. First, it must define specific rules for all who operate personal information systems. Second, it must require the appointment of a "responsible person" in each organization who can ensure that the appropriate steps are being taken to be in compliance with the law. That person should be responsible for overseeing all aspects of system design, security safeguards, and information flow; the individual should also be as independent from management and policy-making functions as is possible. The advantage of self-regulation is its flexibility; each organization can be left to comply in the most beneficial way. Record-keeping relationships are different from organization to organization. Self-regulation does not interfere with professional norms and existing codes of practice, nor does it require the establishment of a costly external apparatus to monitor compliance. Data protection policy can be introduced

2. Hondius, *Emerging Data Protection*, p. 120.

with a certain sensitivity to specific organizational needs and to the necessary advances in technology.

Voluntary control does not guarantee, however, that personal data protection interests will prevail when confronted with the quest for efficiency and cost-effectiveness. As Simitis argues, the responsible keeper "as an insider will choose criteria for his evaluation which are necessarily influenced by the activities and purposes of the firm. The responsible person can therefore never act as an impartial outsider."[3] In practice, voluntary self-regulation means control by those with interests and obligations that will inevitably conflict with rights to personal data protection. Even if one could define a distinct group to be responsible solely for information management in an agency, there is no guarantee that privacy will prevail over the values of the organization. As information control is central to any organization's identity and function, the conflict of interests is inescapable.

The Subject Control Model

All laws grant the individual to whom the information pertains (the "data subject") certain rights vis-à-vis the record-keeping institution. Hence, the second form of control is naturally based on the active participation and intervention of those persons directly affected by record keeping. This model is what others have named the "self-help solution"[4] or the method of "subjective external control."[5] Subject participation takes two forms under personal data protection policy. The first consists of the specified rights of access and correction. The second is the enforcement of data protection rights through the courts.

The right of the data subject to see his or her information and to correct any part of it that is not accurate, timely, relevant, or complete allows individuals themselves to control the processing of data which relates to them. The "right to know" is based on the assumption that openness discourages the misuse and abuse of personal data. In addition, subject control assists the record-keeping organization itself to maintain accurate data for decision-making purposes. The "right to

3. Simitis, "Establishing Institutional Structures," p. 86.
4. Sieghart, *Privacy and Computers*, p. 123.
5. Hondius, *Emerging Data Protection*, p. 215.

know" entails three interrelated processes. First, people must be told about the existence of databanks and their purposes and contents. Operators of record-keeping systems therefore have a duty to publish (in a special register, an official gazette, or public notices) the name, location, and contents of databanks. Second, individuals have the right to be informed on their request of the information registered about them. This process entails a duty to notify the data subject about the way to gain access (i.e., where to write to) and to establish administrative procedures for meeting citizen requests. The third process is that of correction or erasure if the data can be proven to be inaccurate, obsolete, or incomplete.

The subject control model assumes that through access rights the nature of personal data can be constantly monitored and its accuracy and integrity ensured. Moreover, access may have a salutary effect on the organization and may reduce the suspicions and fears of the individual.[6] Yet rights of access to personal data can never be absolute. Exceptions are normally included to protect law enforcement and national security functions as well as to protect the efficiency of the administrative process. Thus many schemes impose an access fee to ensure that the functioning of the organization is not unreasonably hampered by an overwhelming number of (maybe frivolous) requests.

This solution also encompasses action taken through the courts to seek judicial enforcement of data protection principles. In this respect, the courts act as institutional mechanisms brought into the process by the assertion of privacy rights by the data subject. Under this scheme, however, "control" effectively means an individual's quest for remedial action in the event of a violation. More specifically, a civil remedy may be available if data subjects have suffered actual injury as a consequence of the wrongful collection, storage, maintenance, use, or disclosure of their data. In extraordinary circumstances, criminal penalties might also be imposed. However it is accomplished, enforcement is *post facto*, and the individual must initiate any action.

The subject control model, therefore, is naturally dependent on an activist and litigious citizenry that is concerned about privacy and willing to assert its rights either directly with the record-keeping organization or indirectly through the courts. It relies on individuals

6. Flaherty, *Protecting Privacy in Surveillance Societies*, p. 401.

being cognizant of their rights at every stage of the process, from the data's initial collection to its subsequent uses and disclosures. The individual thus carries an enormous burden. Moreover, the rights of access and correction are only relevant to the specific information requested; they do not ensure that further misuses will not occur or that similar wrongs will not be committed against others. Finally, the courts are often inadequate mechanisms through which to seek remedial action or judicial enforcement given the often expensive nature of the litigation process and the other costs in terms of time, effort, and expertise. Many judges are also not expert in the technical computing issues on which they often have to decide.

Subject control entails some enormous disadvantages, relying as it does on very unrealistic assumptions about the participatory inclinations and abilities of the average citizen. Regan characterizes it as a "symbolic" response to the problem, more an "advertizing gimmick that bureaucracies can use to 'symbolize' their concern with these issues."[7] It nevertheless constitutes one possible approach to the implementation of data protection policy, and it contrasts in significant ways to the last three institutional instruments of protection.

The Licensing Model

Rejecting the assumptions behind voluntary compliance and self-help, the last three models are based on the assumption that personal data protection is too important a value to be left to the voluntary actions of the record keeper or to the self-help of the unskilled, and often incapable, data subject. The weaknesses of the above two models lead us to an approach where the relationship between the record keeper and the data subject is mediated by a separate institution that can both regulate the record keepers and assist the data subjects in the pursuance of their rights.

Fair information principles are enforced under the first approach by the requirement of licensing for every databank that processes personal data. The process requires the establishment of a separate agency with whom all operators must register their information systems and

7. Priscilla M. Regan, "Public Uses of Private Information: A Comparison of Personal Information Policies in the United States and Britain" (Ph.D. diss., Cornell University, 1981), p. 114.

without whose permission no personal data may be processed. The act of licensing allows the agency to stipulate specific conditions on the collection, storage, manipulation, and disclosure of personal data. The need for a license also means that personal data processing is subject to conditions of openness. The essential characteristics of record-keeping systems (their size, the types of information they maintain, their authority for collection, their duration of data storage, and the organizations to which they may transmit data) are recorded and open for inspection. If there is a subsequent change in practice, this must be approved by the licensing authority and publicized accordingly. The licensing agency also serves to inform the public of its access and correction rights and how these might be exercised. Generally, the license would be issued on payment of a fee, thus giving the licensing authority the potential to be self-financing.

The licensing model has several attractive features: the provision of the license may be tailored to the specific information system in question; the license can be provided before the system is established, when it is easier and cheaper to make the necessary adjustments; licensing creates a guarantee that information technology will not only be regulated but will also be investigated and serves as a strategy for gaining crucial insights into the state of the art and into the new problems created by technological developments. But enormous numbers of personal record-keeping systems may exist, and not all can be licensed without imposing absurd burdens on organizations and on the authority itself. Where, then, does one draw the line? According to the nature of the organization, the information, or the technology? Licensing may be considered an overly bureaucratic and cumbersome solution that creates more organizational problems than it solves.[8]

The Registration Model

Registration differs from licensing only in the sense that the control agency would have no authority to block the creation of an information system. The enforcement of data protection principles is more remedial than it is anticipatory. Registration is, of course, a central component of the licensing approach. The very process of applying for

8. Flaherty, *Protecting Privacy in Surveillance Societies*, p. 395.

a license serves to place on record the essential information about the record-keeping system. The pure registration approach, however, merely stipulates that anyone processing personal data should register with the registration authority and in so doing, describe the nature, contents, and purpose of the information system.

Once that notification is provided and the fee is paid, the record keeper would be authorized to process personal data. The act of registration entails a commitment to processing personal data according to the data protection principles. On registration, the organization specifies from where personal data are collected and to where they will be disclosed. But no permission or license, as such, is required. Provided the organization continues to register and publicize its data handling procedures, it may legitimately process personal data. Record keepers may be "deregistered" only in the rare cases when complaints are received and investigations reveal a failure to adhere to the data protection principles.

The Data Commissioner Model

The final approach requires neither licensing nor registration. Derived from the more general ombudsman concept as applied to other areas of administration, it establishes a commissioner's office that acts (normally as an agent of the legislature) as an intermediary between the citizen and the record keeper. The office could be run by a plural executive of some kind (a "commission"), but it is more likely to be run by a single person (a "commissioner"). Without powers of regulation, the commissioner relies on complaints from citizens. The principal task is to investigate those complaints, but this primary function requires the exercise of other powers and responsibilities. The commissioner would also require the production of internal papers; enter premises in order to inspect the data processing operations; give expert advice on the improvement of personal data handling; issue reports; and closely follow advances in technology and make proposals for its effective and secure application.

Without specific enforcement powers, however, the data commissioner relies on either cultivating a relationship of mutual trust with the record-keeping organization or on the publication of abuses, with all the legislative, press, and public pressure that could result. This model also relies on a vigilant and concerned citizenry. Furthermore, its success, as is the experience of ombudsmen in other areas, depends heavily on the personal characteristics of the data commissioner—his or her experience, expertise, aggressiveness, diligence, and organizational abilities.

The Swedish Choice: Licensing the Computer

In Chapter 2 we identified a number of reasons why Sweden was a pioneer in personal data protection. Foremost is the fact that Sweden experienced a relatively earlier and more widespread computerization of its small population than did other countries; this computerization was facilitated by Sweden's already highly developed system of personal identifiers. The uniquely open system of administration also explains why the problem was perceived as acute at such an early stage. More generally, certain structural features of the Swedish state support an anticipatory policy style and an ability to innovate that is not evident elsewhere.

The uncontentious passage of the Data Act is also attributable to the technical terms in which the data protection problem was defined. This influenced the future direction of Swedish data protection policy in some crucial ways. First, the proposed Data Act was to apply only to computerized data. Manually recorded information could, by inference, be adequately protected through the existing framework of publicity and secrecy laws. Second, as it was the technology that posed the new threat, the regulatory scheme would have to apply to both public and private organizations; the danger did not stem, in other words, from specific organizational uses and disclosures of personal data. Third, and in consequence, the implementation scheme had to be prospective and preventive rather than remedial. Therefore, personal data files had to be regulated at the point of collection rather than after visible abuses occured. Thus, as argued by Claes-Goran Kallner, the first Director General of the Data Inspection Board, "by regulating what data may be put into a public computer, privacy can be protected without conflict with the free access principle, because there is no access to what is not put in."[9]

9. Claes-Goran Kallner, "Personal Data: The Open Access Approach," in OECD, *Policy Issues in Data Protection and Privacy*, p. 62.

The regulation of "what is put in" implicitly means a rejection of voluntary control and subject control. The framers of the Data Act thus shunned the notion that the adverse effects of computerization could be mitigated either by the record-keeping organizations themselves or by the individual citizen. Even though it is hard to find a clear statement and discussion of alternative options, from the start it was assumed that as the computer entailed new dangers, it would have to be regulated through some form of institutional control. In the Swedish context that form of control meant licensing.

The central stipulation of the Swedish Data Act is that "a personal register may not be started or kept without permission by the Data Inspection Board."[10] The DIB was established concurrently with the Data Act; in fact, the DIB began its life in July 1973, a year before the act's full provisions came into effect. A "personal register" means any index, list, or other notes "made by automatic data processing and containing personal information that can be assigned to the individual concerned."[11] "Personal information" embraces any particulars concerning an individual. Hence even registers of property or motor vehicles are considered personal registers if they contain any information by which the owners can be identified.

The only exceptions to the need for a license are personal registers compiled under the instructions of either the cabinet or the Riksdag. In these cases, the DIB has a consultative rather than a regulatory role. Freese suggests that "both branches of government must as a practical matter obtain a statement of opinion from the Data Inspection Board before taking any such decision."[12] It should also be noted that cabinet ministers in Sweden are not responsible for routine administration, which is performed by a complex network of semi-autonomous administrative boards. Most public registers in Swedish administration are under the jurisdiction of one of these boards and require DIB permission. On the other hand, the government has created some of the largest and most sensitive information systems. The exemption for the approximately six hundred databanks established by the cabinet and the Riksdag constitutes a significant restriction on the DIB's power.[13]

10. Data Act, Sec. 2.
11. Ibid., Sec. 1.
12. Freese, "The Swedish Data Act" (1977), p. 2.
13. Flaherty, *Protecting Privacy in Surveillance Societies*, p. 116.

The DIB will grant permission if "there is no reason to assume that . . . undue encroachment on the privacy of individuals will arise."[14] The law also gives the DIB wide powers to issue and enforce regulations relating to the method of collection and storage, the technical equipment, the manipulation of personal information, the rights of access and correction, the disclosure of information to others, the time limitations on storage, and basic security questions. Special reasons are required for the establishment of registers concerning criminal activities, personal health, or political and religious convictions. The act also established a completely new category of crime known as "data trespass" for those who unlawfully gain access to personal registers or who interfere with or obliterate the information contained therein. Such activity has since been regarded as a form of computer crime rather than an invasion of privacy, and it carries stiffer penalties in Sweden than it does elsewhere. The Data Act also includes an indemnity rule that requires the responsible keeper to pay compensation to individuals who have suffered damage because a personal register contains incorrect information about them.

Any decision of the DIB can be appealed to the government. The Ministry of Justice then consults with the DIB, the Attorney General, and the authority that desires a resolution. From 1982 to 1988, only eighty-eight of the eighteen thousand decisions issued by the DIB resulted in appeal. There have been on average only ten appeals each year since the DIB began operation in 1974: most have related to the cost of the license fee, but a few have involved the DIB in some controversial disputes.[15] This low number of appeals is attributable to the conciliatory approach taken by the DIB: rather than turning down applications forthwith, the DIB suggests constructive alternatives that would allow a license to be issued.

The DIB, like most other government agencies in Sweden, is autonomous in the sense that it is not responsible to any individual member of the cabinet but only to the King-in-Council (the formal ratifying body for executive actions). This is a "distinctive feature of the Swedish system of public administration" in that "once policy decisions have been reached through executive-legislative channels the ministers

---

14. Data Act, Sec. 3.

15. Correspondence, Data Inspection Board, 22 December 1988; Flaherty, *Protecting Privacy in Surveillance Societies*, pp. 118–19.

and the departments [relatively small bodies] exercise no direct authority over the actual implementation of policy."[16] It has been estimated that there are now approximately two hundred of these autonomous boards in the Swedish administrative system.

Like its counterparts in other policy areas, the DIB is under the guidance of a directorate appointed by the government and headed by a Director General (who in this case is expected to have judicial experience). The other ten members of the DIB are appointed from the various parliamentary parties, from the business community (particularly the computer industry), from the trades unions, and from other interest groups. There are also eight deputy members. Both members and deputies serve four-year terms. The Director General's period of service is unlimited. From 1977 to 1986, the position was held by Jan Freese, who is widely considered to be one of the major pioneers of data protection in the world and an avid and effective publicist for privacy rights in the computer age. He was replaced in 1986 by Mats Borjesson, formerly the Director General of the National Court Administration, who in turn was replaced in 1989 by Stina Wahlstrom, former permanent undersecretary at the Ministry of Labor.

The DIB's head office in Stockholm is comprised of three divisions and employs around thirty-five people: a licensing division, a supervisory division, and an administrative division. The board itself meets only about once a month to settle major cases and permit applications. Routine licensing decisions are delegated to lower levels. It should be noted that the DIB is also responsible for the implementation of the Credit Reporting Act and Debt Collecting Act, both of which protect privacy in these more limited areas. The DIB's annual budget for 1987/88 was 12.7 Swedish krona (around $2 million); only about 10 percent of the annual budget is offset typically by the license fees that are paid by the "responsible keepers."[17] The amount of this offset is a continuing source of disappointment to those who would prefer the DIB to finance itself more completely from its own revenues and to secure, therefore, a greater independence.

Without going too deeply into the experience of implementation, I should note that the burden of work associated with licensing all Sweden's automated personal data systems has been considerably

16. Hancock, *Sweden*, p. 205.
17. Correspondence, Data Inspection Board, 22 December 1988.

greater than was originally expected. As of July 1989, the number of licenses stood at 35,500, an inaccurate reflection, however, of the actual number of personal information systems in Sweden.[18] Over the first few years, the process of granting licenses inevitably became so routinized that "in reality it was more a formality consisting of straightforward registration."[19] About 65 percent of the licensing applications could be dealt with under a "simplified procedure."[20] Hence there developed a standardized process for the majority of routine applications and a specialized procedure for the more unique, sensitive files. A handbook issued by the DIB informs users of the category under which their license applications fall.

This two-tier system was institutionalized in the revised Data Act of 1982 after a lengthy analysis of the operation of the act by the Parliamentary Commission on Revision of the Data Act (DALK), and a controversial parliamentary passage.[21] The "simplified procedure" is used to register those files which are noncontroversial (e.g., those pertaining to salaries, personnel, clients, employees) but which also proved to be the most time-consuming to register in the early years of the act's implementation. Such files must be registered, but they are now exempt from the permit requirement. The change was intended to reduce costs and red tape, to make the system self-financing, and to free the DIB's staff for supervision, inspection, and response to complaints. Flaherty concludes that "the 1982 act significantly turned away from the system of universal advanced licensing of all personal information systems to become primarily a registration system."[22]

While Swedish data protection policy relies most heavily on the licensing approach, there are also aspects of the data commissioner model present. Sweden is the source of the institution known as the

---

18. *Transnational Data and Communications Report* 12 (November 1989): 16. Flaherty reports that the DIB has established the existence of fifty thousand personal information systems: see *Protecting Privacy in Surveillance Societies*, p. 96.

19. Jan Freese, "Freedom of Information and Privacy Protection in Sweden," in *Accès à l'Information et protections des renseignements personnels*, ed. Pierre Trudel (Montréal: Les Presses de l'Université de Montréal, 1984), p. 24.

20. Freese, "The Swedish Data Act" (1977), p. 6.

21. The DALK Report on Revision of the Data Act, *Statens offentliga utredningar* (Stockholm: 1978). The amendments were adopted by the Riksdag with a one-vote majority. The minority (Social Democrats and Communists) wanted to postpone a decision pending the introduction of a bill containing more sweeping provisions. Freese, "Freedom of Information and Privacy Protection in Sweden," p. 24.

22. Flaherty, *Protecting Privacy in Surveillance Societies*, p. 116.

"ombudsman" and has lengthy and valuable experience with enforcing judicial and administrative accountability through use of this device. There are now three *Justitieombudsman*, each charged with investigating written complaints and determining whether civil and military officials "in the execution of their official duties have, through partiality, favoritism, or other causes, committed any unlawful act or neglected to perform their official duties properly."[23] Clearly, at least with regard to public administration, the misuse and abuse of information technology falls within this area of responsibility. Given the technical nature of computer supervision, however, the DIB also plays an ombudsmanlike role. Freese explains:

> The DIB is not merely a sanctioning authority. It also has supervisory duties and serves as a "wailing wall" for the general public. It is therefore empowered to inspect computer centres and other premises where computer processing is undertaken or where equipment for computer processing or other data media are stored. The right of inspection covers all computer installations, not merely those regularly used for processing personal information. But of course the right of inspection is confined to ensuring that computer processing does not entail any improper infringement of personal privacy.[24]

The DIB is therefore granted wide powers of admission and inspection as well as access to relevant documents relating to automatic data processing. Its powers are only qualified by the proviso that "the supervision shall be executed in such a way that it does not cause greater costs or inconvenience than is necessary."[25] In practice, however, the licensing responsibilities of the DIB have tended to swamp its small staff; as a result, the DIB has not performed its supervisory function with the vigor that many desired. The inspection department performs up to one hundred inspections per year; perhaps only one-half of these involve site visits.[26] Since 1982 the DIB has tried to

---

23. Hancock, *Sweden*, p. 236.
24. Jan Freese, "The Swedish Data Act," *Current Sweden* 4 (Stockholm: The Swedish Institute, July 1973), p. 5.
25. Data Act, Sec. 15.
26. Herbert Burkert, "Organization and Method of Operation of the Data Protection Authorities," vol. 2 of *Data Security and Confidentiality*, Report to the Commission of the European Communities (Manchester: National Computing Centre, 1980), p. 165; Flaherty, *Protecting Privacy in Surveillance Societies*, p. 133.

expand this side of its operation but with very mixed success. Experience has also shown that the number of citizen complaints is not that great; Freese suggests it to be about five hundred each year.[27] Many of these do not require a follow-up inquiry; others can be more effectively dealt with by other ombudsmen. Stories in the media of wrongdoing often serve as effective indicators of the major trouble spots in personal data processing.

Probably a more significant "ombudsman" function is the advisory one. The DIB is often involved in a consultative capacity in the setting up of major new information systems, especially in the public sector. Its views are also sought when new technologies are being introduced. Privacy considerations are thus taken into account from the outset, and users save themselves the trouble of making subsequent modifications as a means to conform to DIB regulations. The staff of the DIB are invited to sit on various committees and boards and are consequently involved in the development of information processing in both public and private sectors. The DIB is also used as a body to which draft legislation is submitted for consideration.

The concept of the "responsible keeper" indicates that data protection in Sweden also relies to a large extent on voluntary compliance, especially since the 1982 amendments. The explicit identification of the responsible keeper through the licensing process is implicit admittance that the DIB cannot possibly oversee and enforce all data processing activity. The responsible keeper concept clearly refers to the party that not only houses the register but also is responsible for the decisions which are made about its contents.[28] The responsible keeper is therefore accountable for the accuracy of personal information; for its completeness; for providing procedures for citizen access; for ensuring that data are not transmitted to anyone who might disobey the provisions of the act, including foreign organizations; for maintaining the confidentiality of stored personal information; and for undertaking to inform the DIB whenever the circumstances or contents of the personal register change.

There are, of course, penalties for noncompliance. On the other hand, it is clear that the granting of a license is considered to place an

27. Freese, "Freedom of Information," p. 22.
28. Per-Gunnar Vinge, *The Swedish Data Act* (Stockholm: Federation of Swedish Industries, 1973), p. 9.

obligation on the responsible keepers to keep their own houses in order. The development of standard operating procedures for the processing of applications institutionalizes a trust between the DIB and the responsible keeper and increases the significance of the voluntary control model in the overall implementation framework. As Freese argues: "It permits the law to retain its strength, at the same time as it permits self-policing under self-assumed responsibility in lieu of the comprehensive licensing control which the legal text seems to demand."[29]

The individual citizen is also a player in the implementation scheme, a situation that introduces an element of subject control into the scheme. The licensing process ensures a registration of databanks, and through the general presumption of publicity, individuals may determine the extent of personal record keeping. In this way the openness principle, or the need for "transparency," is satisfied. But data subjects are also granted the right to know information relating to them. Section 10 states that "at the request of an individual registered the responsible keeper of the register shall as soon as possible inform him of the personal information concerning him in the register." Unless the DIB specifically permits the levying of a fee, this information should be given free of charge. The right of access theoretically allows the data subject to verify the accuracy and completeness of personal information and generally to ensure that it is being handled and disseminated in compliance with the law. The access principle is justified because "justice must not only be done but must manifestly be seen to be done."[30]

I should note, however, that the access provisions are not phrased in terms of a right of the individual but in terms of a duty of the responsible keeper. Indeed, most of the statute is devoted to specifying either the powers of the DIB or the duties of the record keepers. The individual is mentioned as an incidental actor in the process. Moreover, although individuals can complain to the DIB, they have no right under Swedish law to apply for injunctions or other interventions by the DIB. The board acts on its own initiative most of the time and has the power to fine a data user without resort to the courts. The citizen has a civil remedy in that he or she may apply for compensation for

29. Freese, "The Swedish Data Act" (1977), p. 6.
30. Sweden, *Computers and Privacy*, p. 8.

actual damages resulting from the processing of incorrect information. But neither civil nor criminal prosecutions through the Swedish court system are considered the major method of enforcement. The threat of the loss of license from the DIB is normally sufficient motivation for compliance. Thus while the citizen can be a help to the DIB in locating and investigating abuses, subject control per se plays only an incidental role in the entire process. In any case, most organizations have received very few access requests over the years.[31]

To summarize, Swedish data protection policy is based principally on a model of institutional control that relies on the licensing of automated personal data processing systems. The ombudsman and supervisory functions are provided in the law but have been subordinated in actual practice to the bureaucratic demands of the licensing procedure. Voluntary compliance by the responsible keeper and self-help by the data subject aid the DIB in the performance of its duties, but neither are central to the operation of the policy. Under the amended simplified procedure, it could be argued that "registration" may be a more accurate title for the implementation scheme for the vast majority of personal registers. In any event, the licensing model was the centerpiece of Swedish data protection policy at the time of enactment. Indeed, the dual procedure, recommended in the Royal Commission Report, was rejected during the final drafting of the law.[32] The main policy choice, therefore, was licensing. It is that choice that I have to explain in the next chapter.

The Swedish law is a typical "framework act" in the context of Swedish administrative law: it contains broad guidelines rather than detailed regulations regarding the definition of privacy and the manner in which the DIB should protect it. The DIB has discretion and flexibility—not only valuable assets in a changing technological climate but also ones that might lead to unpredictability and legal uncertainty. Too, the board is granted some enormous powers, which without a responsible approach could produce highhandedness and rigidity. A recent analysis of DIB decision making has concluded, however, that the DIB has agreed on a working definition of "undue encroachments upon personal privacy" that brings some predic-

31. Flaherty, *Protecting Privacy in Surveillance Societies*, p. 136.
32. Vinge, *Experiences of the Swedish Data Act*, (Stockholm: Federation of Swedish Industries, 1975), p. 35.

tability and continuity to DIB decision making.[33] Data protection has clearly become "institutionalized" in Sweden.

The American Choice: Voluntary Compliance and Self-Help

Throughout the debates on the U.S. Privacy Act, the major dispute centered not on questions of principle but on the method of implementation. The fair information principles were widely accepted in themselves as necessary safeguards. The majority of legislative time was devoted to arguing over the most effective way to ensure their compliance within the bureaucracy.

Advocacy for a privacy commission with regulatory powers over the collection, use, and dissemination of personal information can be traced to the early deliberations and hearings of the Senate Subcommittee on Constitutional Rights in the late 1960s. By the early seventies, as Regan notes, congressional sponsors of privacy legislation, including Senator Ervin and Representatives Koch and Goldwater, were convinced that an oversight agency was required to monitor federal agencies' collection and use of personal information.[34] In fact, there was a broadly recognized need for an agency somewhere in government to give constant and expert oversight and advice on this rapidly developing problem.

Concurrently, opposition to such an idea emerged from a number of sources. The interdisciplinary committee that reported to the Secretary of Health, Education, and Welfare, for example, doubted that "the need exists or that the necessary public support could be marshalled at the present time for an agency of the scale and pervasiveness required to regulate all automated personal data systems." The committee believed that privacy safeguards "require the establishment of no new mechanisms and seek to impose no new constraints on the application of electronic data processing technology beyond those necessary to assure the maintenance of reasonable standards of personal privacy in record-keeping."[35]

33. Sten Markgren, *Datainspektionen och Skyddet av den Personliga Integriteten* (Lund: Studentlitteratur, 1984).
34. Regan, "Personal Information Policies," p. 25.
35. U.S. HEW, *Records, Computers, and the Rights of Citizens*, p. 43.

The primary Senate bill (S. 3418) introduced by Senator Ervin on 1 May 1974 provided for the five-member Federal Privacy Board, which was empowered to inspect personal data-keeping systems, to subpoena the production of documents, to issue cease and desist orders in the event of violation, to hold public hearings on violations and exemptions, and to consult and advise on the establishment and operation of personal record-keeping systems. The bill gave the board virtually full regulatory powers over federal, state, and local agencies. It was also to maintain a register of personal information systems and to conduct certain research activities.

In the hearings on S. 3418 all agency spokespersons testified that responsibility for personal information should reside with the agencies themselves. They argued this position on grounds of cost and on their belief that an additional layer of bureaucracy would be a cumbersome and unnecessary solution to a modest problem.[36] For example, the then director of the Office of Management and Budget, Roy Ash, advised the committee to scrap any notion of an independent commission and to restrict its coverage to the federal government. The Senate Committee on Government Operations, in response to these criticisms, complained that "nothing but deletion of the major provisions of the bill will satisfy some people in the executive branch." The committee reaffirmed the need for a privacy commission: "It is clear that many of the information abuses over the last decade could have been avoided with the help of an independent body of experts charged with protecting individual privacy as a value in government and society."[37]

In the bill that finally passed the Senate on 21 November 1974, however, the powers of the proposed commission were significantly weakened in response to executive branch pressure. It was still to have the power to monitor and inspect, to hold hearings, to publish an annual directory of information systems, and to develop "model guidelines for implementation." But the commission was denied the power to issue cease and desist orders, and hence it was viewed more as an investigative and advisory body than as a regulatory one. In addition, the bill was restricted to federal agencies. On the House side, representatives were more persuaded by agency arguments against a commission; as a result, the bill reported out of committee

36. Regan, "Personal Information Policies," p. 27.
37. U.S. Congress, *Legislative History of the Privacy Act*, p. 772.

(H.R. 16373) did not provide for any independent oversight body. An amendment to reinstate the commission was defeated on the floor of the House on the grounds that it had already been voted down in committee, that it was excessively costly and bureaucratic, that the President was against it, and that the court system was the natural American way to provide redress of individual grievances.[38] H.R. 16373 was passed by the House without an external oversight agency.

On 17 December 1974, Senator Ervin announced that he had accepted a compromise between the different House and Senate versions. As noted in Chapter 2, this agreement was the result of an ad hoc meeting one night in Senator Ervin's office. First, the proposed Privacy Protection Commission was transformed into the Privacy Protection *Study* Commission (italics mine), which devoted the next two years to examining the record-keeping practices of a wide variety of organizations in both the public and private sectors. Its 1977 report *Personal Privacy in an Information Society* contains over 160 recommendations to Congress and the president for improved safeguards. Second, the oversight function was given to the OMB. Inserted at the end of the statute is a stipulation that "the Office of Management and Budget shall—(1) develop guidelines and regulations for the use of agencies . . . and (2) provide continuing assistance to and oversight of the implementation of the provisions."[39]

A number of pressing factors forced Senator Ervin to back down on his insistence that an independent commission with oversight and investigative powers was a sine qua non of effective Privacy Act implementation; the most commonly cited factors are the pressures on congressional time, the drive to pass some privacy legislation in the wake of the Watergate affair, the resistance to the creation of more bureaucracies, and the risk of a presidential veto.[40] The fragmented implementation structure that resulted was the outcome of a typically American process of bargaining between a number of authorities that all operate under the guiding principle that "half a loaf is better than none" (see Chapter 7).

Without an institutional mechanism solely responsible for privacy, primary responsibility for implementing the Privacy Act rests with the

38. Flaherty, "The Need for an American Privacy Protection Commission", p. 239.
39. Privacy Act, Sec. 6.
40. Flaherty, "The Need for an American Privacy Protection Commission," p. 240.

federal agencies themselves. Hence, the law places a duty on agencies to promulgate effective rules for the application of the fair information principles. They should restrict and make an accurate accounting of all disclosures of records, establish procedures for individual access and correction, maintain only such information as is "relevant and necessary" to accomplish a legitimate purpose, and annually publish details of each record-keeping system. With the exception of the Department of Defense, which established the special Defense Privacy Board in 1975,[41] all other agencies implemented these safeguards through a Privacy Act officer, who is generally not highly placed in the agency and who often has other responsibilities. Moreover, no new funds were appropriated for implementation of the Privacy Act. It is chiefly up to the agencies themselves to comply in the way they see most fit. According to our framework of analysis, the American policy relies heavily on voluntary control.

To the extent that they exist, external sanctions are provided through judicially assertible rights of enforcement. Section 2 stipulates that federal agencies are "subject to civil suit for any damages which occur as a result of willful or intentional action which violates any individual's rights under this Act."[42] Thus, the creation of individual rights and the reliance on the courts to ensure the exercise of those rights constitutes the only method of regulation. Subject control, therefore, is also central to the overall implementation scheme. I have already argued that this model suffers certain critical shortcomings in relation to data protection policy. It relies on a participant and litigious citizenry and on the ability of an inexpert judiciary to decide on quite technical issues. The drafting of the United States Privacy Act provides further restrictions, however. The act stipulates that damages can only be awarded if it can be demonstrated that the plaintiff has suffered actual injury from an intentional agency action. This injury is virtually impossible to prove given the intangible and speculative nature of the harm that might result from the unfair use and transmittal of personal information. The inherently restrictive remedial scheme has severely limited the development of case law and has prevented all

41. The Defense Privacy Board has senior-level representatives from all parts of the Pentagon and the armed forces as well as an executive secretary and four full-time officials. It is probably the most successful example of Privacy Act implementation.
42. Privacy Act, Sec. 2(b) (6).

but a few successful actions for damages. Most litigation under the Privacy Act relates to the interpretation of the exemptions to access and to their relationship with those under the related Freedom of Information Act (FOIA).[43]

Furthermore, the courts have not broadly recognized a right to privacy for information held by third parties. In *United States v. Miller* the Supreme Court held that an individual has no Fourth or Fifth Amendment interest to assert when the government demands access to the records an organization maintains about him or her (in this case, bank records).[44] An individual's expectation of privacy for records held by any third party is not legitimate, warranted, or enforceable under the Constitution. While Congress subsequently enacted the Right of Financial Privacy Act of 1978[45] to protect the confidentiality of bank records, in terms of Privacy Act implementation the *Miller* decision reduced the applicability of judicial enforcement.

Subject control also encompasses, of course, the exercise of access and correction rights. The act entitles any individual to see, copy, and correct a record pertaining to him or her, unless it is contained in a system of records that is of a particularly sensitive nature (e.g., relating to law enforcement or national security). While on paper these provisions seem extensive, the rights of individual access and correction are less important than many had expected them to be. Virtually nothing is retrievable under the Privacy Act that cannot also be obtained through the FOIA. Consequently, as the PPSC found, "the number of Privacy Act access requests (i.e., requests specifically citing the Privacy Act) has not been great and most have come from agency employees or former employees."[46] For instance, in the calendar year 1983, OMB reported 204,460 access requests to federal agencies for personal records. Ninety percent of these were granted in whole or in part.

---

43. Richard Ehlke, *Litigation Trends under the Privacy Act* (Washington, D.C.: Congressional Research Service, 1983).

44. 425 U.S. 435 (1976).

45. *Right to Financial Privacy Act of 1978*, 12 U.S.C. 3401 et seq. This legislation requires federal agencies that request access to private financial records either (1) to provide notice of the purpose for which the records are sought, or (2) to obtain a court order for direct access to the records. It was proposed as part of President Carter's 1979 "Privacy Initiative," which also included bills on medical records, research records, and media information.

46. PPSC, *The Privacy Act of 1974*, p. 83.

Of all requests, 4,466 were for the amendment of records, of which 94 percent were granted in whole or in part.[47]

The above data should be treated with considerable caution as it is far from clear how much of this activity is the direct result of the Privacy Act. Most agencies operating public assistance programs already had procedures to allow record subjects' access to their files as part of the eligibility verification process. And since 1967 access to personal records could be gained through the FOIA. Moreover, there are insurmountable problems of definition and quantification. The majority of requesters do not cite the Privacy Act, let alone a specific system of records. Some cite both the FOIA and the Privacy Act (as the civil liberties groups advise). Most just ask to see "their file on. . . ." Although there are no pre-1974 figures on access requests, it is unlikely that the Privacy Act ushered in a completely new spirit of openness. The OMB has concluded that the main result of the access right "has been to give the agencies a uniform set of procedures for handling requests for record subjects . . . even when the requests do not cite a specific Act."[48] The Privacy Act did not grant the American citizen a completely new tool with which to take on "big government."

Finally, the Privacy Act reveals aspects of institutional control, though the final provisions represent only a vestige of the full-fledged Privacy Protection Commission that was proposed in the original Senate version of the bill. The compromise in the final days of the Ninety-third Congress resulted in this permanent commission being transformed into the temporary Privacy Protection Study Commission. At the same time, the role of monitoring record-keeping organizations was given to the OMB. Flaherty notes that this implementation framework was "largely a matter of historical accident."[49] As the political will to establish an independent body was absent, and given the notable unwillingness to give the job to the Justice Department in view of its less than enthusiastic administration of the FOIA, the responsibility

---

47. OMB, *President's Annual Report on the Privacy Act of 1974* CY 1982–83 (Washington, D.C.: OMB, 1985), pp. 17–18.

48. OMB, *Fifth Annual Report of the President on the Implementation of the Privacy Act of 1974* (Washington, D.C.: OMB, 1980), p. 12.

49. Flaherty, "The Need for an American Privacy Protection Commission," p. 236.

fell to the OMB almost by default.[50] While it can be argued that the OMB's central position in the Executive Office of the President grants it an institutional independence that other agencies lack, the OMB certainly did not seek the job. Consequently, there was disagreement about the role that Congress expected it to perform.

Congressional intent regarding the role of the OMB is obscure, with no clarification of the words "develop guidelines and regulations" and "provide continuing assistance and oversight." In practice, the OMB has not interpreted this role in a positive and active manner: it has issued few guidelines to help federal agencies apply the act; it has exhibited a weak and declining interest in submitting the annual report that the President is expected to provide to Congress each year; and it has adopted a very passive and reactive stance with regard to oversight.[51] Critics have pointed to the fact that the location of responsibility for the Privacy Act in the OMB would provide few incentives for aggressive oversight. The OMB's primary mission as coordinator of the President's budget and as fiscal watchdog is directly incompatible with many of the programmatic goals of the Privacy Act. The use and disclosure restrictions as well as the granting of access and correction rights impose direct costs on agencies. The Privacy Act has been monitored to the extent that it provides statutory support for the OMB's emphasis on economy and efficiency in government.

Moreover, the OMB has devoted little of its staff and resources to Privacy Act oversight. This situation became particularly acute after the reorganization pursuant to the passage of the Paperwork Reduction Act in 1980 when responsibility for Privacy Act oversight became diffused within the newly created Office of Information and Regulatory Affairs (OIRA). Each OIRA desk officer is responsible for all the information resources management activities of his or her agency. These include forms clearance, the checking for onerous regulations, the acquisition of automatic data processing equipment, and the mon-

50. U.S. House of Representatives, *Oversight of the Privacy Act of 1974*, Hearings before a Subcommittee of the Committee on Government Operations, House of Representatives, 98th Cong., 1st sess. (Washington, D.C.: Government Printing Office, 1983), p. 43. The Justice Department plays virtually no role in the implementation of the Privacy Act. Its Office of Information and Privacy concentrates on FOIA.

51. U.S. House of Representatives, *Who Cares about Privacy? Oversight of the Privacy Act of 1974 by the Office of Management and by Budget and by the Congress*, Report by the Committee on Government Operations, House of Representatives, 98th Cong., 1st sess. (Washington, D.C.: Government Printing Office, 1983).

itoring of Privacy Act compliance. The former administrator of the OIRA, Christopher DeMuth, claimed that "this has meant a strengthening and enlargement of the scope of our review. An agency's Privacy Act activities are examined within the context of other relevant information resources management activities."[52]

Conversely, this reorganization means that no one person in the OMB has had complete responsibility for Privacy Act oversight. Privacy questions have been subordinated to the programmatic goals of reducing federal regulations and paperwork. In this regard the act has contributed to some reduction in unnecessary information collection and to the consolidation of a number of duplicate record-keeping systems. Although this goal is compatible with the aim of the Privacy Act to limit information collection to that which is "relevant and necessary," the net effect has been to render the Privacy Act a "records management statute" rather than a mechanism to protect individual rights. These observed deficiencies have led recent commentators to call for the establishment of an independent commission similar to that proposed in the original Senate bill introduced by Senator Ervin.[53]

Finally, institutional control in the American case also encompasses congressional oversight. Congress is specifically granted two oversight mechanisms in the law. The first is the annual report, which the OMB is expected to compile and submit but which in recent years has been largely uninformative. The second oversight mechanism is the requirement that agencies give prior notice of the creation or alteration of any system of records. To the extent that oversight exists, it centers on the examination of these system notices before they go to the *Federal Register* by the staff of the Subcommittee on Government Information of the House Government Operations Committee.[54] Their review involves checking that the system notices accurately describe the nature, purpose, and scope of the system and, most controversially, the "routine uses" to which the records may be put. Insofar as these formal descriptions reflect the actual personal information practices of an

52. U.S. House of Representatives, *Oversight of the Privacy Act of 1974*, p. 72.
53. PPSC, *The Privacy Act of 1974*; U.S. House of Representatives, *Who Cares about Privacy?*; Flaherty, "The Need for an American Privacy Protection Commission."
54. See, for example, U.S. Office of the Federal Register, *Privacy Act Issuances*, 1980 Compilation (Washington, D.C.: Government Printing Office, 1981).

agency, the staff will have a fairly comprehensive view of what is going on. On the other hand, such a massive activity as the collection, use, and disclosure of billions of personal records can only be reflected to a very limited extent in a system notice. Congressional oversight is hindered by the size of the task, the speed of technological progress, the inadequacy of the resources, and the few incentives for congressmen to investigate an issue that has little, if any, electoral payoff.

The number of days devoted directly to formal hearings on the implementation of the Privacy Act has been low—three, specifically. In June 1975 the Government Information and Individual Rights Subcommittee conducted a day's hearings to ensure that agencies were preparing to meet their obligations. They found that, with the exception of the Department of Defense, which had decided to establish a separate Privacy Board, agency preparations were less than enthusiastic.[55] The major effort of two days of hearings in November 1983 had a symbolic significance as well as an investigative purpose, especially given the approach of 1984 with its literary significance for surveillance and intrusiveness by the "Big Brother" state.[56] But nothing particularly surprising surfaced from this oversight effort. The tractability of the problem, the inherent statutory weaknesses, and the structural and motivational barriers to successful implementation had been recognized by several other bodies: by the Privacy Protection Study Commission, by the General Accounting Office, and by other congressional committees that had been looking into related issues (e.g., medical records, international data flow, and computer matching).[57]

From time to time, there have also been legislative attempts to give

55. U.S. House of Representatives, *Implementation of the Privacy Act of 1974: Data Banks*, Hearings before a Subcommittee of the Committee on Government Operations, House of Representatives, 94th Cong., 1st sess. (Washington, D.C.: Government Printing Office, 1975).

56. U.S. House of Representatives, *Oversight of the Privacy Act of 1974* and *Who Cares about Privacy?*

57. PPSC, *The Privacy Act of 1974*; U.S. General Accounting Office, *Agencies' Implementation of and Compliance with the Privacy Act Can Be Improved* (Washington, D.C.: General Accounting Office, 1978); U.S. House of Representatives, *Privacy of Medical Records*, Hearings before a Subcommittee of the Committee on Government Operations, House of Representatives, 96th Cong., 1st sess. (Washington, D.C.: Government Printing Office, 1979); U.S. House of Representatives, *International Data Flow*; U.S. Senate, *Oversight of Computer Matching to Detect Fraud and Mismanagement in Government Programs*, Hearings before a Subcommittee of the Committee on Governmental Affairs, Senate, 97th Cong., 2d sess. (Washington, D.C.: Government Printing Office, 1982).

the Privacy Act some teeth. At the same time as the 1983 hearings, Congressman Glenn English, Democrat of Oklahoma, introduced a bill to establish a small privacy commission along the lines of that originally proposed by Senator Ervin.[58] A similar bill to establish a "Data Protection Board" was introduced in 1990 by Congressman Robert Wise, a Democrat from West Virginia.[59] By far the most significant reform has been the enactment of the Computer Matching and Privacy Protection Act of 1988. Computer matching, the comparison of different record systems to expose instances of fraud and wrongdoing, has been a controversial practice that the Privacy Act has been notably incapable of regulating. The 1988 legislation sets up Data Integrity Boards in each department to review and approve matching programs and activities.[60]

In summary, the weakness of external institutional control of the bureaucracy, from the OMB, the Congress, or the courts, means that the central model of implementation is one of voluntary compliance and self-help. The dominance of these approaches is discernible in the language of the law. Later experience merely reinforces the nature and importance of the policy choice made in 1974. It is that choice that differs from the experience of other countries and requires explanation.

The German Choice: A Data Protection Commissioner

On the insistence of the Bundestag in the long and complicated legislative history sketched in Chapter 3, a Federal Commissioner for Data Protection (*Bundesbeauftragte für den Datenschutz*, or BfD) was established to oversee the operation of the federal law. The decision represented a rejection of the self-control model of implementation in favor of an institutional approach in the form of a complex and unusual agency. It is crucial to bear in mind that the office of the BfD

58. *A Bill to Establish a Privacy Protection Commission*, H. R. 3743, 98th Cong., 1st sess. (Washington, D.C.: Government Printing Office, 1983).

59. *A Bill to Establish a Data Protection Board*, H. R. 3669, 101st Cong., 2d sess. (Washington, D.C.: Government Printing Office, 1990).

60. *Computer Matching and Privacy Protection Act of 1988*, 5 U.S.C. 552a. See Flaherty, *Protecting Privacy in Surveillance Societies*, Chap. 29.

is just one institution within a fully integrated network of data protection authorities throughout the Federal Republic. The Federal Data Protection Act applies to the federal public sector and the whole of the private sector. The data protection laws of the eleven Länder apply to the public sectors of the respective Land administration. The supervisory authorities at the Land level are also responsible for the implementation of the federal law inasmuch as it applies to the private sector. They are, therefore, in the position of enforcing two sets of law, a situation that arose from the compromise that was reached between the Bundestag and the Bundesrat in the final days of the law's passage. This integrated scheme clearly necessitates constant cooperation between federal and Land data protection authorities, a relationship that will also be complicated by the reunification of Germany.

At the federal level, the BfD occupies an unusual and ambiguous place in the administrative and political system. This person is nominally an agent of the federal government, appointed by the federal president on the government's suggestion for a period of five years. The commissioner's office is part of the executive branch and is organizationally within the Ministry of the Interior. It is subject to the supervisory control (*Dienstaufsicht*) of the federal administration. The BfD has to negotiate with Interior for his or her budget and reports to its minister. The staff, moreover, are civil servants within the overall payroll and promotion structure of the federal civil service. Career prospects lie within the federal bureaucracy rather than within the office of the BfD. Ambitious staff members sense that antagonizing their superiors within the ministry may not do much for these prospects.[61]

On the other hand, the commissioner is expected to be "independent in the performance of his duties and subject to the law only."[62] The potential conflict of interest between the BfD and data users and the inadequacy of traditional legislative oversight convinced many that the principle of independence should be embodied in the BDSG. Thus the Minister of the Interior cannot instruct the BfD in his or her duties but can ensure that the commissioner is acting according to the law. Hans Peter Bull, the commissioner from 1978 to 1983, saw himself as a professional civil servant with comparable status to a govern-

61. Flaherty, *Protecting Privacy in Surveillance Societies*, p. 41.
62. BDSG, Sec. 17 (4).

ment minister. The office is an independent authority within the executive branch.[63]

On the other hand, like other "ombudsmen" the BfD also has ties and responsibilities to the legislature and is required to submit an annual report[64] and other opinions when requested; in addition, the Bundestag may request the BfD to investigate specific matters as they arise. Through its Interior Committee, the Bundestag may also help the BfD put pressure on an agency, though this is definitely the commissioner's last resort. Moreover, at the federal level, unlike in Hesse for instance, there is no legislative committee with sole responsibility for data protection. Spiros Simitis has maintained that in Hesse, where the legislature elects the commissioner on the advice of the government, the system is more likely to ensure not only that the BfD is independent of government but also that the BfD is seen to be independent.[65] On the other hand, if the federal BfD were, in fact, attached to the Bundestag, there would be less direct access to the offices of the federal bureaucracy.[66]

So the BfD is in a unique and ambivalent position within the federal institutional framework. The independence of the office is provided for in the law but at the same time is compromised by the ties that have to be maintained with the permanent bureaucracy. The independence of the office is ultimately contingent on the attitudes and behavior of the individual commissioners. Hans Peter Bull (1978 to 1983), a renowned legal scholar, became a forceful advocate for data protection and a strident enforcer of the law; his term was not renewed in 1983. He was replaced by Reinhold Baumann (1983 to 1988), whose civil service background raised fears, many of them unfounded, that he would not be such an effective and enthusiastic watchdog. Baumann was replaced in 1988 by Alfred Einwag, a former official in the Ministry of the Interior, who had been closely involved with issues of internal security and whose appointment raised similar misgivings.[67]

The BfD's office has had a staff of about thirty-five; these individu-

---

63. Flaherty, *Protecting Privacy in Surveillance Societies*, p. 40.
64. To date there have been twelve annual reports, the latest being *Zwölfter Tatigkeitsbericht des Bundesbeauftragten für den Datenschutz* (Bonn: BfD, 1990).
65. *Transnational Data and Communications Report* 10 (November 1987): 9.
66. Flaherty, *Protecting Privacy in Surveillance Societies*, p. 43.
67. *Transnational Data and Communications Report* 11 (November 1988): 26.

als are organized into five different divisions (*Referat*), each of which is functionally responsible for the range of financial, social, personnel, health, transportation, educational, planning, statistical, and security activities for which personal data are processed. Many of the staff have a legal background; an increasing number over the years are trained in computer science and information processing. The office takes pride in the considerable expertise that they now employ in their oversight of personal data processing.

The commissioner is to ensure adherence to the provisions of the BDSG and to other laws and regulations pertaining to data protection in the federal agencies. Unlike Sweden's DIB, the BfD's primary role is that of adviser who can investigate and try to persuade but who does not have the authority to issue binding regulations. The assignment is a complex and heterogeneous one, as the office has to become familiar with the functions, responsibilities, and statutory obligations of every federal agency. These duties call for regular and meticulous attention to technical and organizational details as well as a certain sensitivity to the wider political implications of data processing.

Since the BDSG's enactment, the BfD's major method of supervision has been the audit—the investigation of all phases of personal data usage. This inquiry involves the inspection of the hardware and software configurations, the security measures, the procedures established for access and correction, and, generally, the attention paid to data protection principles. Trouble spots are pinpointed and solutions are developed in conjunction with the user. The office conducts an average of thirty audits a year.[68] Although the audit function is normally performed in a consensual and constructive atmosphere, the BfD has legal powers to demand information and to gain access to premises. The commissioner can be refused only if the inspection would endanger the security of the Federal Republic or one of the Länder. But the clear presumption is that the BfD should play a mediating role between the citizen and the federal bureaucracy. Thus while the right of supervision and inspection is virtually unlimited, this right affords little power of enforcement. The BfD can only submit complaints regarding violations to the relevant authority and then hope

68. Ulrich Dammann, "Auditing Data Protection," *Transnational Data Report* 6 (1983): 161.

that political, public, and media pressure will force agencies to correct the irregularities.

The office also takes pride in the fact that it serves an educative and advisory function: it shows the authorities that data protection can be in their interests as well and educates the general public about its rights under the law.[69] The BfD's advice is also sought in the planning of information systems. Indeed, ministries are expected to submit drafts of these plans to get the BfD's feedback on the privacy implications. This process is now routinized, although inevitable conflicts have arisen from time to time, especially in previously unregulated fields. By insisting on data protection safeguards from the outset, the BfD, like the DIB in Sweden, claims to have an important prophylactic effect.

This activity signifies, of course, that the implementation of the law relies a great deal on voluntary compliance rather than on external sanction and control. As we saw in Chapter 3, the BDSG reads as a very detailed and explicit set of obligations for personal data users. The entire scheme rests on the notion that each agency has clearly defined responsibilities and that the collection, storage, use, and dissemination of individually identifiable data may occur only in conformity with these duties. Hence, the basic obligation to see that the BDSG is enforced resides with the head of the agency concerned. Most agencies have appointed data protection officers, similar to the Privacy Act officers in the United States, who are the principal contacts for the commissioner's staff. The compliance of civil servants to these regulations is generally expected in what Flaherty has described as a "law-driven society, meaning that almost every information-collection activity of government is regulated by a particular statute, and every civil servant acknowledges a direct legal responsibility to implement general and specific data protection measures."[70] While the data commissioner approach is the main theory behind data pro-

---

69. A number of public information booklets have been published and eagerly sought after. See *Der Bürger and Seine Daten: Eine Information zum Datenschutz* (Bonn: BfD, 1980); *Bürgerfibel Datenschutz* (Bonn: BfD, 1982); and *Der Bürger und Seine Daten: Im Netz der Sozialen Sicherung* (Bonn: BfD, 1984).

70. David H. Flaherty, "Data Protection and Privacy: Comparative Policies," A Report to the Government Information Technology Project, Office of Technology Assessment, U.S. Congress (Washington, D.C.: U.S. Dept. of Commerce, National Technical Information Science, 1985), p. 7.

tection implementation in West Germany, the BfD could not operate without the compliance and good sense of the thousands of officials that handle personal information.

Other models of control are not stressed. The notion of subject control, for instance, is not relied upon to the extent that it is in Sweden and the United States. To some extent, the BfD relies on the complaints of citizens to identify wrongdoing and to be alerted to the main trouble spots in the federal establishment. Involvement of the citizenry was particularly important early in the commissioner's history. Some one thousand enquiries and complaints came in during the BfD's first year of operation alone.[71] Now, however, most complaints are of a routine nature and tend not to alert the officials to new cases of wrongdoing. Moreover, direct citizen action, either through the rights of access or the courts, is not significant. The access and correction rights, as noted above, are not as extensive as those in Sweden or the United States. Broad and vague exemptions make access a time-consuming and frustrating process. An agency is not obliged to respond to a request within a specified time. Experience has shown that these rights have been little used.

The choice of the data commissioner approach in Germany also represents a rejection of licensing, the system already established in Sweden. The licensing approach was considered overly bureaucratic and extremely impractical in a country of sixty million people, even though there are occasional suggestions that it should be introduced for the most sensitive types of file. There are, however, certain registration requirements. Public authorities are expected to announce in the official bulletin (*Bundesanzeiger*) the type of data they store, the tasks for which these data are used, the persons on file, the authorities to which they regularly communicate personal data, and the type of data communicated. The federal government is authorized to issue regulations concerning the procedures for publishing this information. Again, however, experience has demonstrated that the register of about fifteen hundred databanks is rarely consulted and little used.

The distinctive German method of implementation, therefore, consists of supervision by a publicly appointed data protection commissioner with few enforcement powers, who must consequently use po-

71. Federal Republic of Germany, Press and Information Office, *Data Protection*, p. 6.

litical skill to infuse the minds and actions of federal officials with data protection principles. An office of thirty-five staff members, however, cannot effectively oversee the operation of all personal data systems in the federal bureaucracy. Self-enforcement, therefore, plays a crucial role in the process. The commissioner can advise, consult, and publish wrongdoing in the annual reports. But effective implementation clearly necessitates a cooperative rather than an adversarial relationship with the data user. The BfD requires a delicate blend of technical and policy expertise, political skill, and favorable public opinion to succeed in the complex and sensitive tasks associated with this position.

The British Choice: Registering the Computer

The policy process in Britain was characterized by more procrastination and controversy than was the process in the other three countries. Over this period (the late 1960s until 1984) every type of policy instrument was advocated at some point. The final choice of a system of registration has to be understood in the context of this drawn-out and contentious process.

The Younger Committee of 1972, for instance, recommended that the fair information principles should be voluntarily adopted by all computer users. The only method for attaining compliance was contained in the recommendation that "the Government should legislate to provide itself with machinery for keeping under review the growth in and techniques of gathering personal information and processing it with the help of computers. Such machinery should take the form of an independent body with members drawn from both the computer world and outside."[72] The proposed body would only have powers of review and recommendation. A procedure that was essentially discretionary dominated British official thinking at this time.

The 1975 White Paper (Cmnd. 6353) narrowed the choice in one sense: it rejected the American solution of a detailed statute that left enforcement up to the individual and the courts. The Labour government had apparently resolved that some form of permanent statutory

72. Great Britain, *Report of the Committee on Privacy (1972)*, p. 191.

authority would be needed "to oversee the use of computers, in both the public and private sectors, to ensure that they are operated with proper regard for privacy and with the necessary safeguards for the personal information which they contain."[73] Beyond that, the document was vague. Two possible approaches were envisaged: a registration and licensing agency similar to that of Sweden, or a kind of ombudsman with investigative and advisory powers.

The nature and powers of the new authority were left up to the newly appointed Lindop Committee, which essentially recommended in 1978 a system of voluntary compliance with a Data Protection Authority (DPA), which in turn was to prepare codes of practice for data users.[74] Given the various data practices of different organizations and the rapid progress of the technology, these codes would have the force of law but the advantage of flexibility. Registration of databanks was required, however, in order to keep the situation under review, but this did not mean Swedish-style licensing. The DPA would also have certain "ombudsman" functions, but the powers of inspection and oversight were not as extensive as those in the German legislation. Self-help effectively meant registering a complaint with the DPA rather than engaging in litigation as in the United States. Moreover, enforcement by civil suit would be far more uncertain in the United Kingdom than in the United States: in Britain, individuals are liable for their opponent's legal costs and have limited eligibility for legal aid.

When the Conservative administration entered office, the first indications from the Home Secretary in 1981 were that the government would *not* seek to establish an independent Data Protection Authority along the lines of the Lindop recommendations in any legislation that it might introduce.[75] Conservative politicians viewed the Lindop Committee as a "Labour-inspired" group and were distrustful of any effort to establish another quango (quasi-autonomous nongovernmental organization). Indeed, Mrs. Thatcher's perceived mandate was to diminish the number of such bodies. At the same time, however, the government signed the Council of Europe Convention with the knowledge that ratification could not take place without "credible" data

---

73. Great Britain, *Computers and Privacy*, p. 9.
74. Great Britain, *Report of the Committee on Data Protection*.
75. Cornford, "The Prospects for Privacy," p. 295.

protection legislation, which was taken to mean the statutory implementation of the fair information principles overseen by some sort of
independent authority.

Because of the international economic arguments increasingly coming to official attention and the lobbying from the computer industry,
the government was forced to act. The first idea for enforcement was a
public register of databanks to be located in the Home Office. Widespread suspicion of this incredible idea generated the proposal in an
April 1982 white paper of a more independent Data Registrar. The
government rejected the notion that the whole field of data processing
could be regulated through statutory codes of practice. Instead, the
proposal relied on the "requirement that—with the possible exception of small scale users who keep data for domestic purposes—all
users of data systems which process automatically information relating to identifiable individuals should register."[76] The Registrar would
oversee the formulation of the register and ensure that registered data
users would comply with data protection principles. It was this policy
instrument that eventually found its way into the 1984 Data Protection Act.

The choice of registration represents a distinctively British approach
to implementation in the comparative perspective of this book. It was
first advocated in the Data Surveillance Bill introduced by Kenneth
Baker in the Commons in 1969. It is the central proposal of a draft
bill proposed by the British Computer Society in 1972. Registration is
mooted in the 1975 white paper, and advocated in the Lindop Report.
It is the proposal that appears the most consistently throughout the
long debate on data protection. The central theory is that all "data
users" (those who automatically process personal data) must register
by applying to the Registrar and providing this person with a notification of the data held and the purposes for which they are held, a
description of the sources and recipients of the data stored, and an
address to which subjects may write for access to their data. Failing to
register, or operating outside the terms of the register entry, are criminal offenses. The notion of registration can be traced to the very first
stages of the British debate.

After the controversial and halting parliamentary passage, the Data

---

76. Great Britain, *Data Protection*, p. 4.

Protection Act finally received royal assent in July 1984. Shortly thereafter, the government announced that Eric Howe, then deputy director of the National Computing Center, would be the first Data Protection Registrar. Many read the appointment as a signal that the technical requirements of the law would be emphasized over the civil libertarian ones. Computer users were given six months from November 1985 in which to register with the new Registrar's office, located in Wilmslow, just south of Manchester. Failure to register by May 1986 made anyone processing personally related data guilty of an offense and liable to a fine of up to £1000. Initially, there was much confusion over who was supposed to register as well as a great deal of ignorance about the existence and scope of the law.[77] By June 1986, of the 300,000 applications that had been expected, only 136,000 had been received.[78] The office initiated a checking procedure to rectify this considerable shortfall. By the end of 1988, the number of applications received had risen to 170,000.[79] A microfiche version of the register containing about 150,000 entries was put in place in about 170 libraries throughout the United Kingdom.[80]

If the Registrar is satisfied that a registered person is in contravention of the data protection principles, that individual may be served an "enforcement notice." Any person failing to comply will be guilty of an offense. Under extreme circumstances the Registrar may serve a "deregistration notice," which states that the user will be removed from the register and thus prohibited from processing personally related data. The law provides a special Data Protection Tribunal to hear appeals against the decision of the Registrar. On paper these powers constitute a considerable inducement to comply; without the ability to process personal information, some organizations may just as well not exist. In 1989, nine enforcement notices and fourteen notices of refusal of application for registration were served, all of which arose in connection with the collection of personal information to implement the government's new community charge (the poll

77. "Data Protection: Crashed," *The Economist*, 19 April 1986.
78. Data Protection Registrar, *Second Report* June 1986 (London: HMSO, 1986), p. 22.
79. Data Protection Registrar, *Fifth Report* June 1989 (London: HMSO, 1989).
80. It should be noted, however, that this register has been little used, and its generation and updating have been time-consuming. The Registrar's office has decided to keep just one updated master file in Wilmslow, which can be accessed online for telephone enquirers, and simply an index to this file in the nation's libraries.

tax).[81] But no deregistration notice has yet been issued. It is clear that with regard to enforcement, Eric Howe regards these powers as a means of last resort. Over time, the use of these notices and the pursuance of prosecutions will obviously depend on how certain statutory language is interpreted in the courts.

Many critics have argued that the Registrar and the office's small staff (the law provides for only twenty people) will be so swamped with applications that registration will constitute the only major activity of the office. Early experience did indeed demonstrate that a far larger operation was necessary. In the first years, the number of staff members rose to as many as ninety-four, sixty-six of whom were engaged on registration tasks. The total permanent staff requirement was about seventy in 1989. The expenditure of the office for FY 1989-90 amounted to £2.98 million, which was more than offset by receipts of £5.43 million from the registration fees (now set at £75) that each user is expected to pay every three years.[82]

The Registrar is also expected to fulfill certain "ombudsman" functions, such as receiving complaints from the general public and investigating perceived trouble spots. From June 1988 to May 1989, 1122 complaints had been received by the Data Protection Registrar's office, a large proportion of which related to the receipt of unsolicited mail.[83] The Registrar has begun to develop the office's investigative capacity to determine the facts surrounding individual complaints and to identify data users who have failed to register. The ombudsman activity is, as the Registrar admits, "still in its infancy."[84] Yet, as opposed to registration, it is this function of the office that Eric Howe regards as the most significant.

Like other ombudsmen, Howe is expected to perform an educative function. In the first place, he is required to report annually to the House of Commons. But beyond this activity, valuable efforts have also been made to publicize the existence and requirements of the law. An extensive publicity campaign, involving the dissemination of informational booklets, newsletters, press releases, and newspaper adver-

81. Data Protection Registrar, *Sixth Report* June 1990 (London: HMSO, 1990), p. 21.
82. Ibid., p. 28. It should not be inferred from this passage that the Registrar is self-financing, because 1989 was the year during which most data users had to reregister. In most years, receipts do *not* cover expenses.
83. Ibid., p. 11.
84. Data Protection Registrar, *Third Report*, p. 7.

tisements, was conducted in the first two years of implementation. The Registrar and his deputies spent much time giving interviews and addresses to different groups. A special telephone enquiry service was also established and has dealt with an enormous number of calls, especially when deadlines for registration were approaching. The Registrar himself places a great emphasis on both educating the general public about data protection and on finding out the nature and the extent of public concern.

A distinctive feature of the British approach to data protection during both the formulation and implementation of the law has been the continual emphasis on promoting "good computing practice." The data protection principles are advocated not only to protect individual privacy but also to "ensure that the automatic processing of personal data is carried out in a sound and proper manner."[85] Clearly the Registrar sees data protection as a vehicle to instill a range of good working techniques into the minds and behavior of computer users. This may reflect the more technical orientation of both the British law and the people implementing it.

The main method of promoting "good computing practice" (apart from the educational efforts mentioned above) has been the "code of practice." Unlike the Lindop solution, however, the Registrar is empowered only to "encourage trade associations or other bodies representing data users to prepare, and to disseminate to their members, codes of practice for guidance in complying with the data protection principles."[86] The clear intention is to avoid the legal obligation inherent in the Lindop scheme but to retain the flexibility that codes of practice offer to the various needs and problems of different data users. The Registrar has developed, in consultation with the concerned associations, codes for travel agencies, the direct marketing industry, police offices, universities, and local authorities. Many other codes are envisaged in the future. This emphasis on good computing practice does indicate, however, how important voluntary compliance is to the overall scheme.

Because the Registrar's office is beginning to be seen as a permanent and institutionalized feature of the British political landscape, other departments have sought its views on the planning of information

85. Data Protection Registrar, *Second Report*, p. 16.
86. Data Protection Act, Sec. 36 (4).

systems or on draft legislation that involves the collection of personal data. Throughout 1988 to 1989, the views of Eric Howe and his staff were sought on such issues as the community charge, a bill to register football spectators, a new system of driver and vehicle licensing, and computer hacking. This early consultation, however, is not as routinized as it is in Germany. Howe has expressed a desire for a more active and regular consultation when political and administrative initiatives have clear privacy implications.[87]

Traces of the subject control model are also present in the British approach to data protection, but are much qualified. Data subjects are allowed a right of access to data stored about them and a copy of that information upon payment of a reasonable fee. There are broad exemptions, however. First, the act does not cover manual files. Moreover, there are few other public access provisions (such as a Swedish or an American freedom of information act) through which to obtain such material. In addition, broad exemptions exist for personal information held for the purposes of safeguarding national security, preventing or detecting crime, apprehending or prosecuting offenders, and assessing the collection of taxes. Too, the act gives the Home Secretary wide powers to exempt health and social work records or any other information on the physical or mental health of the data subject. Citizens may be entitled to correction or erasure of inaccurate data and to compensation from data users for damages resulting from the processing of such data.

The access provisions did not come into effect until November 1987. At the moment, it is not clear whether these rights amount to a genuine instrument of control or whether people will indeed have the knowledge or inclination to use them. In a public opinion survey conducted in April 1987, 46 percent of those polled responded that they would be very or quite likely to use these provisions.[88] As the first comprehensive access to information law in Britain, it may have a novelty appeal and promote wide usage during its first few years. Subsequently, given the exemptions, the fees that will be charged (up to £10), and the experience of other countries, it is difficult to conclude that subject access will constitute an effective and widely used means of control.

87. Data Protection Registrar, *Sixth Report*, p. 2.
88. Data Protection Registrar, *Third Report*, p. 45.

To summarize, the policy instrument chosen in the British law relies principally on a process of registration. In fact, the Registrar has only two positive duties under the law: to submit an annual report to the Parliament and to maintain the register. Everything else is a discretionary responsibility. However much the Registrar would like to focus on other tasks, it is the registration function that dominates these other tasks and defines the character of the institution. As Nigel Savage and Chris Edwards conclude, registration assists "the Registrar in promoting the compliance with the principles by placing the onus on data users to identify themselves and to specify their processing activities. Second, it is intended to serve as an 'audit trail' to assist data subjects who wish to track down their personal data."[89] As we have seen elsewhere, this policy instrument could not function without the good sense and voluntary cooperation of the thousands of computer users.

In one sense, each national law is a hybrid of different policy instruments. To differing degrees, most of these instruments are apparent in all four pieces of legislation and in the practices of the agents of implementation. But each is also based on a dominant approach to implementation around which the whole data protection policy is centered: Sweden licenses, the United States relies on individual self-help and the courts, West German policy operates through a data commissioner, and British policy is implemented through a registration system. Other functions are secondary to, and dependent on, the effective operation of these respective instruments.

At a deeper level, each national choice reflects something about the political system in question. A clear, if complicated, variation in policy instruments suggests a relationship between the content of each choice and the context from which it emerged. Political science can offer a more thorough theoretical understanding of that relationship. In Chapter 6 I try to reach a more profound understanding of why virtually the same statutory principles are implemented through such different means.

---

89. Nigel Savage and Chris Edwards, "The Legislative Control of Data Processing: The British Approach," *Computer Law Journal* 6 (1985): 150.

6

Explaining the Divergence

A fruitful way to look at modern government, according to Christopher Hood, is to examine its "toolkit." All governments have a range of "detecting tools" which they use for taking in information and "effecting tools" which they can use to try to make an impact on the outside world.[1] Hypothetically, the toolkit varies from country to country. Different states may each have distinct "policy equipment," a repertoire of instruments or "inventory of potential public capabilities and resources that might be pertinent in any problem-solving situation."[2] This variance is one important justification for comparative policy analysis according to Theda Skocpol: "Cross-national comparisons are necessary to determine the nature and range of institutional mechanisms that state officials may conceivably be able to bring to bear on a given set of issues."[3]

The study of "policy instruments" has found a place in the political science of certain individual states, a circumstance that not only reflects different national traditions of policy analysis but also different styles of policy making.[4] But so far there have been few attempts to set such an analysis within an explicit and systematic comparative frame-

1. Hood, *The Tools of Government.*
2. Charles W. Anderson, "Comparative Policy Analysis: The Design of Measures," *Comparative Politics* 4 (1971): 122.
3. Theda Skocpol, "Bringing the State Back In: Strategies of Analysis in Current Research," in *Bringing the State Back In,* ed. Peter B. Evans, Dietrich Rueschemeyer, and Theda Skocpol (Cambridge: Cambridge University Press, 1985), p. 18.
4. Michael Howlett, "Policy Instruments, Policy Styles, and Policy Implementation: National Approaches to Theories of Instrument Choice," *Policy Studies Journal* (1991): 1–21.

work.[5] In the case of data protection, the neat equivalence of the problem, the time frame, and the statutory principles presents an interesting opportunity to explore the reasons for the different choices of policy instruments and to investigate whether data protection agencies were indeed chosen from distinct Swedish, American, German, and British "toolkits."[6]

Regardless of how these instruments have operated in practice, the dominant methods of implementation vary in significant ways. The explanation of these choices logically requires us to identify plausible relationships between variation in policy content and variation in context. If, as we saw, the most contentious issue in each country was, not the principles, but the means of enforcement, then our understanding of the causes of that variation must lie at the domestic level and not in any overwhelming transnational force. It will also be recalled that one justification for the selection of the United States, Sweden, West Germany, and Britain is that these states display a wide and interesting range of contextual features which were hypothesized to be significant potential forces for divergence.

Five explanations for this divergence are examined: (1) the formal constitutional norms within the state (the toolkit argument); (2) the preferences and influence of dominant social groups; (3) the electoral politics and partisan ideology; (4) the position and power of national bureaucracies; and (5) the economic constraints. As with the arguments for convergence, it is plausible to assume that no one all-embracing explanation will allow us to understand the many aspects of the complex choices made. Moreover, variation in content may easily be attributable to events that did *not* happen, to forces that played *no* role, or to actions that were *not* taken. The plausibility of one explanation, therefore, may rest in a complementary fashion on the implausibility of others. In this spirit, I proceed to examine each of these five arguments in turn, to paint a composite picture of why different instruments were selected.

5. A notable exception is Peter J. Katzenstein, ed., *Between Power and Plenty: Foreign Economic Policies of Advanced Industrial States* (Madison: University of Wisconsin Press, 1978).
6. For a fuller discussion of this point, see Bennett, "Regulating the Computer: Comparing Policy Instruments."

Constitutions and Toolkits

Legal scholarship would argue that data protection law has to be compatible with the constitutional system in which it is to operate. Any structure or process established to implement or enforce the law must also "fit." Given the legalistic orientation of much of the current literature on data protection, this argument is a commonly stated one. Jon Bing, for instance, comments that "privacy law is part of a national legal system and must be fitted into this system with proper respect to its legal environment and national institutions."[7] Knut Selmer, chair of the Norwegian Data Inspectorate, asserts that "any regulatory agency set up by a contracting state must fit into the general pattern of public law and institutions of the country in question."[8] More specifically, Hondius distinguishes between common-law countries (such as the United States and the United Kingdom), which will normally prefer customary or case law, and the civil and Nordic law systems (i.e., of West Germany and Sweden), which tend toward a more specific definition of rules and exceptions within the statutory instruments themselves. In the former countries, the courts will play the major role in implementation; in the latter, regulatory bodies will be charged with enforcing a more defined set of regulations. The policy instruments chosen for the implementation of data protection policy, Hondius argues, are compatible with the existing legal framework.[9]

Considered out of vogue for some time, such explanations of policy differences have enjoyed a recent renaissance in the literature that has attempted to "bring the state back in" to the realm of empirical political science. The frame of reference has broadened to what Margaret Weir and Theda Skocpol call the "structural features of states and the pre-existing legacies of public policies."[10] But the central proposition is no different from the more simple legalistic notions of

7. Bing, "A Comparative Outline of Privacy Legislation," p. 149.
8. Knut Selmer, "Data Protection Policy Trends," *Transnational Data and Communications Report* 11 (December 1988): 19.
9. Hondius, "Data Law in Europe," p. 97.
10. Margaret Weir and Theda Skocpol, "State Structures and the Possibilities of 'Keynesian' Responses to the Great Depression," in *Bringing the State Back In*, ed. Evans et al., p. 109.

traditional constitutional or public law scholarship. Each state has a relatively fixed way of dealing with public problems that is mandated by the structures and rules which govern the exercise of power. These structures and rules then create legacies and perceptions that constrain a choice to solutions which are consistent with tradition and past practice—solutions which are within the "toolkit."

We have already seen, however, that the incorporation of fair information principles into national legal systems proceeded without particular regard for different legal and constitutional traditions. The question now is whether the choice of policy instruments was constrained by such factors. Two specific questions arise. How typical are the policy instruments within the political system, or in other words, are there parallels in other regulatory fields? And how did policy makers in different countries perceive the choices available—were the choices on the agenda confined by preformed beliefs about the "proper," "natural," "traditional," or "constitutional" way to solve such problems in the country concerned?

Let us begin with the British case. Throughout the twelve years from the publication of the Younger Report to the passage of the legislation, every conceivable instrument was seriously debated; self-help and judicial enforcement, voluntary codes of practice, registration, licensing, and a data commissioner were all suggested and discussed at some stage. Virtually the full repertoire of instruments was on the agenda from the outset. It is impossible to detect any preconceived notion among policy makers that there was a typically "British" way to implement such a statute. The typically British way is probably to avoid such issues altogether.[11] Over the years of the debate, many arguments were advanced that one proposal or another was not consistent with that amorphous and elusive thing called the "British Constitution." For example, giving the courts too much power was considered too "American"; giving responsibility to a separate agency to oversee bureaucratic information practices supposedly conflicted with the principle of ministerial responsibility and was dismissed as too "continental." The British Constitution was used in this reform, and in many others, as an expedient. Time-honored principles

---

11. Priscilla M. Regan, "Protecting Privacy and Controlling Bureaucracies: Constraints of British Constitutional Principles," *Governance* 3 (1990): 33–54.

were cited repeatedly by those who wished to maintain the status quo for other reasons.

Inasmuch as the Registrar, either alone or through the courts, can oversee the information practices of the civil service, the law does compromise the convention that administration is solely accountable to Parliament through ministers. The fact that this convention is an anachronistic reflection of the realities of power in a modern industrial welfare state does not alter the fact that it provided very little guidance for the choice of an appropriate policy instrument. When the government was forced to legislate for economic reasons, it produced the Data Protection Act, which is very much a hybrid. The diversity of the Registrar's responsibilities reflects this complexity: the Registrar is to oversee the compilation of the register, investigate citizen complaints, advise data users, construct codes of practice, and the like. The Office of the Data Protection Registrar has few, if any, precedents in other regulatory fields. It joins the large and disparate family of public and semipublic boards, commissions, and agencies that go under the broad heading of "quasi-autonomous nongovernmental organizations," more usually referred to by the acronym "quangos."

There is evidence that the West Germans, too, were not guided by constitutional precedent in establishing the BfD. Housed within the Ministry of Interior yet responsible to the Bundestag, the BfD occupies a unique position in the federal administrative system. It is, in fact, the only institution in the German administrative system that like a "child of divorced parents" has formal links with both the executive and legislature. The establishment of a separate oversight institution is quite peculiar even though the ombudsman concept has been introduced in some narrow areas of financial and military administration.

Perhaps the more expected form of implementation in Germany would be the voluntaristic self-control model. Administrative accountability is normally achieved through the strict discipline of the civil service culture. West German civil servants are trained in law and are expected to pay strict attention to the legalities of their work. The precise codification of expectations in the BDSG reflects this orientation. Moreover, the Basic Law provides that no one in government has the ultimate power to order ministries to do anything except for the ministers themselves. This provision explains the rejection of a regulatory body like that of Sweden in favor of a commissioner with only advisory powers. Overall, however, the BfD, like the Data Protection Registrar, was not created through pressures to conform to legal and constitutional imperatives but through a process of political bargaining. And it is this process that accounts for the uniqueness of the institution.

The constraints imposed by constitutional precedent were more clearly apparent in the United States. In this country, many have made a strong case that the solution of self-help through the courts was the "American way of dealing with such problems." The most convincing source was President Gerald Ford himself, who in his statement to Congress endorsed the House version of the bill (H.R. 16373) over that of Senator Samuel Ervin (S. 3418). Ford's reason had much to do with Ervin's proposal for an independent privacy board:

> I do not favor establishing a separate Commission or Board bureaucracy empowered to define privacy in its own terms and to second guess citizens and agencies. I vastly prefer an approach which makes Federal agencies fully and publicly accountable for legally mandated privacy protections and which gives the individual adequate legal remedies to enforce what he deems to be his own privacy interests.[12]

The United States was subsequently subjected to European criticism for not establishing an independent data protection authority. In response, the National Telecommunications and Information Administration (NTIA) published a study to explain and defend the American approach to privacy protection. The report stressed the traditional importance of the individual's right to seek redress of grievance: "Primary authority for enforcing United States privacy law is situated in the courts. The enforcement role of the courts, highly important in the United States legal system as a whole, is even more so in the case of privacy law, because the courts have traditionally been perceived as the most reliable guardians of constitutional liberties."[13] Earlier in the policy process, the ombudsman concept was rejected by the HEW committee because "the function is not well understood or widely

---

12. U.S. Congress, *Legislative History of the Privacy Act*, p. 956.
13. Robert Aldrich, *Privacy Protection Law in the United States* (Washington, D.C.: U.S. Department of Commerce, NTIA, 1982), p. 8.

198

accepted in America, and some observers feel it has severe limitations in the context of American legal, political and administrative traditions."[14] The ombudsman concept was not in America's toolkit.

Sieghart also observes that the "self-help solution is of course very much in the American tradition, which dislikes paternalism and prefers to leave the citizen to pursue his rights through the courts."[15] As he goes on to point out, however, this practice may be more attributable to the practical advantages of going to court and to a political culture that many have described as litigious. It is also worth noting that American privacy law (and by inference the self-help solution that it embodies) is more firmly grounded in constitutional principles than are laws in other countries. The Privacy Act does not constitute a new legal regime. Rather, the protections that it affords are based squarely on the notion that "the right to privacy is a personal and fundamental right protected by the Constitution of the United States."[16]

While the subject control model is clearly typical and consistent with the American way of implementing such policy, alternatives are not inconceivable or necessarily unconstitutional. A federal privacy board with oversight and regulatory powers was advocated in the Senate bill but defeated, and it continues to be proposed. We can also note that New York State's 1983 Personal Privacy Protection Law establishes a State Committee on Open Government to ensure its effective implementation.[17] On the whole, however, self-help and judicial enforcement, while ineffectual in practice, are perceived as the natural American solution. Perceptions of tradition played an important part in preventing the creation of a separate, nonjudicial institution to mediate between citizens and their government.

Perhaps the country in which the choice was most restricted by these considerations was Sweden. The agenda here permitted no other solution except licensing. There was a clearly recognized need to make the Data Act of 1973 conform to the publicity principle mandated by the Freedom of the Press Act. Indeed, a constitutional amendment was needed before the data protection principles could attain statutory force. The nature of the Swedish response can be attributed to the

14. U.S. HEW, *Records, Computers, and the Rights of Citizens*, p. 42.
15. Sieghart, *Privacy and Computers*, p. 124.
16. Privacy Act, Sec. 2(a) (4).
17. New York, *Personal Privacy Protection Law* L. 1983, c. 652, para. 1.

legacy of open government and the problems that the computer created for the publicity principle. The DIB is, therefore, a typical agency in the context of the fragmented administrative system and the tradition of framework law. The response is thoroughly consistent with regulatory practice in other sectors. It is difficult to find in any of the debates on the Data Act, or in the deliberations of the Royal Commission, any serious consideration of alternatives. Licensing was the natural solution given the past information policy, the regulatory approaches in other areas, and the fragmented nature of the Swedish state.

The Swedish case, more than any other, demonstrates the constraints imposed by the "structural features of states and the pre-existing legacies of public policies." In the United States, a real choice (a privacy board) was on the agenda, but the result was heavily biased by the perceptions of established constitutional imperatives. In Germany, the traditional solution was rejected in favor of the data commissioner. In Britain, it is hard to find any clear understanding of the typically British way to implement such a law. The agenda was, therefore, muddled, and the final choice was a hybrid one. Contrary to the arguments of legal scholars, constitutional constraints provide only a partial explanation of the choice of policy instrument. The argument is most plausible in the cases of Sweden and the United States. For Britain and West Germany we need to look elsewhere for an explanation.

Pressure from Group Forces

The second argument can be equated with a rejection of the static, legalistic frameworks of formal instititional relations in favor of the more dynamic and reciprocal models of the policy process. The approach can be contrasted with the statist orientation because it looks "primarily, often exclusively, to civil society in order to understand what the state does and why it does so."[18] We can hypothesize with much support from many schools of thought in political science that a

18. Eric Nordlinger, *On the Autonomy of the Democratic State* (Cambridge: Harvard University Press, 1981), p. 44.

necessary condition for the choice of one policy option over another is the backing from influential social groups. To make policy choices that will command support, politicians and bureaucrats have to marshal these forces behind them, forming bargains and tradeoffs. Policy output at any one time, therefore, will be dependent on the prevailing constellation of group forces and the resources these forces can muster to influence public policy.

Besides the strong pressure in Britain from the computer industry, outside groups played only a minor role in the formulation of fair information principles and in their application to different countries. Can the choice of different policy instruments, however, be understood in terms of the existence, or conversely, the absence, of influence from interest groups? In this policy sector, we would expect the civil liberties groups to be the central channel of influence, because personal data protection (and privacy, more generally) would be likely to be a focal issue for this lobby. Let us begin here and examine other associations later. A guiding hypothesis might be that the stronger the civil liberties lobby, the stronger the instrument of enforcement.

Civil liberties groups were not relevant in Sweden. Interest groups of all types did indeed play a consultative role in the Royal Commission on Publicity and Secrecy. But this process was typically depoliticized and consensual, a situation that was facilitated by the elaborate remiss advisory procedures. Civil liberties groups played a minor role at this time, as did representatives from business (particularly the Association of Swedish Industries) and the unions (the *Landorganisations*). The highly institutionalized corporatist model of interest intermediation is not without reciprocal advantage for the government: it gives them expertise and information; it legitimizes the final policy choice; and it supposedly eases the process of implementation.

In West Germany, which has a less formalized process of group consultation, it appears that group lobbying was even less evident. An organization entitled *Die Deutsche Vereinigung für Datenschutz* (DvD) was founded in 1977 to try to strengthen the law during its legislative passage. But the DvD's influence was negligible, as leaders of the association readily admit. To this day, it only has eight hundred subscribing members. Occasional outbursts of popular resentment against intrusive governmental practices, most notably over the censuses of 1983 and 1987, demonstrate that *Datenschutz* is a salient concern. But there has never been a strong tradition of civil liberties associations in West Germany, and as a result, such outbursts have never been channeled into a strong coalition of data protection advocates. In the United States and the United Kingdom, by contrast, the American Civil Liberties Union (ACLU) and the British NCCL each waged a long-term campaign for privacy. Their experiences have been very similar.

In Britain, the NCCL has been a prominent actor since the late 1960s when privacy first reached the political agenda. The group formulated a draft bill that was submitted to the Younger Committee.[19] It later published a number of widely cited publications on surveillance and personal information abuse in Britain.[20] These long-term efforts, however, clearly did not produce legislation that was to their liking. The 1984 Data Protection Act was described in an NCCL briefing sheet as "ineffective in safeguarding personal records, inefficient in operation, and it will not meet the requirements of our European trading partners."[21] Thus, while the NCCL served to publicize the problem, it had a negligible impact on the content of the law. The experience of the ACLU has been very much the same. Its lobbying strategy has been similar to that of the NCCL—it has drafted bills, published literature, commented on federal information practices, and given testimony to committees. It has waged a long-term campaign for privacy rights in all spheres since the time the issue made its way onto the agenda in the 1960s. The experience of the NCCL and ACLU demonstrates a number of inherent problems and dilemmas in the lobbying for privacy legislation.

First, personal data protection law is an indivisible, public good; it applies to the whole society. Consequently, interest groups cannot attract members and support by offering benefits (or the prospect of benefits) that are available to only their members. Acting rationally, an individual will see no marginal benefit in participating in group activity if the gain is an indivisible political benefit. This rationale

---

19. Great Britain, *Report for the Committee on Privacy*, pp. 278–80.
20. See, for example, NCCL, *Privacy: The Information Gatherers*; NCCL, *Legislating for Information Privacy*; Cohen, *Whose File Is It Anyway?*; Cornwell and Staunton, *Data Protection*.
21. NCCL, *Data Protection Bill*.

produces a large number of "free riders," people who will potentially receive benefits from the group's activity regardless of their own membership status.[22] Civil liberties groups face this dilemma on most of the causes for which they lobby.

Second, privacy always has to be balanced against other competing values. The mass public wants privacy protection, as we have seen from the opinion polls. But members of the public also want government fraud and abuse cleared up; they want effective law enforcement, good schools, efficient social insurance programs, and the like. All these functions require personal information. Thus privacy always conflicts with some other value. Most people are not so concerned about their privacy that they are willing to forego the benefits which accrue from surrendering personal information in an incremental fashion to a variety of public and private organizations.

Third, privacy is even perceived to contradict other values espoused by the civil liberties groups. Freedom of speech and of the press, for instance, are sometimes considered (erroneously, in many cases) to be values contrary to privacy. This perception is a particular problem in the United States where the issue entitled "data protection" has never been separated from the wider and more nebulous issue known as the "right to privacy." That broader right still encompasses controls on intrusive press practices, thereby creating tensions within the civil liberties coalition. As a result there was, and still is, enormous opposition within the civil liberties community in Washington to a privacy commission. Opponents agree that such a commission, rather than being a watchdog for the citizen, could be susceptible to manipulation from a variety of antiprivacy interests in government. This possibility raises concerns among, for instance, press organizations and major newspapers, which are allies of the ACLU on First Amendment questions but are more ambivalent on privacy-related issues. There were similar tensions in Britain before the data protection problem (relating to computers) was separated from the wider issue of privacy and thenceforth (from 1975) had its own dynamics and momentum as a distinct public-policy question. For example, many newspapers and press associations were highly suspicious of the Younger Committee

22. Mancur Olsen, *The Logic of Collective Action* (Cambridge: Harvard University Press, 1971).

Report and of its predecessor, the report entitled *Privacy and Computers* written by Justice.[23]

Finally, as data protection is a very abstract issue, people are generally not concerned with a heuristic set of fair information principles. They only become interested when they are subjected to personal harm as a result of a specific violation of these principles in specific contexts at specific times. Consequently, to increase public awareness requires the collection and publication of a series of individual and largely disconnected horror stories about how people can be denied rights and privileges through the violation of fair information practices. This task would be a difficult and painstaking effort: the whole point about surveillance risks is that 999 out of 1000 times one has no idea who has what on what computer and who discloses what to whom. Much of the advocacy, therefore, must argue about the future risks, rather than the past and present harm, and takes on a very hypothetical quality.

Despite all these real and imagined reasons, nowhere did a "privacy constituency" emerge—one that had a coherent view of the subject; an established set of policy goals; strong and widespread support; and effective tangible and intangible resources. The absence of such a group was lamented most noticeably in the United States, where the existence of a clientele or a constituency is regarded almost as a prerequisite for effective policy formation. Personal data protection policy sits uneasily within the dominant style of American policy making. That style involves a fragmented system in which "subgovernments" or "issue networks"[24] interact within more or less clearly defined policy sectors to convey tangible government benefits to subsidized individuals, groups, and corporations.[25]

It is clearly not the case that pressure from civil liberties groups materially affected the content of data protection policy. Conversely, like Sherlock Holmes's curious story of the dog that did not bark in

23. The written and oral evidence presented by the media to the Younger Committee reflects this opposition. There were fears that the press would become vulnerable to malicious actions, which would have a chilling effect on press investigation. The shortcomings of some reporters were not "so outrageous that the very principle of freedom of speech needed to be subordinated to a general right of privacy." Great Britain, *Report of the Committee on Privacy* (1972), pp. 38–39.

24. Ripley and Franklin, *Congress, the Bureaucracy, and Public Policy*; Heclo, "Issue Networks and the Executive Establishment."

25. Theodore J. Lowi, *The End of Liberalism* (New York: Norton, 1969).

the night, the absence of strong and effective advocacy for a privacy commission in the United States does help us understand why one was *not* created. Had the pressure been more forceful, perhaps Senator Ervin would not have been compelled to back down. The lack of a coherent privacy constituency allowed other arguments, particularly the constitutional one, to hold sway.

Conclusions about the weakness of social groups are easier to derive when one is just dealing with the public sector, as in the United States. Although outside my framework, data protection in the private sector obviously raised concerns and objections from a wide variety of professional associations and business interests. The Swedish licensing and British registration schemes, in particular, continue to raise disquiet about burdensome regulation and undue governmental intrusion into private organizational affairs. In a few, isolated circumstances, pressure from professional or private-sector interests secured exemptions or special provisions for particular categories of personal data. The British law in particular is cluttered with a variety of exemptions from the act as a whole and from its subject access and nondisclosure provisions in particular: the legal profession secured from subject access the confidentiality of the lawyer/client relationship; the medical profession received the provision that the Secretary of State may exempt from access "data concerning physical or mental health or social work"; police and criminal justice interests secured exemptions for information relating to law enforcement; and business interests obtained exemptions from the registration requirements for data related to payrolls, pensions, and accounts. Professional associations and private sector interests also played a visible role in the battles over the German Data Protection Act and the powers of the BfD. Here, however, they were less successful in weakening the supervisory institutions; like the federal bureaucracy, private interests would have preferred a voluntary system. The law also reflects fewer special provisions or exemptions than does the British law.

In general, the role of interest groups has been marginal in all countries. Nowhere can one conclude that a different policy instrument would have been chosen had it not been for the activities of dominant groups. Whether we look at the privacy advocates, such as the civil liberties associations, or the privacy opponents, the same constraints are visible. Privacy invasions are specific and context-related. The harm to be remedied is variable because the value of personal information changes from time to time, from person to person, and from organization to organization. Statutory protections are seen to be of value only when specific, tangible harm is demonstrated. Thus nowhere do we find a coherent coalition of interests that has been able to affect the content of the law or the nature of the policy instrument in any significant way.

Partisan and Electoral Competition

It was shown in Chapter 4 that personal data protection has not been an election issue anywhere. The reason is not because the issue is nonideological but because it spans all ideologies (with the possible exception of those on the extreme Right and extreme Left). It is not an issue, therefore, that supports an "end of ideology" thesis but one which is embedded in the belief systems of all advanced liberal democratic states. Thus an attempt to place the issue on a continuous liberal/conservative or left/right dimension would be mistaken and impossible. We noted that the perceptions of the utility of these laws may differ in some subtle ways, but the policy received strong cross-party support in all countries. Consequently, it would be surprising if there were significant partisan battles over the question of implementation.

In Britain, however, it is plausible that the Labour party, had it won the election in 1979, would have produced an implementation instrument rather different from the Registrar. The Conservative government entered office in 1979 with many suspicions of the Lindop Report and the proposed Data Protection Authority. They definitely saw the report as a Labour-inspired initiative, and at first had no intention of acting on it at all. Part of the distrust was prompted by the Thatcher government's electoral commitment to reduce regulation and the number of administrative bodies (especially "quangos"). By 1983, however, the pressure to ratify the Council of Europe Convention had overwhelmed the neoliberal faith in reducing regulation and bureaucracy. Ironically, it could be argued that the Data Protection Registrar is the most bureaucratic instrument in the four states under consideration.

In the United States, the differences in conception were divided more on House/Senate, rather than party lines. On the final Senate vote on the version of S. 3418 that included the Privacy Commission, the bill received wide bipartisan support from 74 senators. The initial House version (H. R. 16373) without a commission received support from 192 congressmen of both parties. The final version was passed by a vote of 353 to 1.

The Swedish DIB was devised and established through a highly depoliticized process of accommodation between the Royal Commission and a variety of affected interests from government, industry, the professions, and unions. In West Germany, the Christian Democratic party objected to the organizational location of the BfD within the Ministry of the Interior. But the major battles were drawn along Bundestag/Bundesrat and legislative/executive lines. In conclusion, nowhere did partisan disagreements force compromises on the powers and location of the policy instrument. And nowhere, with the possible exception of Britain, can it be said that the intervention of an election that delivered a different party to power changed or influenced the final choice of the policy instrument.

Bureaucratic Politics and Bargaining

Next we move to the argument that government bureaucracies have been the decisive factor which has determined the nature of the different policy instruments. All bureaucracies are expected to regard information as critical to their internal dynamics and to their relationship with other organizations, individual clients, and citizens. Information is a crucial resource that contributes to organizational autonomy, prestige, stability, predictability, and efficiency. Personal information is no different.

Under data protection policy, bureaucracies are expected to surrender their exclusive control of this vital resource. They face potential limitations on its collection, storage, retrieval, and transmittal. There is a qualitative difference between expecting a public agency to alter its standard operating procedures to distribute or redistribute goods and services, or to regulate an outside activity, and expecting it to submit to the regulation itself. Along with other attempts to "open up" government, data protection policy, at least as it relates to the public sector, has a somewhat peculiar characteristic: the policy's target group is mainly the bureaucracy, and its "impact" is defined and evaluated in terms of reducing bureaucratic power. Bureaucracies would therefore be inclined to resist the efforts of outside bodies to enact these laws and would try to ensure a weak enforcement framework. In other words, they would prefer voluntary control over subject control and would prefer both over institutional control. Policy variation is then dependent on the ability of national bureaucracies to defend their interests by engaging in the political process.

That ability may be associated with a number of interrelated factors. First, there are structural considerations: bureaucracies that are more integrated, hierarchical, and centralized may be able to resist the imposition of outside control more effectively than those that are nonintegrated, decentralized, or characterized by a high rotation of outside personnel. Second, there are cultural or attitudinal factors: some bureaucracies are characterized by a "civil service mentality," a penchant for secrecy, a deep sense of loyalty to the organization, and an oligarchic belief in the power of the state over individual rights. These are all reasons why the "government's privilege to conceal" may be valued more highly than the "public's right to know."[26] They are also all reasons why we might expect resistance to have been higher in Britain and Germany than it was in the United States and Sweden.

The importance of personal information (and particularly computerized personal information) to bureaucracies is recognized and emphasized in all countries, with no noticeable national variation. Data protection officials everywhere have complained of the "inherent tendencies" of bureaucracies to collect vast quantities of information, the incessant drive for efficiency, and the increased dangers posed by computerization. In all four countries, data protection was resisted as a radical departure from traditional bureaucratic norms that view the control of information as central to the organizations' values. The question is how, and with what effect, such resistance entered the political process.

26. Itzhak Galnoor, ed., *Government Secrecy in Democracies* (New York: Harper Colophon, 1977).

Gauged in terms of constant opposition over time, the strongest resistance to data protection came in Britain. It was demonstrated in Chapter 2 that in the United Kingdom there was a significantly longer period between the first appearance on the political agenda of data protection legislation and its enactment than there was in any other country that had yet legislated. This lengthy process of attrition is attributable not to intractable constitutional dilemmas but to civil service, and particularly Home Office, resistance. The policy process since 1970 can be characterized by a gradual breaking down of this opposition.

This resistance began in 1970 when Brian Walden introduced his privacy bill and the Home Secretary was sent to the House of Commons to block the bill at any cost. It continued over the terms of reference of the Younger Committee and was instrumental in excluding the public sector from its remit. The Home Secretary did relent by setting up within Whitehall an internal "Shadow Younger Committee" (whose report has never been published), which by most accounts was conservative, cautious, and resistant to any external control. The obstruction continued after the Younger Report was published. When the next Labour government was faced with producing a white paper on the subject, the new Home Secretary had to bring in an outsider to write it because of official intransigence; *Computers and Privacy* (Cmnd. 6353) was essentially published over the heads of Home Office civil servants. The resistance continued in official testimony to the Lindop Committee and in the early months of the new Conservative government.

Once the new government (in 1981) became convinced that data protection was necessary for purely economic reasons, the bargaining reached a new intensity. There was a cabinet decision that a bill would be introduced, and this decision was announced in a very curious way in response to a parliamentary question. It is probable that the Home Office first heard about the bill at this time; they were then put in the extraordinary position of having to present a bill that they did not really want. The first proposal contained the suggestion that the Registrar should be a Home Office official, an idea that was unacceptable to the medical profession, to European data protection officials, and to practically everyone else. Then the principle of independence was established in the white paper of 1982. And so it went on, with the Home Office gradually relenting on one small point after another until final enactment.

It should be stressed that opposition to data protection was by no means constant across all Whitehall departments. The Department of Trade and Industry, and its Secretary of State Kenneth Baker, were particularly insistent that data protection legislation was necessary for Britain's commercial interests. Most ministries, however, would have been happier without it. This sentiment can be attributed to the same uniquely British attitudes toward secrecy that have asserted themselves to block other attempts to open up British government. The highly elitist and centralized administrative culture in Britain has been notably resistant to outside attempts to change administrative practices, especially where information is concerned.

The particular opposition of the Home Office in this case is also attributable to certain functional reasons. Sir Norman Lindop explains:

> Over twenty years . . . the attitude of the Home Office has been consistent and on the whole negative. It is easy to see why, because the Home Office has a dual role. It is not only a Ministry of Justice, concerned with the liberties of the subject, but it is also a Department of the Interior, and it is concerned with the internal security of the State. It has direct concern for example with immigration, with drugs control, with prisons, with the Metropolitan Police, the Special Branch, and so on. What would the Home Office—that part of it—want with data protection, of all things? It wants it like a hole in the head.[27]

His point is well taken. This peculiar combination of responsibilities, not apparent elsewhere, fortified the resistance to and lengthened the delay of data protection legislation.

Beyond this inconsistent combination of functions, however, is a wider structural consideration that allowed a department such as the Home Office to successfully resist the will of democratically elected governments for over a decade. The integrated nature of the British

---

27. Sir Norman Lindop, "Data Protection: The Background," in *Data Protection*, ed. Bourn and Benyon, pp. 25–26.

bureaucracy (its hierarchy, specialization of function, and low rate of personnel exchange with outside bodies) produced an ability to confront an incoming minister with a coherent "departmental view." Those structural characteristics, combined with a general civil service penchant for secrecy and a particular Home Office reluctance to surrender control of its own personal data systems, motivated the observed bureaucratic behavior.

The character of the policy instrument that finally emerged in the Data Protection Act is largely due to this long-term bargaining process during which the Home Office steadfastly attempted to defend bureaucratic autonomy over personal data systems. This resolute opposition tended to frame the debate and define the policy instrument in terms of what could be "won" politically from the Home Office. On one level, this resistance explains the blanket exemptions for systems dealing with law enforcement and national security (within the jurisdiction of the Home Office) and for manual records on the whole. More generally, it explains the hybrid nature of the Registrar's responsibilities. The imperative that motivated the proponents of the law was not, therefore, a "rational" one, that is, one to secure the most coherent and effective instrument to enforce data protection in British circumstances. Instead, the imperative was a "consensual" one, namely, one to obtain agreement on a minimal set of powers that would satisfy both bureaucratic and legislative actors and would conform to the Council of Europe Convention.

West Germany provides another case of a highly integrated bureaucracy underpinned by the Prussian civil service tradition and a strong legalistic mentality. At the same time, behavioral research has shown that attitudes of loyalty, objectivity, and instrumentality among German civil servants are being replaced by a keener awareness of the political nature of their positions and by a growing tendency to engage in political transactions. Robert Putnam's study of the political attitudes of civil servants in Western Europe found a higher acceptance of conflict as a part of the political process in Germany than in the past.[28] In Germany, as in Britain, we would expect to see the

---

28. Robert D. Putnam, "The Political Attitudes of Senior Civil Servants in Western Europe: A Preliminary Report," *British Journal of Political Science* 3 (1973): 257–90. See also Joel D. Aberbach, Robert D. Putnam, and Bert A. Rockman, *Bureaucrats and Politicians in Western Democracies* (Cambridge: Harvard University Press, 1981).

ability and the will to resist the demands for personal data protection. The policy not only challenged an inherent bureaucratic motivation to collect and control personal information, however, but it also attacked the heart of the German system of administrative responsibility. German public officials (*Beamte*) are expected to serve the state loyally and with impartiality. The practices and procedures of public service are explicitly prescribed in law and in the *Common Code of Administrative Procedure*. Adherence to these legal norms is sustained by the dominant influence of lawyers in the higher levels of the civil service. In return for their loyalty and obedience to the state, civil servants receive lifetime tenure and a salary that permits a very comfortable lifestyle.

The notion of a semi-independent oversight body was therefore considered not only alien but also unnecessary. The idea that the bureaucracy, on both the federal and state levels, needed external control challenged deep-seated beliefs about the public service. This combination of administrative values, a growing perception of the political character of the bureaucracy, and the more general threat to information management produced a stiff resistance first to the concept of data protection and then to the idea of external control. And this resistance produced in turn the delays and the protracted process of bargaining with the Bundestag, which insisted on some form of independent authority.

The bargaining ability of the bureaucracy was also enhanced by the role of the Bundesrat, whose influence in the policy-making process has steadily increased since 1969.[29] As representatives of the Länder governments, Bundesrat delegates have traditionally been concerned with examining legislation from the standpoint of how it would be implemented at the local level. Much of this work is delegated to civil servants who deputize for the regular members in the Bundesrat's committees. The opposition to the BDSG during the legislative passage was motivated, therefore, not only by a skeptical administrative mentality, but also by the desire to protect the interests of the Länder.

As they did in Britain, the cultural and structural characteristics of the bureaucracy led to predictably strong opposition to data protection policy. In political-bargaining terms we can conclude that the

---

29. David P. Conradt, *The German Polity* (New York: Longman, 1978), p. 136.

German federal bureaucracy lost its fight to institute a voluntaristic model of implementation. The establishment of the Federal Data Protection Commissioner reflects the result of a long process of bargaining in which the Bundestag, operating within a political culture and climate of opinion very favorable to civil liberties issues, eventually won the day. This bureaucratic-politics model does help us understand the choice of the BfD, an institution with virtually no precedent within the German administrative system, and its location in the Interior Ministry, its jurisdiction over the federal public sector, and its blend of powers and responsibilities. The resulting institution was a reflection of what could be won in a battle against entrenched bureaucratic forces.

As we have already determined, the constitutional and legal tradition in the United States accounts for the choice of judicial enforcement and self-help, a policy instrument that is culturally consistent with the American tradition of protecting civil liberties. Strong arguments were advanced that any alternative would be unworkable and alien to this tradition. The American administrative system is both structurally and culturally different from either the British or German models. Government departments are umbrella organizations for a diverse, nonintegrated, and decentralized collection of bureaus. Political direction is attempted through some nine hundred presidential appointees, whose tenure is normally short-lived and who generally find it difficult to energize the permanent members of the civil service with the President's ideas and programs before they leave for the more lucrative pastures of the private sector. The federal establishment has been described as a "government of strangers" characterized by a high rotation of personnel, weak lines of communication, and the consequent difficulty of advancing a coherent bureaucratic or even departmental view on anything.[30]

Yet the Privacy Act, which applies to the entire federal bureaucracy and which challenged long-standing information policy, did arouse bureaucratic opposition, if not to the same extent as similar legislation did in Britain and Germany. The pattern of resistance displayed in testimony before congressional committees is like that already seen.

---

30. Hugh Heclo, *A Government of Strangers: Executive Politics in Washington* (Washington, D.C.: Brookings, 1977).

At first the very need for a statute was questioned. Then, as legislation was perceived as being inevitable, opposition was directed toward the implementation framework. Six recurring arguments were advanced against a commission: its cost would be enormous; an additional layer of bureaucracy would be burdensome; a separate oversight agency would be like using a hammer to crack a nut; its start-up time would delay the realization of the programmatic goals; a privacy commission would fragment responsibility; and congressional oversight of voluntary compliance would be sufficient.[31] Federal agencies (led by the Treasury, the Office of Management and Budget, and the Department of Commerce) advanced these arguments over a period of years before various congressional bodies. As late as 1974 in the committee hearings on S. 3418, agencies displayed unified opposition to the privacy commission idea. As Regan argues, this resistance exposes the dilemma of trying to decide implementation questions during the legislative process: "When implementation questions are left unresolved in policy design, bureaucratic concerns will dominate the implementation stage, but when implementation questions are resolved in policy design, bureaucratic concerns will dominate the formulation stage."[32]

The eventual triumph of bureaucratic interests was also facilitated by some other factors. First, advocates were by no means unified on whether an institutional mechanism was necessary, and if it was, on what form it should take. Second, Congress was divided on the same issue, with the House producing a bill that was far more acceptable to bureaucratic interests. And finally, there was the overwhelming, if dubious, argument that the privacy board was an unnatural, "un-American" way to solve the problem. Bureaucratic opposition, therefore, needed powerful allies in both the White House and the Congress. It is unlikely that the bureaucracy could have thwarted the idea on its own. So it would be wrong to conclude that these efforts were directly and solely responsible for the absence of a separate privacy board in the final legislation. Yet the bureaucratic-politics model does contribute to our understanding of the bargaining process that took place in the final hours of the Ninety-third Congress. The fear of bureaucratic noncompliance was one reason why Senator Ervin backed down. It was one reason why the implementation scheme was diluted and the Privacy Protection Commission became a Privacy Pro-

31. Regan, "Personal Information Policies," p. 27.
32. Ibid., p. 36.

tection Study Commission with responsibility for its regulation going to the OMB. At the end of the bargaining, however, was a typical solution that rejected paternalism and left the onus where it had always been—with the individual.

Government bureaucracy in Sweden is the most fragmented. Departments are very small, and the implementation of policy is carried out through a complex network of autonomous boards; they are not accountable to cabinet ministers but are responsible for the control of most personal data systems in the Swedish public sector. As expected, bureaucratic resistance in Sweden was the weakest. This fact is consistent with our expectation that the bureaucracy would not be structurally equipped to confront elected politicians with a civil service view on the question. The policy problem in Sweden was not framed in terms of attacking or reducing bureaucratic power. Rather, the major difficulty was seen as making the Data Act (generally regarded as necessary) consistent with existing information policy. The problem was defined in technical and legalistic terms rather than in political ones. Furthermore, it is possible that Swedish bureaucrats saw very little to defend, given the already extremely open system of administration mandated by the Freedom of the Press Act.

In Britain and Germany, data protection policy confronted a basic presumption of secrecy. In the United States, despite the enactment of the Freedom of Information Act in 1967, there were still battles over the desired degree of openness in American administration. In Sweden, by contrast, the starting presumption was one of publicity; hence, bureaucratic "control" of information meant less, there was less ground to defend, and there were far fewer incentives to resist data protection. In this atmosphere, the structure and the powers of the DIB emerged more from a rationalistic and depoliticized process of study and analysis than from a confrontation between civil libertarian interests on the one hand and entrenched bureaucratic forces on the other.

Economic Constraints

While economic considerations played little role in the choice of principles to be legislated, they were of some importance in the structuring of the policy instrument. Nowhere does the implementation of data protection policy entail the expenditure of vast sums of public money. Nevertheless, the 1970s were times of economic recession and austerity, of reaction against burdensome regulatory bureaucracies, and of a greater realism about what governments could achieve. Evidence of these themes is implicit, and in some countries explicit, in the debates over the choice of policy instrument.

In Sweden, for instance, the system of licensing was partly chosen because it was thought that the payment of license fees over time would render the DIB self-financing. The DIB has not reached this state, although it claims that the principle of licensing, and, of course, the comprehensive coverage of both private and public record-keeping systems, allows for the recovery of most of the costs of enforcement. This desire to recover enforcement costs was more clearly discernible in the British case. The government was insistent in the white paper of April 1982 that,

> in accordance with the Government's objective of keeping the burden of resources to a minimum, everything possible will be done to ensure that neither the legislation nor the regulations made under it impose unnecessarily costly requirements. In the public sector, costs and manpower will have to be contained within existing planned totals, even if this means deferring application of the legislation in some areas. The initial cost of the Registrar and his staff . . . is likely to be in the order of £500,000 a year at 1981/2 prices. It is the intention that the fees charged by the Registrar will recover all the costs, including those of setting up the register.[33]

In this context of stringent public expenditure controls, we can more easily understand the choice of a system of universal registration that had already been demonstrated in Sweden to be slow and cumbersome. All personal data users, regardless of their size or the scope and sensitivity of the data, have to pay a standard fee in order to comply with the law.[34] The British expenditure for FY 1989–90 amounted to £2.98 million.

In other countries, considerations of public expense had a less substantial impact. Federal agencies in the United States did raise objec-

---

33. Great Britain, *Data Protection: The Government's Proposals for Legislation*, p. 7.
34. Originally set at £22, the charge is now £75.

tions to Ervin's proposed Privacy Protection Commission on grounds of cost; they saw it as an unnecessary administrative layer that was imposed to deal with a relatively minor problem. The Privacy Act was passed without any additional funds being appropriated for its implementation. Today, economic considerations might play a more significant part in defeating the commission idea given the record budget deficits and the antiregulatory stance of the Reagan and Bush administrations.

Ministries in West Germany also objected to the BfD on the largely unsubstantiated grounds of cost. The BfD operates on funds appropriated for the Ministry of the Interior. And while the system of regulation at both state and federal levels is the most costly of all four countries because the offices cannot rely on license or registration fees, the BfD's staff and budget are modest. Moreover, many data protection officials would contend that the BfD's work leads to a rationalization in the collection of personal data, thus leading to significant, if unquantifiable, savings.

Conclusion: Explaining Divergence

In summary, we can paint a composite picture of why different instruments were selected by various countries to implement virtually the same statutory principles. No one explanation suffices for all states. Choice is also attributable to factors that had *no* influence as well as to those that did. In no country was a synoptic view of the problem taken, a view by which all possible solutions within the international repertoire were carefully and rationally considered. For Sweden, licensing seemed the natural solution from the outset, and other alternatives were never seriously considered. In the United States, the choice came down to self-help and judicial enforcement versus a type of data commissioner; licensing and registration were never options. Nor were they seriously on the agenda in Germany, where the choice was restricted to voluntary compliance or a data commissioner. Only in Britain does one find a consideration of most approaches. But this fact is more attributable to the protracted time between the appearance of the issue on the agenda and the final enactment than to any deep-seated commitment to rational decision making by British policy makers. Rather, the picture is one of a range of alternatives that were relatively clear at the beginning of the process (in the early 1970s), and of a filtering through constitutional, structural, and economic constraints. This filtering restricted the agenda and narrowed the choice.

We saw that in Sweden the DIB is a typical agency in the context of the fragmented administrative system. The constitutional tradition of publicity was threatened by the introduction of computers. The technology was the problem rather than the individual rights or the bureaucratic pathologies. Regulating the computer, therefore, was the only feasible solution. Licensing also had a particular appeal because of economic considerations. The choice was made in a typically (stereotypically) Swedish style—it was consensual, rationalistic, and depoliticized. The speed and smoothness of the legislative process was facilitated by the weakness of interest group divisions, by the absence of partisan or ideological feelings, and by the ineffectiveness of bureaucratic resistance.

In the United States, strong attachments to constitutional norms also filtered out "unacceptable" or "unnatural" American solutions. The resulting instrument is again very typical of a system of separation of powers where rights are individually asserted to the courts and administrative accountability is achieved through congressional oversight. The United States arrived at this solution after greater controversy had occurred than had in Sweden. Conflict is institutionalized in the American system and led, in this case, to an uneasy compromise whereby the Office of Management and Budget and a Privacy Protection Study Commission assumed central enforcement, investigative, and analytical tasks. Nevertheless, the strong bias was for the tried and tested solution. Absent any coherent privacy constituency or clientele, this presumption prevailed.

The German policy instrument is atypical. Its location, jurisdiction, and responsibilities are attributable to a series of compromises between the bureaucracy and the Bundestag. Within a strongly statist tradition and an overall presumption of secrecy for government-held information, data protection was inevitably seen as a threat. Only because of the insistence of the Bundestag within a climate of public opinion favorable to civil liberties interests was a separate policy instrument established. Both the immediate realization on enactment that the solution was imperfect and the consequent attempts to amend the federal law are reflections of this uneasy and rushed compromise.

In Britain, too, bureaucratic resistance, principally from the lead department, the Home Office, produced an instrument that many have described as "minimalist"; it reflects the least the government needed to do to conform to the Council of Europe Convention. While a formidable coalition of private and professional groups supported the law, most were content with a provision that would simply allow the United Kingdom to join the European "data club"; they were not overly concerned about the resulting policy instrument becoming so burdened with registration duties that it would be unable to act as a watchdog for civil liberties. Economics influenced British data protection policy at every turn, from the decision to legislate to the content of the statute to the choice of an instrument that could be self-financing.

There is no central theory of divergence, therefore. Explaining policy choice is a complex and multifaceted task. No single explanation suffices. Arnold Heidenheimer and his colleagues came to the same conclusion in their comparative analysis of American and European social policy. Each structural, institutional, cultural, ideological, or economic explanation may be useful, "but arguing about their relative merits is like arguing about which is the most important leg of a three-legged stool. Each explanation in isolation seems inadequate for coping with the complex mesh of forces creating modern social policies."[35] Only through a juxtaposition of various theoretical perspectives can we approach an understanding of how and why "different governments pursue particular courses of action or inaction." Thus we come full circle to the declared purpose of comparative policy analysis defined at the outset.

35. Heidenheimer et al., *Comparative Public Policy*, 1st ed., p. 260.

7

Policy Determinants, Styles, and Predictions

The data protection issue has manifested a richness and a complexity and has led to some profound and perennial questions about the determinants of public policy. Our "answers" have not been definitive findings of causation but rather more qualified statements of probable relationships. The methodology is one of judging, in the light of the empirical evidence, whether the different arguments for convergence and divergence simply make any sense. Consequently, a summary of the most plausible explanations is now appropriate. I will then discuss the implications of the argument with particular attention to what these conclusions say about the relative autonomy of the contemporary democratic state.

The issue has also presented an interesting juxtaposition of policy-making styles. One justification for exploring this issue was that it would allow us to more sharply contrast how these equivalent systems have dealt with the same problem within a common time frame. What does this account tell us about the problem-solving capabilities of these four states in more general terms? Which have been able to anticipate the problem, and which have been more reactive? In which countries was the process more consensual, and in which was it more conflictual? These are questions that are subsumed in current literature under the appellation "policy style."

In a similar vein, the argument about convergence and divergence has implications for the way these policies have been implemented. For the most part, our treatment of this issue has been confined to the "how" and "why" questions and has left the "to what effect" aspect alone. I would be remiss, however, to omit any reference to how these laws have been implemented. The way that these policies were formulated has a lasting influence on the way they are being applied. Thus while we can note some lessons for the successful implementation of data protection, we can also attempt to understand this experience in relation to the domestic and international forces that have guided this study so far. This analysis will also allow us to speculate on the future of data protection and to determine whether this issue is one whose time came and went or whether it will stay with us as long as we have complex organizations and high technology.

Convergence and Divergence in Public Policy

Over time different states came to agree on the statutory principles that comprise data protection, a process I have interpreted as policy convergence. Some commentators have found the convergence to be both striking and surprising. Yet in a policy-making climate of bounded rationality, of imperfect information about the nature and future development of the technology, and of growing interdependence within the information society, convergence can probably be expected, despite overt national differences. The critical question is, why?

The most all-encompassing explanation is the technology. Commentators from all countries have stressed the computer's pervasiveness and speed of development. Others have also spoken of its enigmatic character and thus of the need to render the data processing environment "transparent." The acceptance of this interpretation leads inevitably to a set of fair information principles that logically cannot display much variation. The argument has force, especially in the early stages of policy formation (through 1975). Evidence points to an intense process of internal study and debate in all four countries. There was a clear awareness of overseas developments and a keen desire to learn, but the construction of the national policies in the first states to legislate was mainly based on this indigenous analysis and discussion.

International contacts at this stage were of an ad hoc and bipartite nature. As more analysis was completed, however, more formal and

221

institutionalized contacts also arose; as a result, those observing the process could identify a "policy community," a core group of maybe six to ten knowledgeable individuals who shared a common concern and motivation as well as increasingly regular contacts with each other through international organizations. As communication and lesson drawing intensified, the recognition of the commonality of concern broadened as well. Pressure was placed on international organizations to codify this consensus in both nonbinding guidelines (in the case of the OECD) and in a full convention (in the case of the Council of Europe). I should emphasize that such action was prompted by this small network of experts rather than by a widespread understanding of interdependence. From the mid-1970s onward, however, data protection is more properly regarded as an international issue on an international agenda. Domestic policy makers had to pay increasing heed to this wider program; the result was the more penetrative process that is observed in the countries which have legislated more recently.

At the level of the principles, broad transnational forces transcended national characteristics. Furthermore, different forces had a variable impact over time. For the pioneers, the United States and Sweden, the convergence resulted from independent and indigenous analyses that traveled along the same learning curve and arrived at the same conclusion. For West Germany, and other countries such as Canada, France, Norway, Denmark, and Austria that legislated in the late 1970s, the convergence followed from the mutual process of lesson drawing within an international policy community. For Britain, and other laggards such as the Netherlands, Japan, and Australia, the convergence has resulted from a pressure to conform to international standards for mainly commercial reasons.

At the level of the policy instruments, however, national forces surfaced and produced a significant variation. Although the enforcement framework in each country reflects a combination of processes, each is also based on one dominant approach underpinned by a distinctive theory of individual and organizational behavior: Sweden chose a licensing system, the United States selected individual self-help and enforcement through the courts, West Germany appointed a data protection commissioner, and Britain opted for a registration system.

In Sweden and the United States, the instruments selected were typical of their respective systems. Powerful historical forces have produced policy legacies and notions of the "natural" or "traditional" way to enforce administrative law in both countries. In Britain and Germany, on the other hand, the instruments chosen were atypical, if not unique. Constant and forceful opposition from national bureaucracies defined the policy as an attack on the control of information, a virtually sacrosanct area of administrative responsibility. Thus, the agenda was confined, not by historical legacies, but by what could be won from entrenched bureaucratic forces. The resulting authorities were, therefore, the products of bargaining and compromise and had few, if any, precedents in their respective systems. In Sweden and particularly in Britain, economic considerations motivated the choice of instruments that had the potential to be self-financing.

The overall finding of a convergence on one aspect of the policy and divergence on another is consistent with those in several other recent comparative policy studies that have found interesting combinations of variation and similarity across different dimensions of the same policy.[1] Findings of convergence and divergence are intrinsically interesting, and this study is at least as revealing for the divergence of policy instruments as it is for the convergence of principles. But if case studies are to say anything about the autonomy and problem-solving capabilities of different states beyond the immediate issue at hand, then what is significant is not the evidence of convergence and divergence but the explanation thereof. As Douglas Ashford asks: "Is the most interesting thing about the modern state that it encounters similar conflicts and must make similar choices, or is it that it has done these things in a variety of ways?"[2]

1. See David Vogel, *National Styles of Regulation: Environmental Policy in Great Britain and the United States* (Ithaca: Cornell University Press, 1986), who finds a divergence of policy style and a convergence of outcome in British and U.S. environmental regulation; Jerold L. Waltman and Donley T. Studlar, eds., *Political Economy: Public Policies in the United States and Britain* (Jackson, Miss.: University Press of Mississippi, 1987), who detect a strong convergence of policy goals between British and American neoconservative administrations in the 1980s, but very mixed evidence as far as policy content is concerned; and, more generally, Hoberg, "Technology, Political Structure, and Social Regulation," and Bennett, "Review Article: What Is Policy Convergence?"
2. Douglas E. Ashford, "The Structural Analysis of Policy or Institutions Really Do Matter," in *Comparing Public Policies*, ed. Douglas E. Ashford (Beverly Hills: Sage, 1978), p. 81.

Convergence, Divergence, and State Autonomy

The answer to Ashford's question depends, as with so many questions in political science, on one's view of the state. It would be tempting to conclude, along with the "convergence theorists," that the similarity in data protection principles is further evidence of the lack of state autonomy. And yet it is time, many argue, to "bring the state back in"—to formulate research designs and develop theories on the assumption that states are significant, independent actors in the policy processes of advanced democratic countries. Looking to the actions and preferences of state actors has as much inherent plausibility as does looking to society or the "environment" for an understanding of policy decisions.[3]

If we first address the broad response to the problem, it can be noted that the data protection case seemingly contradicts the prevailing picture of policy making in the 1970s, a picture that has generally portrayed the democratic state as highly constrained. By most accounts, the democratic state was becoming harder to govern in the 1970s, and the autonomy of state officials was being progressively reduced. Some authors have pursued these arguments at the level of individual nation-states; for example, Theodore Lowi spoke of a "crisis of public authority" within the United States because of the effort to please and appease every interest.[4] Parallel arguments have been expressed in Britain: Anthony King introduced the concept of "overload" to denote the "combination of increasing demands on government and government's increasing inability to cope";[5] Samuel Beer wrote in a similar vein of "pluralistic stagnation" to describe the proliferation of group demands and the consequential "paralysis of public choice."[6] Other authors have written in more general language about a "crisis of democracy"[7] or a "legitimation crisis."[8] Still others

3. See, for example, Evans et al., *Bringing the State Back In; Nordlinger, On the Autonomy of the Democratic State*; Stephen D. Krasner, "Approaches to the State: Alternative Conceptions and Historical Dynamics," *Comparative Politics* 16 (1984): 223–46.
4. Lowi, *The End of Liberalism.*
5. Anthony King, "Overload: Problems of Governing in the 1970's," *Political Studies* 23 (1975): 284–96.
6. Samuel H. Beer, *Britain against Itself: The Political Contradictions of Collectivism* (New York: Norton, 1982).
7. Michel Crozier, Samuel Huntington, and Joji Watanuki, *The Crisis of Democracy* (New York: New York University Press, 1975).
8. Jurgen Habermas, *The Legitimation Crisis* (Boston: Beacon Press, 1975).

have spoken in economic terms about the restriction of the "policy space" and about the fact that austerity will force governments to avoid innovation.[9] From a number of theoretical and ideological perspectives, writers have agreed that it is becoming harder to solve the problems of the advanced democratic state. Several have even predicted a condition of "ungovernability."

The data protection case contradicts this general picture. This case is an example of democratic states responding to a commonly perceived problem, largely in anticipation of future technological advances and without prior clamoring from outside groups. These states have responded to different prompts, with different timing, and according to their own distinctive styles. But they have responded. Even in Britain, which has adopted a more reactive posture, the stalemate was broken. The data protection case may not be typical in that it does not require the outlay of vast sums of public money. Nevertheless, it does suggest that the prognostications of "overload, ungovernability, and delegitimation" have been exaggerated. In any event these predictions do not have the universal validity that has sometimes been claimed for them.[10]

Moving to an analysis of the causes of how and why these four states have converged, we have observed that the principal policy-making actors have been a technocratic elite. Policy convergence is at least as attributable to the actions and preferences of an international policy community of public, or quasi-public, officials, as it is to anything else. The distinction between the state and society can never be sharply drawn and embodies a variety of controversial theoretical assumptions. Nevertheless, we can conclude that the data protection case does provide support for Eric Nordlinger's basic point that "explanation" can be provided as much by the conscious investigations, puzzlements, and choices of authoritative state actors (either acting in the domestic or the international arenas) as by "environmental" forces.[11] The issue demonstrates, therefore, that convergence should not be regarded as the antithesis to autonomous state action. We

9. Hugh Heclo, "Frontiers of Social Policy in Europe and America," *Policy Sciences* 6 (1975): 403–21; Brian W. Hogwood and B. Guy Peters, *Policy Dynamics* (Brighton: Wheatsheaf Books, 1983).
10. See Anthony H. Birch, "Overload, Ungovernability, and Delegitimation: The Theories and the British Case," *British Journal of Political Science* 14 (1984): 135–60.
11. Nordlinger, *On the Autonomy of the Democratic State*, p. 28.

argued, for instance, that the coincidence of recognition that information technology could compromise individual privacy should not be interpreted as a "technological imperative." The perceptions of the technology that the policy community developed and disseminated were the critical factor. Those perceptions could vary; they could lead to inaction as well as to action.

Nordlinger's typology of explanations for the authoritative actions of the democratic state helps us construct a more general statement about the relationship between relative state autonomy and the five forces for convergence.[12] He constructs a four-cell framework along two dimensions: first, where state and societal preferences are divergent or nondivergent; and second, where state preferences and authoritative actions are coincident and noncoincident. The lack of autonomy (the societal constraint explanation) is associated with just one cell of the framework: where state and societal preferences are divergent and state preferences and authoritative actions are noncoincident. In these instances, the state is presumed to act in accordance with the preferences of the dominant social group rather than in accordance with its own. The only convergence process that fits this characterization is penetration, which is based on an explicit assumption of constraint imposed by external actors. Britain is the only state where policy makers were forced to pass data protection legislation against their initial preferences.

In the other four processes, we can conceptualize a "state autonomy" variant: the state's preferences do not diverge with societal (external) preferences, and state preferences and authoritative actions are coincident. In other words, states might be willing to formulate similar policies to those of other states: to agree autonomously that there is indeed only one best way to solve a given problem; to surrender willingly to the temptation to emulate action taken elsewhere; to be influenced by the expert and seemingly rational arguments of a transnational issue network; or to submit to the soothing and harmonizing influences of intergovernmental organizations.

There are some enormous problems with Nordlinger's atomistic and homogenous conceptualization of the state, as well as with his distinction between state and society.[13] Nevertheless, the simple, logi-

12. Ibid., p. 28.
13. Krasner, "Approaches to the State."

cal exercise he offers does clarify the researchable hypotheses about the relationship between convergence and state autonomy.[14] Evidence for the convergence of public policy does not signify that the democratic state has been buffeted by an unyielding and inexorable set of transnational forces. Rather, it calls for the examination of alternative hypotheses that rest on different assumptions about the behavior and autonomy of state actors.

The evidence for the divergence of policy instruments also provides some proof of the validity of state-centered explanations. The most powerful explanation in Sweden and the United States was explicitly suggested by the statist literature — "the structural features of states and the preexisting legacies of public policies."[15] Similarly, the conclusion that a model of bureaucratic power has some considerable utility in explaining the choice of policy instruments especially in Britain and Germany might also be cited as strong support for a statist interpretation. There are, however, some important qualifications that need to be made before jumping to the conclusion that this case provides empirical support for "bringing the state back in."

In all countries, with the possible exception of Sweden, different state actors had different interests. In Germany, Britain, and the United States, we found a legislative interest in an effective data protection policy and a bureaucratic interest against one. Moreover, there were different interests within the bureaucracy. In Britain, the Department of Trade and Industry was a strong advocate for data protection, albeit for the "wrong" reasons, while the Home Office was bitterly opposed to such policy. Thus we can conclude, together with Nordlinger, that "public officials have at least as much independent impact or explanatory importance as any and all private actors in accounting for the public policies of the democratic state";[16] this conclusion, however, is based on an overly homogenous view of "the state" that obscures significant variations in the motivations and behavior of different state actors. This difficulty is a perennial one within

14. This view is also Skocpol's conclusion about the value of Nordlinger's work. Skocpol, "Bringing the State Back In," p. 31. Nordlinger can be justly criticized for stretching pluralism to its conceptual limits and for viewing state actors as being on equal terms with any other group in the dynamics of the political process.

15. Margaret Weir and Theda Skocpol, "State Structures and the Possibilities of "Keynesian" Responses to the Great Depression," in *Bringing the State Back In*, ed. Evans et al., p. 109.

16. Nordlinger, *On the Autonomy of the Democratic State*, p. 8.

this literature, especially that which is written from an international relations perspective.

Another problem with this interpretation is exposed by the somewhat peculiar properties of this policy. Confined to the most important motive for data protection in the four countries—controlling the public sector—the policy sets the conditions under which *public* activity should be undertaken. Its purpose is principally to attain a normative value derived from a common set of liberal democratic tenets on the relationship between the individual and the state. The "protected" are all citizens. The "target group" *is* in part the bureaucracy. The "impact" of this policy takes place within the agencies of government. The behavior to be regulated is that of the regulators. Although the private sector is regulated in many countries, in large measure, policy "objectives" do not exist independently of the structures and processes of the public bureaucracy.

We are dealing, then, with an inherently different breed of state action, one that does not fit into the most common typologies of public policy.[17] As there is no identifiable external group that benefits from the production of the policy, there can be no single clientele or constituency. There is no complicated process of resource allocation made through multiple administrative layers and transmitted to remote geographical locations. There is no complex set of intervening interests. Privacy has a certain discrete and uncomplicated quality. As far as the public sector is concerned, the policy-making effort is a classical liberal form of state action in that the attempt is "simply" to protect the relationship between the citizen and the democratic state. For policies where the bureaucracy is an *object* of regulation, can one still say that it is behaving as a "state actor"? Or, do the strong individual and structural motivations for resistance mean that the bureaucracy should be considered as just one other societal group fighting for its interests in a complex, pluralistic policy process?

This study effectively points up the vagueness and ambiguity of the

---

17. It is difficult to place data protection in any of the normally applied typologies. It cannot be classified according to Lowi's original scheme of distributive, redistributive, or regulatory policy: Theodore J. Lowi, "American Business, Public Policy, Case-Studies, and Political Theory," *World Politics* 16 (1964): 677–715. Nor does it fit in the four-cell typologies that later revised Lowi's original idea, for example, in Ripley and Franklin's categorization of distributive, redistributive, competitive regulatory, and protective regulatory policies, in *Congress, the Bureaucracy, and Public Policy*.

distinction between state- and society-centered explanations. In this policy, more so than in most others, it is impossible to make any behavioral distinction between authoritative, public-regarding actions and private, self-regarding ones. The internal focus of the regulation makes the distinction not only blurry (as statist theorists admit) but also tautological. And as a result, then, the location of responsibility within the "state" is rendered less meaningful. In other words, the general conclusion that a model of bureaucratic power is useful in explaining the divergence between national policy instruments holds no validity unless motives are taken into account. We can then expose the more self-regarding incentives as well as the fact that the bureaucracy is acting, not as an authoritative allocator of values, but as just one group, albeit a powerful one, within the "contours of civil society." The bureaucracy's resistance to data protection in Britain, in Germany, and to a lesser extent in the United States, simply constituted the action of the politically weightiest group, which may explain the content of the respective policies in some important respects. But it is precisely the explanation of policy choice that the statist theories, such as those of Skocpol and Nordlinger, are explicitly trying to steer away from.

Thus, in the attempt to evaluate the empirical utility of "bringing the state back in," our study has also served to expose some profound contradictions within the literature. Admittedly, we may be dealing with a special form of regulatory policy that immediately inspires bureaucratic resistance and thus a distinctive set of policy dynamics. It would be valuable to examine in further research whether comparable issues have been characterized by similar patterns of policy making; freedom of information, "sunshine," and ombudsman laws are the ones that readily come to mind.

Convergence, Divergence, and National Policy Styles

The novelty and peculiarity of the issue also mean that it could not be placed within a previously defined policy sector, one with its own group dynamics or previous patterns of decision making. The "sectorization" of policy making is a familiar phenomenon that may invalidate any attempt to detect an overall British, American, German, or Swedish "policy style" or to detect "standard operating procedures for handling issues which arrive on the political agenda."[18] As Jeremy Richardson and his colleagues write: "If each policy area develops into a semi-watertight compartment, ruled by its own 'policy elite,' then quite different policy styles may develop within the same political system."[19] Policy style is a notoriously elusive concept, and any conclusions regarding distinctive styles must inevitably be qualified. Nevertheless, the absence of a clear sector into which data protection fits allows us to juxtapose at least the policy responses and to examine whether the quintessential policy styles described in current literature are manifested in this relatively new issue. The case, as Regan also concludes, "could be considered a 'pure' test of policy convergence or divergence as its placement in an established policy arena was not obvious."[20]

The following depiction of the Swedish policy style of the late 1960s could almost have been a description of the construction and passage of the 1973 Data Act:

> Swedish policy-making is *extraordinarily deliberative*, involving long periods of time during which more or less constant attention is given to some problem by well trained specialists. It is *rationalistic*, in that great efforts are made to develop the fullest possible information about any given issue, including a thorough review of historical experiences as well as the range of alternatives suggested by scholars in and out of Sweden. It is *open*, in the sense that all interested parties are consulted before a decision is finally made. And it is *consensual*, in that decisions are seldom made without the agreement of virtually all parties to them.[21]

It is not true that there was a "thorough review" of the "range of alternatives . . . in and out of Sweden," because the options were relatively unknown at the time. The Swedish work was very exploratory. In all other respects, the above depiction is accurate.

18. Jeremy Richardson, Gunnel Gustafsson, and Grant Jordon, "The Concept of Policy Style," in *Policy Styles in Western Europe*, ed. Richardson, pp. 1–16.
19. Ibid., p. 3.
20. Regan, "Public Uses of Private Information," p. 351.
21. Thomas Anton, "Policy-making and Political Culture in Sweden," *Scandinavian Political Studies* 4 (1969): 94.

Recent writers on Sweden have observed that this policy style has been eroded in the less sure economic atmosphere of the late 1970s and 1980s.[22] This deterioration has led to a more conflictual and less confident Swedish mood, one characterized by an increase in scandals and most dramatically, of course, by the assassination in 1986 of Olaf Palme and by the subsequent failure to find his assailant. A major controversy entered the data protection area also. In 1986 a story broke in the press concerning "Project Metropolitan," a long-term research project conducted by Carl-Gunnar Janson of the Department of Sociology at the University of Stockholm. This project was a longitudinal study of some fifteen thousand people born in Stockholm in 1953. Data collected included a range of sensitive information about various items (for example, illnesses and criminal activities), data that were collected mainly from administrative records without the knowledge of the data subjects. The ensuing controversy, which involved the government, the DIB, the university community, the press, and some of the "53s," as the subjects of the project were called, lasted a year and raised some fundamental, if misinformed, fears about the purposes of social science. Similar controversies about other social science research as well as the 1980 and 1985 censuses were also a reflection of the politicization of data protection and of the declining trust for institutions within the Swedish political culture.[23]

Thus the textbook view of Swedish politics as enlightened, consensual, depoliticized, and innovative is only partially true today. A recent study of Swedish politics suggests that these tensions have always been present but were just less latent in recent years: "Swedish public life exhibits a paradoxical combination of adaptability and rigidity, of innovation and highly structured behavior."[24] This ambiguity ("principled pragmatism") is observed with data protection. The innovativeness is apparent in the early attention to the problem. The consensual, accommodating style is visible in the structured consultation with affected groups before the Data Act was passed. But this style may also lead to a rigidity of process in which "pressures in the political system

22. Ruin, "Sweden in the 1970s," in *Policy Styles in Western Europe*, ed. Richardson.

23. Tore Dalenius, "The Debate on Privacy and Surveys in Sweden," *Chance: New Directions for Statistics and Computing* 1 (1988): 43–47; Flaherty, *Protecting Privacy in Surveillance Societies*, p. 384.

24. Hugh Heclo and Henrik Madsen, *Policy and Politics in Sweden: Principled Pragmatism* (Philadelphia: Temple University Press, 1987), p. 5.

231

are organized and channeled in quite stable, predictable, and orderly ways."[25] It is that rigidity which leads to a high-handed and bureaucratic licensing process for personal data systems. The search for a "rational solution" to a highly subjective problem produced a regulatory framework that is more inflexible than any other.

The formulation of the 1974 Privacy Act was similarly an archetypal piece of American policy making. Kingdon's theory of how and why issues come to the agenda helps us make some sense of what may be regarded as a seemingly random series of events. His metaphor of the "open policy window" certainly sheds light on the role of Watergate in the formulation of privacy policy. "Open windows" are opportunities for advocates to push their ideas and to raise attention to special problems: "Predictable or unpredictable, open windows are small and scarce. Opportunities come, but they also pass. Windows do not stay open long. If a chance is missed, another must be awaited."[26] The need to take advantage of favorable circumstances partially explains the willingness of Senator Ervin to compromise in literally the final hours of the Ninety-third Congress. We can speculate that he and his supporters knew that they had to take advantage of a congressional and public climate hostile to the executive's abuse of power and information.

Interestingly, when asked today what it will take to get privacy back on the national agenda, commentators point to the occurrence of some random, unforeseen event that might again create an "open window", for instance, a big horror story involving a massive abuse of enormous quantities of personal data, perhaps accompanied by a major class action suit. The system needs a similar episode to that which happened in Canada in 1986 when identifiable tax records on sixteen million Canadians were stolen from a Toronto office of Revenue Canada. Privacy Commissioner John Grace, who occupies a position similar to that of the Data Protection Commissioner in West Germany, later described this as Canada's "Chernobyl for data protection."[27] The United States has never experienced a similar incident. Commentators also pointed to the role of Senator Ervin, the "policy entrepre-

25. Ibid., p. 9.
26. Kingdon, *Agendas, Alternatives, and Public Policies*, p. 213.
27. Privacy Commissioner of Canada, *Annual Report 1986–87* (Ottawa: Minister of Supply and Services Canada, 1987), pp. 2–3.

neur" in Kingdon's terms, as a critical variable. Many saw the emergence of a strong advocate as a prerequisite for privacy to return to the American agenda and for a commission to be established.

To be able to explain any policy outcome in the United States in terms of one institutional or decision-making model is rare. Policy goals are always susceptible to the vagaries of a competitive and fragmented political system in which a diversity of individuals, authorities, and groups are continuously in play. The conclusion of the first edition of *Comparative Public Policy*, by Heidenheimer, Heclo, and Adams, a work with which we began, probably captures the American policy style as well as any other:

> An ideology of pragmatism, bargaining, and mutual accommodation has been extremely valuable in helping Americans use their variegated system to cope with policy problems. American reformers have generally chosen to take half a loaf, enough to meet the claims of all the possible veto groups, rather than strive for an approach that would try for the fairest possible allocation of all loaves. At the same time, the American public philosophy has remained remarkably faithful to its eighteenth-century intellectual origins. Individual, civil society, and state are still regarded as three distinct, somewhat estranged spheres. While all three are considered to be mutually threatening . . . it is the danger to the individual from the state that has generally been of greatest concern in American political thought.[28]

The 1974 Privacy Act was very much "half a loaf."

The West German policy style is more difficult to pin down. The German treatment of the data protection question reveals a blend of ideas and themes. On the one hand, there is a highly "didactic" endeavor to structure a coherent and integrated system of regulation throughout Germany. "Half a loaf" may have been acceptable to American policy makers, but such incoherence has never appealed in Germany. This traditional view of policy making in Germany is expressed by Kenneth Dyson: "One aspect of policy style is the intellectual style of policy, the approach to problem-solving. West Germany is characterized by a high-minded and didactic style of thought about

---

28. Heidenheimer et al., *Comparative Public Policy*, 1st ed., p. 261.

policy that focuses on *Sachlichkeit* (objectivity) and on public-regarding attitudes and that has its cultural roots in a tradition of distaste for the materialism of politicking."[29] There is a conception, rooted in Prussian ideology, of the state versus society in which "the overriding common good must be guaranteed by imposing the technically correct solution."[30] This objectivity is reflected in the confined and elitist participation in the process that led to the enactment of the BDSG.

Against this tradition, however, are ranged two opposing forces that are very clearly manifested in the data protection case. First, the opposition of the federal bureaucracy reflects that greater willingness among high officials to become politically engaged. The imperative then shifted from one of rationalistic problem solving to one of bargaining to reach a consensus. Thus a normative policy style stressing objectivity, duty, stability, standards, and competence is contrasted with the more politically motivated behavior of many modern officials. At another level we see a clash of interests between the didactic, statist concerns of an administrative elite and the postmaterialist values of the postwar generation, of which *Datenschutz* is a perfect, if unrecognized, example. The rise of data protection to the German political agenda reflects as nowhere else a historical fear of state power. The traditional picture of the German political culture—deferential, subject, and satisfied with governmental performance and output—painted in the famous *Civil Culture* study has been redrawn.[31] David Conradt talks of a "remade political culture" that is characterized by higher levels of popular involvement in the political process.[32] Just as the German political and administrative system has had to come to terms with active social movements such as the Greens, so it was forced to respond to a fresh and traditionally un-German notion that public officials could not be trusted with personally related data or with the sole control over new technologies.[33]

29. Kenneth Dyson, "West Germany: The Search for a Rationalist Consensus," in *Policy Styles in Western Europe*, ed. Richardson, p. 17.

30. Ibid., p. 18.

31. Almond and Verba, *The Civic Culture*, p. 312: "German political culture is characterized by a high level of confidence in the administrative branches of government and a strong sense of competence in dealing with them."

32. David P. Conradt, "West Germany: A Remade Political Culture," *Comparative Political Studies* 7 (1974): 222–38.

33. This mood is reflected most strongly in the partially successful campaigns of civil disobedience against the censuses of 1983 and 1987. See Roland Appel and Dieter Hummel, *Vorsicht Volkszahlung!* (Koln: Kolner Volksblatt, 1987).

In conclusion, the West German policy style seems both anticipatory and reactive, consensual and conflictual. As Dyson concludes: "West German policy style exhibits and reflects various political ideas that live in a state of complex tension and, at the same time, lend a certain adaptability to the policy process."[34] The complicated and drawn-out delivery of a data protection policy can best be understood in terms of the clash of these deep-seated and contradictory forces within the German political culture. How, and to what extent, this picture of the West German policy style translates into a *German* policy style with the reunification of the country will be one of the fascinating questions for students of this political system over the next decade.

The words we have used to describe the formulation of the British Data Protection Act also appear in more general depictions of the British style of policy making—words denoting "inertia,"[35] "stagnation,"[36] "intractability,"[37] or "institutional sclerosis."[38] Campbell and Connor argue that the "two decades of non-legislation on privacy are as impressive a textbook achievement of Whitehall delaying tactics as one might hope not to find."[39] "The most god-awful example of prevarication on an important social issue I have ever witnessed," complained Tony Smythe, another civil libertarian.[40] Of our four cases, Britain clearly had the most difficulty recognizing that there was a problem, defining it in clear terms, devising an appropriate solution, and orchestrating the necessary support among groups, legislators, and particularly permanent officials. At this writing, Britain would probably still not have data protection legislation had it not been for the international pressure.

The central feature of British policy making is "bureaucratic accommodation," a pattern of group/departmental relations based on five overlapping features according to Jordon and Richardson: "sectorisation, clientelism, consultation, institutionalisation of compromise and

---

34. Dyson, "West Germany," p. 44.

35. Jack E. S. Hayward, "Institutional Inertia and Political Impetus in France and Britain," *European Journal of Political Research* 4 (1976): 341–60.

36. Beer, *Britain against Itself.*

37. King, "Overload."

38. Mancur Olson, *The Rise and Decline of Nations* (New Haven: Yale University Press, 1982), p. 78: "In short, with age British society has acquired so many strong organizations and collusions that it suffers from an institutional sclerosis that slows its adaptation to changing circumstances and technologies."

39. Campbell and Connor, *On the Record*, p. 23.

40. Online, *Privacy and Computers*, p. 68.

the development of exchange relationships . . . Britain is best characterised as emphasising consensus and a desire to avoid the imposition
of solutions on sections of society."[41] Britain, therefore, normally
indulges almost by default in reactive problem solving. "Indeed," as
the same authors add, "the stress on consensus might lead to the
deliberate non-identification of problems which would de-stabilize
agreement."[42] David Vogel shows in his study of environmental regulation how this style generally leads to a "bias in favor of the status
quo."[43]

This "don't rock the boat" syndrome, so brilliantly satirized in the
BBC series "Yes, Minister," allows us to understand why the British
system appeared so unsuited to dealing with this new policy problem
that required a high degree of innovation. And when the object of
regulation is not some external group but is the public bureaucracy
itself, the motivations for inaction, or even resistance, will be higher.
Furthermore, government growth in the twentieth century has occurred without a commensurate increase in bureaucratic accountability. The nineteenth-century character of British institutions and constitutional principles is not equal to the policy-making needs of the
late twentieth century. In particular, the twin constitutional principles
of ministerial responsibility and civil service anonymity, while they
bear little relation to the real distribution of power in modern Britain,
are still used as convenient excuses for resisting innovative reforms in
British administration.

The protracted process in Britain and the final effort from 1982 to
1984 to provide a legislative response to the Council of Europe leads
us to another interesting feature of the data protection case. By most
accounts, the British government would not have legislated on this
issue had it not been *prompted* to do so by external forces. In this
case, a tangential issue related to the economics of international data
flow and a hypothetical fear of "British computers standing idle"
pressed the government to act. These issues were all highly incidental
to the central civil libertarian nature of the policy problem. They did,
however, act as the "triggering mechanism" that pushed the issue

41. Grant Jordon and Jeremy Richardson, "The British Policy Style or the Logic of
Negotiation," in *Policy Styles in Western Europe*, ed. Richardson, p. 81.
42. Ibid., p. 100.
43. Vogel, *National Styles of Regulation*, p. 272.

firmly onto the institutional agenda.[44] It appears that the British system needed an external prompt to energize elected policy makers and to mobilize the bureaucracy to prepare legislation.

One other country—the United States—required such a prompt. The "triggering mechanism" there was Watergate—not just the break-in of the Democratic party headquarters but the entire panoply of abuses and intrusions by the Nixon administration. The case created a public and congressional mood that was sympathetic toward measures designed to increase executive and bureaucratic accountability. Watergate and its ramifications, however, had very little to do with the direct abuse of personal record-keeping systems. Had it been in existence at the time, the Privacy Act would have prevented or deterred few of the actions that took place. Therefore, we again have a situation where an extrinsic set of circumstances, seemingly incidental to the substance of the immediate problem, served to precipitate policy action.

In Sweden and West Germany, by contrast, no such prompts were needed. The substantive problem, defined in civil libertarian terms, was sufficient to motivate policy makers to provide a response. For this type of policy problem, the structural features and the intellectual bases of the German and Swedish systems were more suitable than were the more conflictual and unpredictable conditions within Britain and the United States. And the fact that the United States proved to be a relative "pioneer" in this area had more to do with the coincidental combination of problems, politics, and participants than with the intrinsic problem-solving capabilities of the system. Had Watergate not occurred, we might reasonably ask whether "policy entrepreneurs" ever would have been able to marshal the necessary support to bypass the many veto points in the legislative process to produce a data protection policy.

To summarize, it is probable that the data protection issue has exposed some fairly essential characteristics of national policy styles. But the concept of "policy style" remains problematic because it is difficult to see how these somewhat vague and abstract depictions can ever be disproven. There is an inherent danger of confirming stereotypes without adequate evidence. Nevertheless, these questions about

44. Cobb and Elder, *Participation in American Politics*, p. 84.

anticipatory and reactive policy styles, and about the comparative need for a triggering mechanism, are fruitful subjects for further research, but clearly with a larger sample of countries and over a range of different issues.

Convergence, Divergence, and Policy Implementation

The most obvious area for future research, however, lies in the implementation of data protection policy. Apart from a number of comments in Chapter 5, we have largely ignored two questions: How have these laws been implemented? And what impact have they had on bureaucratic behavior? The promulgation of data protection laws, even those with apparently strong enforcement mechanisms, does not ensure that the fair information principles will be adopted or that the "privacy" of the individual is now being protected.

It is doubtful, however, whether a systematic policy evaluation is possible for data protection. As with many other areas of distributive, redistributive, or regulatory policy, "impact" can be defined in reasonably objective, and sometimes quantifiable, terms—houses built, toxic emissions reduced, childrens' test scores increased, income inequalities diminished, health improved, and so forth. With data protection, however, it is not clear how one could measure or even observe success. Impact has to be evaluated according to complex changes in the treatment of a very intangible, elusive, and ephemeral commodity—personal information. The goal of the legislation is to protect individual privacy, which, as we saw in Chapter 1, is a vague and subjective notion embodying a complex knot of humanistic, political, and instrumental values. Therefore, how do we know when privacy is, or is not, being protected?

David Flaherty's very comprehensive study of the operation of data protection law in Sweden, West Germany, France, Canada, and the United States adopts an "empirical and functional" approach to these questions. Conclusions are reached inductively from a long-term and careful observation of these laws in operation. The lessons he draws about the most successful experiences to date are based on a painstaking accumulation of descriptive evidence about the challenges that "data protectors" have faced and about their relative successes and failures. From these case histories we can infer something about the model for successful data protection.

Flaherty's recipe for success appears to include the following: (1) a constant review, updating, and adaptation of the law; (2) a continuing sensitivity to, and expertise in, new technologies and their application; (3) a separate, institutionalized policy instrument with a permanent, relatively small, dedicated, administratively expert, and technically competent staff whose responsibilities for licensing or registration are minimized; (4) a single privacy advocate at the head of the agency who knows exactly when to use the carrot and when to use the stick, and who is not concerned with balancing data protection with other administrative and political values; and (5) a supportive public opinion and legislature. For these reasons, he prefers the West German model to any of the others.

The purpose here is not to debate these conclusions, all of which seem highly reasonable. Rather, the aim is to demonstrate how the experiences that Flaherty charts and evaluates relate to the story about policy formation told above. The processes by which countries have enacted data protection law, and the patterns of convergence and divergence outlined in the previous chapters, have legacies that carry over into the experience of implementation. Therefore, our attempt to study the formation of these policies in the context of a transnational problem that has had a convergent impact on statutory principles, and a divergent impact on policy instruments, has enormous implications for the present and future implementation of these laws. The dynamics of policy formation do not end with the promulgation of law. Rather, they establish certain national and international legacies that continue to this day. Those legacies can best be defined as statutory, political, technological, and international.

The first legacy is, of course, the set of structures, resources, and incentives provided by the statutes themselves. Implementation theory suggests that these three must be consistent. The statute must coherently prepare the implementation process and ensure that the established structures have the resources to attain the statutory goals.[45] Officials must not only have the means to protect personal

45. See, for example, Jeffrey L. Pressman and Aaron Wildavsky, *Implementation*, 2d ed. (Berkeley: University of California Press, 1979); Robert T. Nakamura and Frank Smallwood, *The Politics of Policy Implementation* (New York: St. Martin's Press, 1980); and Daniel A. Mazmanian and Paul A. Sabatier, *Implementation and Public Policy* (Glenview, Ill.: Scott Foresman, 1983).

data but must also have the desire to do so: "the watchdog must have both a bark and a bite."[46] Yet there is a mismatch of structures, resources, and incentives to a certain extent in all countries.

Nowhere is this seen more than in the function of inspecting and auditing information systems, probably the most important responsibility of data protection authorities. Flaherty shows that fair information practice is probably more effectively established where there is constant interaction between record keepers and data protection officials. Progress is more likely where a regular staff can become aware of the complexities of information processing and of its likely problems and conflicts, and mutually familiar with those responsible for the collection, use, and disclosure of personal information. In Germany, data protection officials pride themselves on the successes they have achieved in auditing personal information systems. Freed from licensing or registration responsibilities, the staff has been able to develop an administrative and technological expertise and thus to gain the trust and respect of the organizations that they regulate. A major motivation of the BfD is to educate officials that data protection can be in their interest too. In this regard, a consensual and accommodating style is more beneficial. But the necessary spirit of trust and cooperation can lead to the familiar problem of the regulators being captured by the regulated, a possibility that is even more likely when data protection officials are still formally part of the civil service hierarchy.

Like their counterparts in Germany, the staff of the Swedish DIB have also seen their role in educative rather than in enforcement terms. They have become functionally responsible for different sectors of society; they know the problems and the likely conflicts and are increasingly consulted at the initiation of new personal information systems. Any task that detracts from the central function of inspection reduces the effectiveness of the agency and compromises data protection. Thus, the bureaucratic burden of licensing has meant that Swedish officials cannot sustain the kind of consistent inspection program followed in Germany. The history of implementation of the Data Act has been to move staff and resources away from licensing and toward supervision. The introduction of simplified and routinized licensing procedures has helped to free staff and resources for this purpose, but

46. Flaherty, *Protecting Privacy in Surveillance Societies*, p. 387.

as a recent annual report of the DIB makes clear, more needs to be done.[47] It appears that the Data Protection Registrar in Britain is moving along the same learning curve. The most recent British reports envisage a gradual increase in supervision and inspection as the formidable burden of registration hopefully diminishes.

The American experience demonstrates, as many have noted, the enormous problems associated with enforcing data protection standards without a commission or some other agency whose sole responsibility is privacy. The implementation of the Privacy Act has been inconsistent and sporadic. Privacy, like many other issues, has been susceptible to the unpredictable vagaries of a competitive and fragmented political system, one that has only managed to provide piecemeal and incoherent safeguards. These protections are often couched in vague language and enforced by institutions that have neither the resources nor the incentives to provide constant oversight of agency behavior. Congressional oversight is hampered by a lack of expert staff, by the enormous scope of federal personal record-keeping operations, and by the absence of any incentive to monitor a policy that has no direct electoral payoffs for the representative. In the OMB, no one official has sole responsibility for Privacy Act enforcement; this office has little incentive to promote data protection when the costs incurred would conflict with its primary mission as the President's expenditure watchdog. The lack of an adequate institutional framework for the implementation of the Privacy Act leads to a conflictual atmosphere and much sniping across the legislative-executive divide.

Flaherty argues that one way to get around these difficulties is to have a strong advocate as the leader of the data protection agency, someone who can break through the statutory constraints: "the ideal data protection commissioner is self-confident, perceptive, experienced, well-connected, reasonable but firm, has a strong presence, and is politically astute. He or she must have an awareness of the multiplicity of implementation games and the devices available to counteract them."[48] Part-time commissioners, or collective committees, such as the Commission Nationale de L'Informatique et Libertés (CNIL) in France, have been less successful. Moreover, data protectors

47. Sweden, Data Inspection Board, *Year-Book 1986/87.*
48. Flaherty, *Protecting Privacy in Surveillance Societies*, pp. 386–87.

should be unashamed privacy advocates whose primary role is to "continue to articulate the interests requiring defense." They should not be a kind of "miniparliament that seeks to settle the appropriate balance internally. . . . Emphasis should be on the antisurveillance side of the balance, since the forces allied against privacy, or at least in favor of efficient surveillance, are generally so powerful."[49]

The relative success of the German and Swedish systems is mainly attributable, according to Flaherty, to the skills of Hans Peter Bull and Jan Freese respectively. But the importance of leadership conversely signifies the fragility of data protection. Both men were replaced by more traditional public servants who have been less open and assertive in the promotion of privacy interests. Again we find a contradiction between structures and incentives. If, as Flaherty argues, one of the key determinants of successful data protection is leadership, then are the qualities he identifies likely to be seen as important by the politicians who appoint data protection officials? Do the regulated have an incentive to appoint regulators who will use the resources at their disposal in such an independent and assertive way? Recent experience in some countries suggests that there is reason to believe that the regulated will not appoint a watchdog who will use the bark or the bite.

These initial conclusions suggest, as have other implementation studies, that the statutory framework is only one determinant of implementation. Moreover, it may be the case that the resources and incentives within this statutory context are less important than other factors. The statutory context is just one legacy of the data protection movement that is situated within a domestic political context, a technological context, and ultimately an international context. There is much evidence from the initial period of implementation that factors largely beyond the reach of the statute are just as important to the prospects for data protection.

In a political sense, one lesson to be drawn seems to be the importance of a conducive legislative and public opinion. Data protection officials need to operate within an atmosphere of support. They require in their battles against powerful arguments for bureaucratic surveillance a strong and clear sense that they are working in the

---

49. Ibid., p. 391.

public interest and that the public is genuinely concerned about its privacy. To this end, symbolic events such as "Orwell's year" serve to enhance public awareness and support the data protectors' roles. The media can also be a significant ally. Part of Hans Peter Bull's reputation was owed to his skillful use of sympathetic newspeople to publicize abuses of personal information and to make the data protection case. Jan Freese was a publicist in the same vein. Eric Howe, less of a publicist, has nevertheless seen the importance of supportive public opinion and has commissioned a number of polls since taking office.

But it is also generally true that the political support for these agencies has waned in the 1980s. The rise in importance of a range of issues has directly confronted the privacy value, especially within the neoconservative administrations of Britain, the United States, and Germany. The general movement toward deregulation, the attempts "to roll back the frontiers of the state," and the anticrime and antiterrorism mood have led to irresistible demands for the more efficient use of administrative resources, including personal information. The argument that data protection can help to increase efficiency and reduce burdensome and intrusive bureaucracy has not generally found a place in neoconservative rhetoric or policy.

Yet the character of the debate that surrounded the formation of these laws was generally very low key. Thus there was no legacy of sustained public interest in these laws. Interest group pressure was confined to civil liberties associations and the most directly affected professional associations. Media interest was sporadic. Data protection law did not emerge in any country out of a ground swell of popular outrage. Data protectors today, therefore, reap few benefits from the opinion polls that consistently show people to be worried about their privacy. These data protectors need a supportive climate, but the elitist and low-key emergence of these laws did not leave a large residue of interest in their success.

A third context that will determine the shape of data protection in the future is obviously the technology itself. Here, too, the legacy of policy formation endures. These "first generation" statutes responded to a political and technological climate that has changed in some important respects. Data protection officials have had to demonstrate an awareness of the privacy implications of a variety of techniques and practices that were not envisaged in the 1970s.

Computer matching, or record linkage, is probably the most serious practice. This technique, which is most developed in the United States and Sweden, involves the comparison of different tapes to identify wrongdoers, recalcitrants, welfare cheats, draft dodgers, or other people of interest to an agency. The comparison may be made by matching names, social security numbers, or any other personal identifier. Where such matching occurs prior to the receipt of a government benefit ("upfront matching") and with the consent of the data subject, it can provide an important check on eligibility for a whole range of services and positions. The problem arises when data collected by one agency are matched against data collected by another without the consent of the individual. This practice then confronts the central fair information principle that personal data should only be employed for the purposes for which they were collected. The dangers become even more acute when individuals are earmarked as wrongdoers on the basis of inaccurate data.

The United States has passed separate legislation in the form of the 1988 Computer Matching and Privacy Protection Act to try to place the whole process on a firmer statutory footing.[50] The extent of automation and the highly developed system of personal identification numbers in Sweden have also caused a proliferation of computer matches. And the linkages here span national, state, and municipal governments as well as the private sector. This networking has caused enormous problems for the DIB and its small staff. In an era in which the cost-effectiveness of administration is high on the agenda of many governments, computer matching has attained a reputation as being a harmless application of high technology. It has been a considerable challenge for data protection advocates in all countries to explain the enormous implications for the privacy of the individual, for legal principles such as the presumption of innocence, and for the enhanced power of the state.[51]

Computer profiling is a related technique with no fewer implications. A more recent application than matching, it involves the search

50. U.S. House of Representatives, *Computer Matching and Privacy Protection Act of 1988* H. R. 4699, 100th Cong., 2d sess. (Washington, D.C.: Government Printing Office, 1988).

51. See John Shattuck, "In the Shadow of 1984: National Identification Systems, Computer-Matching, and Privacy in the U.S.," *Hastings Law Journal* 35 (1984): 991–1005.

of record systems for a particular combination of elements: "profiling involves the use of inductive logic to determine indicators or characteristics and/or behavior patterns that are related to the occurrence of certain behavior."[52] Thus a profile is created, for instance, of the typical "drug dealer" or "tax cheat" or "violent offender." These profiles are then used for investigative purposes. Again the practice is most prevalent in the United States. Again it entails enormous privacy implications, ones that data protection agencies now have to confront.

Machine-readable identity cards, or "smart cards," are also an example of a new application with which data protection agencies have to come to terms. Most of us are familiar with the plastic card, embossed with a magnetic strip and a PIN, used for withdrawing cash from bank machines. But a variety of transactions may be validated in this way. In November 1984 the German government planned to issue such cards for the control of persons crossing national boundaries until the census controversy and objections by the Data Protection Commissioner forced some second thoughts. The British government proposed such a card in 1988 for football supporters in the wake of several incidents of violence. These plans were also postponed. Machine-readable passports have also been proposed in other countries from time to time. Pilot projects in local communities in the United States have introduced smart cards to dispense certain government benefits.[53] Underlying all these issues is the increasing use of PINS, such as the American Social Security Number or the British National Health Insurance Number, as identifiers in circumstances for which they were not originally intended.

The startling thing about the data protectors' concerns in the 1990s is the extraordinary variety of technologies to which they need to pay attention. A 1989 report from the Council of Europe identified three new challenges: telemetry, the remote collection of personal data by automatic means without the intervention of the data subject (e.g., by remote cameras, by sound detectors, or as in the monitoring of television programs); interactive media (teleshopping, electronic fund transfers, cable television); and electronic mail. All have complex, and subtly different, privacy implications to which traditional privacy con-

52. U.S. Congress, OTA, *Federal Government Information Technology*, p. 87.
53. U.S. Congress, OTA, *Electronic Delivery of Public Assistance Benefits: Technology Options and Policy Issues* (Washington, D.C.: Government Printing Office, 1988).

cepts may be insensitive.[54] The breadth and variety of new problems have been reflected at the Annual Conference of the Data Protection Commissioners. In recent years they have discussed, among other things, drug testing, AIDS, artificial intelligence, genetic fingerprinting, the "integrated services digital networks" (ISDN) as well as old favorites such as INTERPOL and transborder data flow.[55] The national reports of data protection authorities also reflect this diversity of problems, ones that were clearly never anticipated at the time of enactment of data protection legislation.

More generally, the information technology of the 1980s and 1990s is more integrated and dispersed than were its predecessors. Most data protection law was designed to meet the challenge of the single, powerful, but bounded "databank." With the proliferation of microcomputers and the convergence of computer and communications technologies, it has become virtually impossible to distinguish where one "databank" of "system of records" begins and another ends. The Council of Europe's report on new technologies notes that "the solutions envisaged in the 1970s were valid insofar as they were brought to bear on the then state of the art, characterised by mainframe/standalone computers with dedicated applications, capable of storing and processing data on 'identified or identifiable individuals' on a 'file' under the authority of a 'file controller' identifiable at will by a 'supervisory authority.'"[56] These developments have led several to conclude that the first generation data protection statutes are insensitive to different organizational and technological contexts. It has led the Council of Europe, for one, to develop a more refined series of recommendations for the protection of data in different fields (e.g., social security, direct marketing, medicine, and scientific research).

This new technological context highlights the importance of continual updating, review, and amendment. In this context the legacy of policy formation has placed some states in a better position than others. The Swedish Data Act, for example, has been amended twice since enactment, first in 1979 and then, more substantially, in 1982. It

54. Council of Europe, *New Technologies: A Challenge to Privacy Protection?* (Strasbourg: Council of Europe, 1989).
55. "Resolutions of the 11th Conference of Data Protection Commissioners," *Transnational Data and Communications Report* 12 (November 1989): 33.
56. Council of Europe, *New Technologies,* p. 5.

is under an almost continuous process of evaluation in response to proposals by different committees as well as to legislative developments in other areas, particularly freedom of information, computer crime, population registration, and computer vulnerability. The Swedish system of institutionalized policy analysis is ideally suited to the constant process of adjustment that data protection requires.

The three other countries have not been so successful in making such adjustments, and none of their laws has so far been substantially amended. In the United States, bills have been regularly introduced in Congress to establish a privacy or data protection commission, but there have been no serious attempts to tackle the inherent statutory flaws or the vague exemptions. Without a permanent data protection commission to articulate privacy interests, responses have been uncoordinated as this multiplicity of problems has come to the attention of a variety of congressional committees. It was recognized from the beginning that amendments would be needed to the German BDSG.[57] This need has been underscored by the 1983 decision on the census by the Federal Constitutional Court and by the German ratification of the Council of Europe Convention. Several bills, however, have been unable to attract the necessary political support for passage into law. The British law, the youngest of the four, has also yet to be revised.[58]

The statutory, political, and technological contexts within which data protection policy will reside in the future will all, of course, be profoundly affected by the growing interdependence of both problems and solutions. It is probably within this international context that the most significant developments in data protection will emerge. Technology, as we have seen, continues to shape the agenda and to have a common impact. Its pervasiveness, rapid development, and mysterious quality still shape the attitudes of the regulators of the 1990s.

57. Spiros Simitis, "Bundesdatenschutzgesetz: Ende der Diskussion oder Neubeginn," *Neue Juristische Wochenschrift* 30 (1977): 729–37.

58. The Data Protection Registrar did, however, begin an extensive process of consultation in 1988 on the assumption that the Data Protection Act required constant review and probable revision. See Data Protection Registrar, *What Are Your Views? Monitoring and Assessment of the Data Protection Act 1984* (Wilmslow, Cheshire: Data Protection Registrar, 1988). A more official review took place from 1989 to 1990 within an interdepartmental committee on data protection that, in consultation with the Registrar, recommended some extensive revisions to the Data Protection Act, including a virtual elimination of registration. The committee's work was shelved, however, when the Draft Directive from the European Commission was published in September 1990 (see note 65 below).

But other forces for convergence also endure. The dynamics that produced the convergence in the original laws continue to have a transcendent impact on the implementation of domestic data protection policy.

For example, the process of cross-national emulation within elite networks, one that began in the early 1970s, has become far more institutionalized. We have already mentioned the Annual Conference of the Data Protection Commissioners, now representing some 18 countries. The Council of Europe's Committee of Experts on Data Protection continues as a forum for cross-national debate and lesson drawing, as does the Information Computer Communications Policy (ICCP) Division of the OECD. In September 1990 the first meeting of *Privacy International* was held, a new, nongovernmental organization involving the leading privacy and data protection advocates in the world. Modelled on Amnesty International, its declared purpose is to improve liaison and communication within this network and to monitor developments in surveillance technologies.[59] These continuing and expanding linkages led one recent commentator to declare that there now exists in Europe a "data protection culture."[60]

Convergence also progresses through harmonization. The force of the Council of Europe Convention, more than that of the OECD Guidelines, has continued to draw new countries into the data protection community. A Consultative Committee was established to oversee its working. By the end of 1990, all member countries had signed the convention; ten countries had ratified it.[61] But there is still a patchwork of international agreements that apply to different groupings of countries. This incoherence is attributable, according to Simitis, to the weaknesses of harmonization as a process to reach common regulation: "Experience shows that harmonization is most of the time not the result of substantial analysis of the particular problems but of a complicated and time-consuming bargaining process, the sole pur-

59. "World Privacy Protection Network," *Transnational Data and Communications Report* 13 (August/September 1990): 25.
60. B. de Schutter, "Europe's Data Protection Challenge," *Transnational Data and Communications Report* 13 (August/September 1990): 16.
61. The ten countries are Sweden, Norway, France, Germany, Spain, Austria, Luxembourg, Denmark, Iceland, and the United Kingdom. There continues to be a question about the validity of Spain's ratification since its data protection measures are within a constitutional provision rather than within a statute.

pose of which is to combine as many as possible of the participants' initial positions."[62]

Nowhere is the interdependence of data protection more apparent than within the European Community (EC), an institution that until 1990 had been overshadowed in this area of law by the Council of Europe, but whose actions carry a number of implications for data protection which have not been lost on data protection officials.[63] In particular, the Schengen agreement of 1985, which eliminates border controls between France, Germany, and the Benelux countries, established a Schengen Information System for the exchange of information on population movement between these five countries. This agreement is seen to presage the kind of transborder data flow problems that will arise when all trade controls are eliminated throughout the community in 1992. "The Europe of trade must not take precedence over the Europe of human rights," declares Jacques Fauvet, the president of the French CNIL.[64] The 1989 Conference of the Data Protection Commissioners urged the EC to adopt the Basic Principles of Data Protection contained in the Council of Europe Convention as binding on all member nations and on the EC institutions themselves.

In September 1990, the Commission of the European Communities published a draft directive to ensure "the protection of the privacy of individuals in relation to the processing of personal data contained in data files." The directive's aim is to establish an "equivalent, high level of protection in all the Member States of the Community in order to remove the obstacles to the data exchanges that are necessary if the internal market is to function."[65] Since some member states (Belgium, Greece, Italy, Portugal, and Spain) still have no data protection legislation, and others provide only partial protections, this directive is having profound and widespread ramifications. If passed by the Council

62. Spiros Simitis, "Data Protection: Transcending the National Approach," *Transnational Data and Communications Report* 12 (November 1989): 27.

63. Action on data protection from EC institutions has until 1990 been confined to two reports from the European Parliament in the 1970s and a major research study commissioned in the early 1980s. See Burkert, *Organization and Method of Operation of the Data Protection Authorities*.

64. Jacques Fauvet, "Privacy in the New Europe," *Transnational Data and Communications Report* 12 (November 1989): 18.

65. Commission of the European Communities, *Proposal for a Council Directive concerning the Protection of Individuals in Relation to the Processing of Personal Data*, SYN 287 (Brussels: EC, September 1990), p. 12; see also "EC Data Protection Package," *Transnational Data and Communications Report* 13 (August/September 1990): 5.

of Ministers in anything like its present form, it will presage a spate of quite rapid and extensive reform throughout Europe. Since its promulgation, the lobbying from member states and from private industry associations has been intense.

The final evidence of the growing interdependence of data relations is in the 1989 *Guidelines Concerning Computerized Personal Data Files* from the United Nations. They were prepared on the initiative of Louis Joinet, one of the architects of the French law, and contain all the familiar fair information principles.[66] It is significant how the logic of convergence set in motion in the 1970s endures. The legacy of that logic is a set of enduring principles that, through the Council of Europe, the OECD, and now the EC and the United Nations, is now advocated for every country in the world. Although it is not likely that data protection legislation will spread throughout the developing world with the same rapidity, it is probable that the same commercial pressures that forced British legislation will be felt elsewhere. The larger the "data club," the greater the incentive to forbid transborder data flows to countries with inadequate protections. Thus the dominant force for convergence for most countries is likely to be a penetrative one. The pioneers of the 1970s remain the pioneers of the 1990s; the laggards remain the laggards.

Conclusion: The Prospects for Data Protection

The success of data protection in the future, therefore, will depend on factors that operate and interact on these four statutory, political, technological, and international dimensions. To a large extent, therefore, the effective implementation of the policy will be determined by developments that are external to the immediate scope of data protection laws and outside the powers of data protection officials. These initial conclusions point to the continuing importance of setting the analysis of this policy within the broader political, technological, and international contexts. The legalistic emphasis of much of the literature has tended to confine our attention to just one dimension and to

66. "UN Guidelines Concerning Computerized Personal Data Files," *Transnational Data and Communications Report* 12 (November 1989): 35–36.

exaggerate the importance of statutory principles and policy instruments over that of the national and international arenas within which they are situated and which they also have to regulate. For ultimately, this study has not only been an analysis of lawmaking but also a reflection on how states manage technological change.

It is not difficult to predict that the various pressures for convergence will continue and probably increase. The technology is becoming more transnational in character; the insecurity about these developments will promote a greater and more regular process of lesson drawing; international regimes will continue to promote harmonization; and countries that have not yet responded will be pressured to conform. Under these circumstances, the differences among policy instruments may become less important. Data protection officials will learn more and more about the approaches of their colleagues overseas and will try to draw lessons about the most effective responses to these common challenges. All policy instruments contain a variety of powers and responsibilities, which will allow their incumbents the discretion to stress the most successful functions as they learn from historical and overseas experiences. This learning is already reflected in the attempts by Swedish and British data protectors to move resources and personnel away from licensing and registration respectively.

The place of data protection on the agendas of advanced industrial states is still fragile and uncertain, however. That central doubt leads Flaherty to conclude that there is a "real risk that they [data protection authorities] will be looked back upon as a rather quaint, failed effort to cope with an overpowering technological tide rather than as a fruitful, successful exercise in promoting the coexistence of competing human and societal values."[67] Ultimately, whether the "problem" can be solved depends largely on how the "problem" is defined. Here we return to the exposition of the issue in Chapter 1. The different prospects for data protection are largely related to whether one views the problem in humanistic, political, or instrumental terms.

From a humanistic point of view, one may very well conclude that the computer and communications revolutions have continued apace and that data protection has been a symbolic attempt to protect a lost

67. Flaherty, *Protecting Privacy in Surveillance Societies*, p. 406.

value. Thus it could be inferred that the force of technology has overwhelmed political and legal controls and has progressively shaped our
institutions according to the exigencies of the latest technology. This
process may be seen as the culmination in the drive for the efficiency
and control that have their roots in the seventeenth and eighteenth
centuries. In the face of such a powerful and inexorable imperative,
personal privacy is an inevitable sacrifice. It is lost as soon as an
automated record-keeping system is established and personal data are
collected and stored. It is this conclusion that leads James Rule to
contend that privacy can only be regained by a dismantling of such
systems and by developing a looser, less efficient, and less discriminating relationship between the individual and the modern organization,
a reversal of three hundred years of bureaucratic development in other
words.[68] Data protectors only serve to legitimate new forms of surveillance; data protection law offers only a symbol of protection to
both individual and organization. It cannot restore a balance between
humanistic privacy interests and bureaucratic power.

From a political point of view, one might conclude that administrative and political power can be circumscribed where strong and effective data protection agencies have developed respect and expertise;
where privacy becomes a more salient value among members of the
mass public; and where cooperation within international regimes
leads to real controls on bureaucratic power. In this case privacy is one
interest among many in a pluralistic political process. Its status as an
issue will then rely on a range of statutory, political, technological,
and international factors. Like other issues, it will enjoy some successes in some places at some times. And it will suffer certain defeats.
At the moment the issue is overshadowed; given some visible scandals
and horror stories, it could return.

In instrumental terms, finally, the prospects rely on the integration
of fair information practice into organizations to promote the value
that the "right data are used by the right people for the right purposes." We encounter here a recent and widespread recognition
among privacy advocates that data protection cannot continue to be
seen as a discrete and separate political issue. Privacy, in an instrumental or strategic sense, is inextricably linked with a variety of other

68. Rule et al., *The Politics of Privacy.*

information policy issues, such as computer crime, international data flow, computer vulnerability, copyright, and access to information. Data protection policy should be conceived and implemented as just one problem among many in the increasingly interdependent and interconnected information society.

The first generation of data protection law was enacted in many countries because the issue was defined separately and given its own political momentum. This study has been conceivable because it has been possible to define a sector with some discrete boundaries. As the technology has taken on a more ubiquitous and interconnected character, other related issues have surfaced, a situation that demands a reassessment of data protection in this new light. The Office of Technology Assessment in the United States reached a similar conclusion at the end of its 1986 analysis of federal government information technology. It called for "systematic study of the broader social, economic, and political context of information policy, of which information privacy is a part."[69] Privacy advocates in other countries have also recognized this need. It leads us to conclude, therefore, that in instrumental terms the prospects for data protection are probably related to the development of a variety of related policy questions.

Yet a fundamental contradiction will remain. Whether viewed in humanistic, political, or instrumental terms, the roots of data protection are individualistic. It is essentially a *preindustrial* liberal value that has risen to the political agenda of the *postindustrial* state. And it has to be translated into public policy through institutions that grew out of the *industrial* age. Yet it is still collective demands and interests that sustain the policies and institutions of the state and of the international regimes within which states participate. It is also these factors that supposedly require the collection and storage of vast quantities of personal information. And it these factors that created the problem in the first place. In more concrete terms, if we as individuals want privacy, we also want welfare, law enforcement, social security, health insurance programs, income maintenance, and all the other collective values that we expect contemporary democratic governments to pro-

69. U.S. Congress, OTA, *Federal Government Information Technology*, p. 100. See also Colin J. Bennett, "Computers, Personal Data, and Theories of Technology: Comparative Approaches to Privacy Protection in the 1990s," *Science, Technology, and Human Values* 16 (1991): 51–69.

vide. And therein lies the contradiction. In that light, this postmaterialistic issue, while peculiar to the postindustrial age, will inevitably be overshadowed as long as predominantly materialistic values and interests elect our democratic governments and sustain the policies that they administer.

Selected Bibliography

Almond, Gabriel A., and Sidney Verba. *The Civic Culture*. Boston: Little, Brown, 1965.

Beer, Samuel H. *Britain against Itself: The Political Contradictions of Collectivism*. New York: Norton, 1982.

Beniger, James R. *The Control Revolution: Technological and Economic Origins of the Information Society*. Cambridge: Harvard University Press, 1986.

Bennett, Colin J. "Different Processes, One Result: The Convergence of Data Protection Policy in Europe and the United States," *Governance* 1 (1988): 415–41.

———. "Regulating the Computer: Comparing Policy Instruments in Europe and the United States," *European Journal of Political Research* 16 (1988): 437–66.

———. "Review Article: What Is Policy Convergence and What Causes It?" *British Journal of Political Science* 21 (1991): 215–33.

Bing, Jon. "A Comparative Outline of Privacy Legislation," *Comparative Law Yearbook* 2 (1978): 149–81.

Bourn, Colin, and John Benyon, eds. *Data Protection: Perspectives on Information Privacy*. Leicester: University of Leicester, Continuing Education Unit, 1984.

Brickman, Ronald, Sheila Jasanoff, and Thomas Ilgen. *Controlling Chemicals: The Politics of Regulation in Europe and the United States*. Ithaca, N.Y.: Cornell University Press, 1985.

British Computer Society, *Steps to Practicality*. London: British Computer Society, 1972.

Bull, Hans Peter. *Datenschutz oder die Angst vor Dem Computer*. Munich: Piper, 1984.

Burnham, David. *The Rise of the Computer State*. New York: Random House, 1983.

Campbell, Duncan, and Steve Connor. *On the Record: Surveillance, Computers, and Privacy*. London: Michael Joseph, 1986.

255

Carmody, Frank. "Background to Data Protection in Europe," *Information Privacy* 1 (1978): 24–29.

Cobb, Roger W., and Charles D. Elder. *Participation in American Politics: The Dynamics of Agenda-Building.* Boston: Allyn and Bacon, 1972.

Cohen, Ruth N. *Whose File Is It Anyway?* London: NCCL, 1982.

Cooley, Thomas M. *A Treatise on the Law of Torts,* 2d ed. Chicago: Callaghan, 1888.

Cornford, James. "The Prospects for Privacy," *The Political Quarterly* 52 (1981): 295–313.

Cornwell, Roger, and Marie Staunton. *Data Protection: Putting the Record Straight.* London: NCCL, 1985.

Council of Europe, *Convention for the Protection of Individuals with Regard to Automatic Processing of Personal Data.* Strasbourg: Council of Europe, 1981.

Dammann, Ulrich, Otto Mallmann, and Spiros Simitis. *Data Protection Legislation: An International Documentation.* Frankfurt am Main: Metzner, 1977.

Danziger, James N., William H. Dutton, Rob Kling, and Kenneth L. Kraemer. *Computers and Politics: High Technology in American Local Governments.* New York: Columbia University Press, 1982.

Data Protection Registrar (UK). *First Report.* London: HMSO, 1985.

———. *Second Report.* London: HMSO, 1986.

———. *Third Report.* London: HMSO, 1987.

———. *Fourth Report.* London: HMSO, 1988.

———. *Fifth Report.* London: HMSO, 1989.

———. *Sixth Report.* London: HMSO, 1990.

Dyson, Kenneth. "West Germany: The Search for a Rationalist Consensus." In *Policy Styles in Western Europe,* ed. Jeremy Richardson. London: Allen & Unwin, 1982.

Evans, Peter B., Dietrich Rueschemeyer, and Theda Skocpol. *Bringing the State Back In.* Cambridge: Cambridge University Press, 1985.

Feldman, Eliot J., and Jerome Milch. *Technocracy versus Democracy: The Comparative Politics of International Airports.* Boston: Auburn, 1982.

Flaherty, David H. *Privacy and Government Data Banks: An International Perspective.* London: Mansell, 1979.

———. "The Need for an American Privacy Protection Commission," *Government Information Quarterly* 1 (1984): 235–58.

———. "Governmental Surveillance and Bureaucratic Accountability: Data Protection Agencies in Western Societies," *Science, Technology, and Human Values* 11 (1986): 7–18.

———. *Protecting Privacy in Surveillance Societies: The Federal Republic of Germany, Sweden, France, Canada, and the United States.* Chapel Hill: University of North Carolina Press, 1989.

France, *Rapport de la Commission Informatique et Libertés* (Tricot Report). Paris: Documentation Française, 1975.

Freese, Jan. "The Swedish Data Act," *Current Sweden* 4. Stockholm: The Swedish Institute, July 1973.

256

———. "The Swedish Data Act," *Current Sweden* 178. Stockholm: The Swedish Institute, November 1977.

———. "Freedom of Information and Privacy Protection in Sweden." In *Accès à l'information et protections des renseignements personnels*, ed. Pierre Trudel. Report of a colloquium held 17–18 November 1983. Montréal: Les Presses de l'Université de Montréal, 1984.

Ganley, Oswald H., and Gladys D. Ganley. *To Inform or to Control? The New Communications Networks*. New York: McGraw-Hill, 1982.

Gourevitch, Peter. *Politics in Hard Times: Comparative Responses to International Economic Crises*. Ithaca, N.Y.: Cornell University Press, 1986.

Great Britain, Home Office. *Report of the Committee on Privacy*, Cmnd. 5012 (The Younger Committee). London: HMSO, 1972.

———. *Computers and Privacy*, Cmnd. 6353 London: HMSO, 1975.

———. *Computers: Safeguards for Privacy* (Cmnd. 6354). London: HMSO, 1975.

———. *Report of the Committee on Data Protection*, Cmnd. 7341 (The Lindop Committee). London: HMSO, 1978.

———. *Data Protection: The Government's Proposals for Legislation* (Cmnd. 8539). London: HMSO, 1982.

Hancock, Donald M. *Sweden: The Politics of Postindustrial Change*. Hinsdale, Ill.: Dryden Press, 1972.

Harris, Louis, and Associates. *The Dimensions of Privacy: A National Opinion Research Survey of Attitudes toward Privacy*. Stevens Point, Wis.: Sentry Insurance, 1979.

———. *The Road after 1984: The Impact of Technology on Society*. New Haven, Conn.: Southern New England Telephone, 1984.

Heclo, Hugh. *Modern Social Politics in Britain and Sweden*. New Haven: Yale University Press, 1974.

———. "Issue Networks and the Executive Establishment." In *The New American Political System*, ed. Anthony King. Washington, D.C.: American Enterprise Institute, 1978.

Heidenheimer, Arnold J., Hugh Heclo, and Carolyn T. Adams. *Comparative Public Policy: The Politics of Social Choice in Europe and America*. New York: St. Martin's Press, 1975 (1st ed.), 1983 (2d ed.).

Hoberg, George, Jr. "Technology, Political Structure, and Social Regulation: A Cross-National Analysis," *Comparative Politics* 18 (1986): 357–76.

Hondius, Frits W. *Emerging Data Protection in Europe*. Amsterdam: North Holland, 1975.

———. "Data Law in Europe," *Stanford Journal of International Law* 16 (1980): 87–113.

Hood, Christopher C. *The Tools of Government*. Chatham, N.J.: Chatham House, 1986.

Jordon, Grant, and Jeremy Richardson. "The British Policy Style or the Logic of Negotiation." In *Policy Styles in Western Europe*, ed. Jeremy Richardson. London: Allen & Unwin, 1982.

Justice (the British Section of the International Commission of Jurists), *Privacy and the Law*. London: Justice, 1970.

King, Anthony. "Overload: Problems of Governing in the 1970's," *Political Studies* 23 (1975): 284–96.

Kingdon, John W. *Agendas, Alternatives, and Public Policies*. Boston: Little, Brown, 1984.

Kirby, Michael D. "Transborder Data Flows and the 'Basic Rules' of Data Privacy," *Stanford Journal of International Law* 16 (1980): 27–66.

Krasner, Stephen D. "Approaches to the State: Alternative Conceptions and Historical Dynamics," *Comparative Politics* 15 (1984): 223–46.

Lijphart, Arend. "The Comparable-Cases Strategy in Comparative Research," *Comparative Political Studies* 8 (1975): 158–77.

Linowes, David F., and Colin J. Bennett. "Privacy: Its Role in Federal Government Information Policy," *Library Trends* 31 (1986): 19–42.

Lowi, Theodore J. *The End of Liberalism*. New York: Norton, 1969.

Madgwick, Donald, and Tony Smythe. *The Invasion of Privacy*. London: Pitman, 1974.

Mallmann, Otto. "Computers and Civil Liberties: The Situation in the Federal Republic of Germany," *Law and Computer Technology* 7 (1974): 2–11.

Miller, Arthur R. *The Assault on Privacy: Computers, Data Banks, and Dossiers*. Ann Arbor: University of Michigan Press, 1971.

National Council for Civil Liberties. *Privacy: The Information Gatherers*. London: NCCL, 1977.

———. *Legislating for Information Privacy*. London: NCCL, 1980.

———. *Data Protection Bill 1983: NCCL Briefing*. London: NCCL, 1983.

Neier, Aryeh. *Dossier: The Secret Files They Keep on You*. New York: Stein and Day, 1975.

Nordlinger, Eric A. *On the Autonomy of the Democratic State*. Cambridge: Harvard University Press, 1981.

O'Brien, David M. *Privacy, Law, and Public Policy*. New York: Praeger, 1979.

Online. *Privacy and Computers*. Proceedings of the Online Conference, London, 23 February 1976. Uxbridge, Middlesex: Online, 1976.

OECD. *Policy Issues in Data Protection and Privacy*. OECD Informatics Studies no. 10. Paris: OECD, 1976.

———. *Guidelines on the Protection of Privacy and Transborder Flows of Personal Data*. Paris: OECD, 1981.

Packard, Vance. *The Naked Society*. New York: Pocket Books, 1964.

Prosser, William. "Privacy," *California Law Review* 48 (1960): 383–423.

Regan, Priscilla M. "Public Uses of Private Information: A Comparison of Personal Information Policies in the United States and Britain." Ph.D. diss., Cornell University, 1981.

———. "Personal Information Policies in the United States and Britain: The Dilemma of Implementation Considerations," *Journal of Public Policy* 4 (1984): 19–38.

258

Richardson, Jeremy, ed. *Policy Styles in Western Europe*. London: Allen & Unwin, 1982.

Ripley, Randall B., and Grace A. Franklin. *Congress, the Bureaucracy, and Public Policy*, 4th ed. Chicago: Dorsey Press, 1987.

Ruin, Olof. "Sweden in the 1970s: Policy Making Becomes More Difficult." In *Policy Styles in Western Europe*, ed. Jeremy Richardson. London: Allen & Unwin, 1982.

Rule, James B. *Private Lives and Public Surveillance: Social Control in the Computer Age*. New York: Schocken Books, 1974.

Rule, James, Douglas MacAdam, Linda Stearns, and David Uglow. *The Politics of Privacy: Planning for Personal Data Systems as Powerful Technologies*. New York: Elsevier, 1980.

Schoeman, Ferdinand D., ed. *Philosophical Dimensions of Privacy: An Anthology*. Cambridge: Cambridge University Press, 1984.

——. "Background to the Issue and the Government White Paper." In *Privacy and Computers*, Proceedings of the Online Conference, London, 23 February, 1976. Uxbridge, Middlesex: Online, 1976.

Sieghart, Paul. *Privacy and Computers*. London: Latimer, 1976.

——. "Information Privacy and the Data Protection Bill." In *Data Protection: Perspectives on Information Privacy*, ed. Colin Bourn and John Benyon. Leicester: University of Leicester, 1984.

Simitis, Spiros. "Establishing Institutional Structures to Monitor and Enforce Data Protection." In OECD, *Policy Issues in Data Protection and Privacy*. Paris: OECD, 1976.

——. "Reviewing Privacy in an Information Society," *University of Pennsylvania Law Review* 135 (1987): 707–46.

Simitis, Spiros, Ulrich Dammann, Otto Mallmann, and Hans Reh. *Kommentar zum Bundesdatenschutzgesetz*, 3d ed. Baden-Baden: Nomos, 1981.

Skocpol, Theda. "Bringing the State Back In: Strategies of Analysis in Current Research." In *Bringing the State Back In*, ed. Peter B. Evans, Dietrich Rueschemeyer, and Theda Skocpol. Cambridge: Cambridge University Press, 1985.

Sweden, Commission on Publicity and Secrecy of Official Documents. *Computers and Privacy* (English translation of the report *Data och Integritet*). Stockholm: Ministry of Justice, 1972.

U.S. Congress. *Legislative History of the Privacy Act of 1974*. Source book on privacy from the Committee on Government Operations, Senate, and the Committee on Government Operations, House of Representatives. 94th Cong., 2d sess. Washington, D.C.: GPO, 1976.

U.S. Congress, Office of Technology Assessment (OTA). *Federal Government Information Technology: Electronic Record Systems and Individual Privacy*. Washington, D.C.: GPO, 1986.

U.S. Department of Health, Education, and Welfare (HEW). *Records, Computers, and the Rights of Citizens*. Report of the Secretary's Advisory Committee on Automated Personal Data Systems. Washington, D.C.: HEW, 1973.

259

U.S. House of Representatives. *International Data Flow*. Hearings before a Subcommittee of the Committee on Government Operations, House of Representatives, 96th Cong., 2d sess. Washington, D.C.: GPO, 1980.

_____. *Oversight of the Privacy Act of 1974*. Hearings before a Subcommittee of the House Committee on Government Operations, House of Representatives. 98th Cong., 1st sess. Washington, D.C.: GPO, 1983.

_____. *Who Cares about Privacy? Oversight of the Privacy Act of 1974 by the Office of Management and Budget and by the Congress*. Report by the Committee on Government Operations, House of Representatives. 98th Cong., 1st sess. Washington, D.C.: GPO, 1983.

U.S. Privacy Protection Study Commission (PPSC). *Personal Privacy in an Information Society*. Washington, D.C.: GPO, 1977.

_____. *The Privacy Act of 1974: An Assessment*. Washington, D.C.: GPO, 1977.

U.S. Senate. *Federal Data Banks and Constitutional Rights*. Report from the Subcommittee on Constitutional Rights of the Committee on the Judiciary, Senate. 93d Cong., 2d sess. Washington, D.C.: GPO, 1974.

Vinge, Per-Gunnar. *The Swedish Data Act*. Stockholm: Federation of Swedish Industries, 1973.

_____. *Experiences of the Swedish Data Act*. Stockholm: Federation of Swedish Industries, 1975.

Vogel, David. *National Styles of Regulation: Environmental Policy in Great Britain and the United States*. Ithaca, N.Y.: Cornell University Press, 1986.

Warner, Malcolm, and Michael Stone. *The Data Bank Society: Organizations, Computers, and Social Freedom*. London: Allen & Unwin, 1970.

Warren, Samuel, and Louis Brandeis. "The Right to Privacy," *Harvard Law Review* 4 (1890): 193–220.

Weir, Margaret, and Theda Skocpol. "State Structures and the Possibilities for 'Keynesian' Responses to the Great Depression in Sweden, Britain, and the United States." In *Bringing the State Back In*, ed. Peter B. Evans et al. Cambridge: Cambridge University Press, 1985.

Westin, Alan F. *Privacy and Freedom*. New York: Atheneum, 1967.

Westin, Alan F., and Michael A. Baker. *Databanks in a Free Society: Computers, Record-Keeping, and Privacy*. New York: Quadrangle Books, 1972.

Index

Library of Congress Cataloging-in-Publication Data

Bennett, Colin J. (Colin John), 1955–
     Regulating privacy : data protection and public policy in Europe
and the United States / Colin J. Bennett.
        p. cm.
     Includes bibliographical references and index.
     ISBN 0-8014-2611-1 (cloth : alk. paper)
     1. Data protection—Europe.   2. Privacy, Right of—Europe.
3. Data protection—United States.   4. Privacy, Right of—United
States.   I. Title.
     KJC6071.B46   1992
     342.4′0858—dc20
     [344.02858]   91-30559